Students' Guide to
Accounting and Financial Reporting Standards

8th edition

GEOFF BLACK

FINANCIAL TIMES

Prentice Hall

An imprint of **Pearson Education**

Harlow, England · London · New York · Reading, Massachusetts · San Francisco · Toronto · Don Mills, Ontario · Sydney
Tokyo · Singapore · Hong Kong · Seoul · Taipei · Cape Town · Madrid · Mexico City · Amsterdam · Munich · Paris · Milan

To Rachel, Susannah, Andrew and Michael

PEARSON EDUCATION LIMITED

Edinburgh Gate
Harlow
Essex CM20 2JE
England

and Associated Companies around the world

Visit us on the World Wide Web at:
www.pearsoned-ema.com

First published 1987
Eighth edition 2002

© Pearson Education Limited 2002

The right of G. H. Black to be identified as author of
this work has been asserted by him in accordance with
the Copyright, Designs and Patents Act 1988.

ISBN 0 273 65538 8

British Library Cataloguing in Publication Data
A catalogue record for this book can be obtained from the British Library.

Library of Congress Cataloging in Publication Data
Black, Geoff.
    Students' guide to accounting and financial reporting standards / Geoff Black. – 7th ed.
        p. cm.
    Includes index.
    ISBN 0–273–65538–8 (pbk.)
    1. Accounting – Standards – Great Britain – Examinations, questions, etc.   2. Financial
statements – Standards – Great Britain – Examinations, questions, etc.   I. Title: Accounting
and financial reporting standards.   II. Title.

    HF5616.G7 B557   2001
    657'.02'1841—dc21

                                                                        2001040316

10   9   8   7   6   5   4   3   2   1
05   04   03   02   01

Typeset by 35 in 10/12.5pt Sabon
Printed and bound in Great Britain by Henry Ling Ltd., at the Dorset Press, Dorchester, Dorset

Contents

Index to standards

Preface

Since 1970, Statements of Standard Accounting Practice (SSAPs) and more recently Financial Reporting Standards (FRSs) have become essential reading for both professional accountants and accountancy students. *Every* financial accounting examination is likely to require knowledge of several standards, and some examinations, for example the ACCA's *Financial Reporting*, have a large proportion of questions on specific details of the standards.

This book has been written to make the standards more accessible to students by highlighting the key points of each standard while using actual company account extracts to show their practical applications. In addition, there are numerous flow charts which illustrate key features and processes, and also selected examination questions and answers.

The depth of understanding required will vary depending upon the syllabus content of the particular examination, and the intention of this book is to cover the main requirements of every standard at levels which are appropriate for students at any stage of their studies. Students should look at the full text of the actual standards where appropriate in relation to detailed syllabus requirements.

The standard setting process is dynamic and standards are being constantly revised, updated and occasionally replaced completely. Because of this, it is vital to keep abreast of developments by reading magazines such as *Accountancy* or *Certified Accountant*. In particular, students are recommended to look at their syllabuses for information regarding the depth of knowledge required for their own courses, and also for information regarding those standards which are examinable at the time that they are due to sit the paper.

Internet links and free updates

This book states the position at 1 May 2001. It is possible to obtain free updated information by accessing the Accounting Standards Board's update service, which is available on its website at http://www.asb.org.uk/. The service is free of charge and will send notifications of latest ASB events to you by e-mail. Other parts of the site are of interest to students, and a separate student's section answers 'frequently asked questions' and gives other information.

Acknowledgements

Extracts from Statements of Standard Accounting Practice and Financial Reporting Standards have been reproduced with the permission of the Accounting Standards Board.

The following professional bodies have kindly granted me permission to reproduce past examination questions:

The Chartered Association of Certified Accountants
The Chartered Institute of Management Accountants
The Association of Accounting Technicians
The Institute of Chartered Secretaries and Administrators

Answers to these questions have not been provided by the professional bodies, but are the author's responsibility.

I would like to thank Jacqueline Senior of Pearson Education for her encouragement, and my wife and family for their support.

Geoff Black

Publisher's acknowledgements

We are grateful to the following for permission to reproduce copyright material:

Kingfisher plc for figures 2.3, 6.2, 7.4 and 8.13; J. Sainsbury plc for figures 3.7 and 4.5; George Wimpey plc for figure 3.8; Pace Micro Technology plc for figure 4.5; Tate & Lyle plc for figures 4.5 and 13.2; Balfour Beatty plc for figure 5.4; British American Tobacco plc for figures 6.1 and 11.5; Wembley plc for figures 8.9, 8.10, 8.11, 8.12 and 10.1, and Manchester United plc for figures 11.3 and 12.4.

Whilst every effort has been made to trace the owners of copyright material, in a few cases this has proved impossible and we take this opportunity to offer our apologies to any copyright holders whose rights we may have unwittingly infringed.

Chapter 1

An introduction to standards

INTRODUCTION

The first Statement of Standard Accounting Practice (SSAP) was issued in 1970. In the preceding decade, the accountancy profession had been coming under increasing pressure to impose standardised procedures upon its members, to avoid inconsistencies between companies and to improve generally the quality and usefulness of the financial statements.

In the 1960s, there were relatively few financial reporting requirements for companies, and although the 1948 Companies Act laid down a small number of minimum disclosures it contained little relating to the valuation of assets and liabilities. The Institute of Chartered Accountants in England and Wales (ICAEW) had issued a series of *recommendations* to its members, but imposed virtually no sanctions where individual accountants chose different methods due to what they saw as special circumstances for their client companies.

One particular factor which brought demands for action from both accountants and non-accountants was a number of highly publicised cases where companies and individuals, having relied upon the work of professional accountants for take-over or investment decisions, found subsequently that certain valuations had been made on the basis of unsound or inconsistent accounting treatments. In 1968 the chairman of Courtaulds wrote to the president of the ICAEW complaining about the wide variations in accounting treatments available to companies when reporting their financial results.

For example, in 1967 Associated Electrical Industries Ltd (AEI) was taken over by the General Electric Company Ltd (GEC) after a hotly contested bid. AEI had forecast a profit of £10m for 1967, and GEC had based its bid price partly on this forecast. The bid was successful, but when the actual results for AEI were announced, a *loss* of £4.5m was reported. The former auditors of AEI defended themselves by issuing a statement saying that AEI attributed: 'roughly £5m to adverse differences which are matters substantially of fact rather than judgement and the balance of some £9.5m to adjustments which remain substantially matters of judgement.'

The confusion of differing treatments such as that displayed in the AEI figures brings the accountancy profession as a whole into disrepute. In his book on *Creative Accounting* (International Thompson 1987), Ian Griffiths suggested that 'Every company in the country is fiddling its profits. Every set of published accounts is based on books which have been gently cooked or completely roasted. The figures which are fed twice a year to the investing public have all been changed to protect the guilty. It is the biggest con trick since the Trojan horse'.

It is not surprising that anything that narrows the areas of individuality available to accountants should be welcomed by users and preparers of accounts. This is not to say that the standards themselves have been untroubled by controversy; there have been and remain specific areas of difficulty, particularly in the field of accounting for inflation. Despite these, however, SSAPs and the more recent Financial Reporting Standards (FRSs) are likely to remain of benefit to users, preparers and auditors of accounting statements for many years to come.

THE STANDARD SETTING PROCESS

The Financial Reporting Council

The standard setting process is performed in the UK by the Financial Reporting Council (FRC), and specifically the FRC's two subsidiary organisations, the Accounting Standards Board (ASB) and the Review Panel. In addition, there is an offshoot of the ASB known as the Urgent Issues Task Force and three specialist advisory committees – the Financial Sector and Other Special Industries Committee, the Public Sector and Not-for-Profit Committee, and the Committee on Accounting for Smaller Enterprises (*see* Figure 1.1).

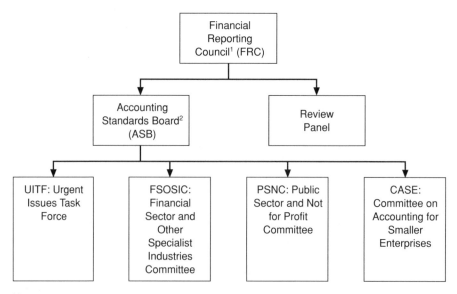

Notes:
1. The FRC is funded by the accountancy profession (CCAB), the Stock Exchange, the Bank of England and the government.
2. The ASB is appointed and funded by the FRC, which also gives it policy guidance.

Fig. 1.1 FRC and subsidiaries

The FRC is responsible for securing finance to operate the standard setting process, and for ensuring that the system is carried out efficiently and economically. In particular, the FRC provides the forum for discussion and support for accounting standards.

Membership of the Council comprises not only members of the accountancy profession but also others who are concerned in some way with the use, audit or preparation of accounting information. This is a significant departure from its predecessor, the Accounting Standards Committee (ASC), which was controlled and financed by the accountancy profession itself. The FRC took over from the ASC on 1 August 1990.

The Accounting Standards Board

The ASB, with only ten members compared with the FRC's twenty, is at the 'sharp end' of the standard-setting process, as it issues standards on its own authority. The FRC has no say over the detail of any individual standard, but the ASB needs to secure the widest possible support for the standards it issues if it is to be successful. The intention is quality rather than quantity, and since its inception in 1990 there has been a steady number of standards published on a variety of issues, as well as a thoroughgoing review of existing standards which the ASB inherited from the old Accounting Standards Committee.

The chairman of the ASB, quoted in *Accountancy Age* (January 1992), said:

'There are two reasons (why) we will change a standard. The first is if we are wrong. If someone comes forward and says you should have done this because logic dictates it, then we shall listen. The second reason is if everybody says it is too expensive to comply with the rules and the information is not particularly useful. But if they oppose it because it is reducing their profits then it is just hard luck.'

Aims of the ASB

The aims of the ASB are to establish and improve standards of financial accounting and reporting, for the benefit of users, preparers and auditors of financial information. It intends to achieve its aims by:

1. Developing principles to guide it in establishing standards and to provide a framework within which others can exercise judgement in resolving accounting issues.
2. Issuing new accounting standards, or amending existing ones, in response to evolving business practices, new economic developments and deficiencies being identified in current practice.
3. Addressing urgent issues promptly.

Targets

In its Annual Review for 1992, the Board's targets were set out. They are:

1. To be aware of the main lines of divergence in accounting standards and their causes.

2. In researching topics to follow as far as possible the relevant International Accounting Standard* and to consider the work of other standard setters, including their reasons for adopting or rejecting certain solutions.

3. To be prepared to offer its own experience and insights as input to international debates.

4. To work with others to improve the structures for international harmonisation.

Guidelines followed by the ASB

The ASB has stated that it conducts its affairs using a number of guidelines, which are reproduced below:

1. To be objective and to ensure that the information resulting from the application of accounting standards faithfully represents the underlying commercial activity. Such information should be neutral in the sense that it is free from any form of bias intended to influence users in a particular direction and should not be designed to favour any group of users or preparers.

2. To ensure that accounting standards are clearly expressed and supported by a reasoned analysis of the issues.

3. To determine what should be incorporated in accounting standards based on research, public consultation and careful deliberation about the usefulness of the resulting information.

4. To ensure that through a process of regular communication, accounting standards are produced with due regard to international developments.

5. To ensure that there is consistency both from one accounting standard to another and between accounting standards and company law.

6. To issue accounting standards only when the expected benefits exceed the perceived costs. The Board recognises that reliable cost/benefit calculations are seldom possible. However, it will always assess the need for standards in terms of the significance and extent of the problem being addressed and will choose the standard which appears to be most effective in cost/benefit terms.

7. To take account of the desire of the financial community for evolutionary rather than revolutionary change in the reporting process where this is consistent with the objectives outlined above.

Furthermore, the ASB has published a *Statement of Principles* (*see* Chapter 2) setting out the concepts that underlie the preparation and presentation of financial statements for external users. Its intention is, *inter alia*, to assist the

---

* *See* p. 11.

Board in the development of future accounting standards and in its appraisal of existing standards.

The development of a Financial Reporting Standard

The process in the development of a Financial Reporting Standard is summarised in Figure 1.2.

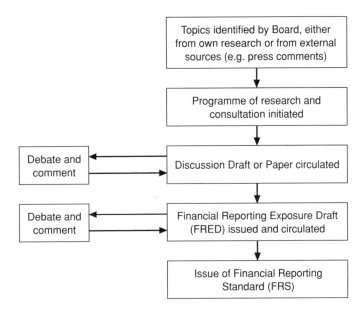

Fig. 1.2 Development of a Financial Reporting Standard

The Review Panel

The 1989 Companies Act requires large companies to state whether their accounts have been prepared in accordance with applicable standards and to give details of any material departures from those standards and the reasons for them. While the Review Panel will not itself monitor or actively initiate scrutinies of company accounts for possible defects, it will look into cases drawn to its attention (e.g. by press comment), giving companies a fair hearing and the chance to put their side of the case.

If the Review Panel rejects the company's defence, then it is able (as is the Secretary of State) under the Companies Act 1989 to apply to the court for an order – based on the premise that the accounts did not show a true and fair view – that the company concerned must prepare revised accounts and circulate them to all persons who were likely to have relied on the original accounts.

The legal option is likely to be a last resort (in fact it has not yet been used), after much discussion with the company, whereby the Review Panel will hope that the company shall voluntarily prepare revised accounts. A major incentive for this could well be the knowledge that the court may order that all or part of the costs of any application to it and any reasonable expenses incurred by the company due to its need to prepare and distribute revised accounts shall be borne by those *directors* who were party to the issuing of the original accounts. Furthermore, if the 'untrue and unfair' accounts were given an unqualified audit report by the company's auditors, some form of disciplinary action can be expected against the audit firm.

During 1999, the accounts of 42 companies were considered by the Panel, and where action was deemed necessary, voluntary agreement was reached between the Panel and the companies' boards of directors. No legal action was taken against companies. Cases reviewed had been brought to its attention in the following ways:

1. through qualified audit reports or disclosed non-compliance with accounting standards or other requirements;
2. by individuals or corporate bodies;
3. through press comment.

The chairman of the Review Panel reported in 2000 that 'since the Panel's inception, 378 cases have been brought to its attention, 142 of which were not pursued beyond initial examination and 181 of which were resolved without the issue of a press notice'.

The Urgent Issues Task Force

This is a committee of the ASB, and brings UK standard setting broadly in line with that of the USA, which has an Emerging Issues Task Force. As its name suggests, the UITF's function is to tackle urgent matters not covered by existing standards and for which the normal standard setting process is not appropriate or practical. Its aim is to assist the ASB in the maintenance and development of good accounting standards and best practice in financial reporting.

Once the UITF has reached a consensus over a particular issue, the ASB will normally accept it, though the Board has the right to reject any decision that it feels is against the law or current accounting standards. The first pronouncement from the UITF came on 24 July 1991 when it issued its Abstract 1 *Convertible Bonds – Supplemental Interest/Premium*. By 30 April 2001 a further 29 Abstracts had been issued (*see* p. 228).

Other Specialist Committees

CASE: Committee on Accounting for Smaller Entities

As its name implies, this sub-committee concentrates on the development and periodic revision of the Financial Reporting Standard for Smaller Enterprises (*see* p. 8).

FSOSIC: Financial Sector and Other Specialist Industries Committee

This reviews Statements of Recommended Practice (SORPs) developed for specific industries and sectors. These are not accounting standards, but give 'best practice' guidance to be adopted. For example, in 2000 a SORP on 'accounting in the oil and gas industry' was issued.

PSNC: Public Sector and Not for Profit Committee

Working with such bodies as local authorities and the Charity Commission, this sub-committee promulgates best practice by reviewing SORPs for the sector. For example, a revised Charities SORP was issued in October 2000.

AUTHORITY OF STANDARDS

The ASB issued a *Foreword to Accounting Standards* in June 1993, in which it set out the authority, scope and application of accounting standards.

Authority

1. FRSs and SSAPs are 'accounting standards' for the purpose of the Companies Act 1985. The Act requires the accounts of 'large' companies to state whether they have been prepared in accordance with applicable accounting standards and to give particulars of any material departure from those standards and the reasons for it.

2. Members of the professional bodies which comprise the Consultative Committee of Accountancy Bodies (CCAB) are expected to observe accounting standards whether as preparers or auditors of financial information.

3. Where CCAB members act as directors or other officers, other than auditors, the onus will be on them to ensure that the existence and purpose of accounting standards are fully understood by fellow directors and other officers.

4. Members should also use their best endeavours to ensure that accounting standards are observed and that significant departures found to be necessary are adequately explained in the financial statements.

5. Where members act as auditors or reporting accountants, they should be in a position to justify significant departures to the extent that their concurrence with the departures is stated or implied. They are not, however, required to refer in their report to departures with which they concur, provided that adequate disclosure has been made in the notes to the financial statements.

In addition to the statutory powers of the Review Panel, the professional accountancy bodies have the sanction of bringing disciplinary action against any of their members who have failed to observe accounting standards or to ensure adequate disclosure of significant departures from standards. Such actions are invariably well-publicised and may result in the member being admonished, fined or, in extreme cases, excluded from membership.

Scope and application

Accounting standards are applicable to financial statements of a reporting entity that are intended to give a true and fair view of its state of affairs at the balance sheet date and of its profit and loss (or income and expenditure) for the financial period ended on that date. Accounting standards need not be applied to immaterial items. They should be applied to UK and Republic of Ireland group financial statements including any overseas entities which are part of those statements, but are not intended to apply where financial statements are prepared overseas for local purposes.

'BIG GAAP v. LITTLE GAAP'

A Discussion Paper *Exemptions from Standards on Grounds of Size or Public Interest* was published in November 1994 by the Institute of Chartered Accountants, which suggested that most accounting standards should no longer apply to small companies. This has become known as the 'Big GAAP/Little GAAP' debate (GAAP = Generally Accepted Accounting Principles). Subsequently, in December 1995, a working party of the CCAB published a paper *Designed to fit – A Financial Reporting Standard for Smaller Entities* (FRSSE), which formed the basis for the FRSSE published in November 1997 and issued in revised form in December 1999. The FRSSE exempts the vast majority of limited companies (estimated at 900,000 of the 1.1 million in existence) from compliance with existing accounting standards and instead gives them a single comprehensive standard containing the measurement and disclosure requirements most relevant to their circumstances.

It applies to companies which meet the Companies Act definition of a 'small company', small groups, and also any other entities which would meet that definition if they were companies. Such smaller enterprises are exempted from approximately three-quarters of existing standards and UITF abstracts. They can, however, choose not to apply the FRSSE in which case they would follow the requirements of all current standards and abstracts. The FRSSE incorporates part or all of the requirements from several standards, with the emphasis on information appropriate to the smaller enterprise. No cash flow statement is required, though voluntary disclosure is encouraged. Several analyses required by FRS 3 (*see* p. 120) are omitted in the FRSSE, including the need to analyse results between continuing operations, discontinued operations and acquisitions.

COMPLIANCE WITH STANDARDS

The *Foreword* (*see* p. 7) explains the circumstances underlying compliance with accounting standards, of which the following is a summary:

1. Compliance with standards will normally be necessary for financial statements to give a true and fair view.

2. In applying accounting standards it is important to be guided by the spirit and reasoning behind them.

3. The requirement to give a true and fair view may in special circumstances require a departure to be made from accounting standards, but the Board envisages that this will only be necessary in exceptional circumstances.

4. Particulars of any material departure from an accounting standard, the reasons for it and its financial effects should be disclosed in the financial statements.

5. The Review Panel and the Department of Trade and Industry have procedures for receiving and investigating complaints regarding the annual accounts of companies in respect of apparent departures from the accounting requirements of the Companies Act, including the requirement to show a true and fair view. The Review Panel can apply to the court to require the directors to prepare revised accounts.

NEW ACCOUNTING STANDARDS AND PRIOR TRANSACTIONS

The *Foreword* addresses the question of the applicability of new accounting standards to transactions which took place before the Standard came into force. In general, the provisions of a new standard should be applied to all material transactions irrespective of the date at which they are entered into. Otherwise, similar transactions might be treated differently in the same set of accounts, and could hinder comparisons between companies.

Note that if a Financial Reporting Exposure Draft (FRED) is issued which would have the effect of amending or replacing an existing standard, the existing standard remains in force until such a time as the FRED is converted into a standard. If companies wish to show the effects of implementing a FRED, they can either:

1. insofar as the information does not conflict with existing accounting standards, incorporate it in the financial statements. However, it should be remembered that the proposals may change before forming part of a FRS and the consequences of a change to the proposals should be considered;

2. provide the information in supplementary form.

STANDARDS AND THE LAW

The first judicial recognition of standards came in the case of *Lloyd Cheyham & Co Ltd v Littlejohn* 1985. The plaintiffs alleged that they had lost money due to placing reliance on financial statements which, they claimed, had been audited in a negligent manner by the defendants. The auditors (successfully) defended their case by attempting to show that their audit was of a proper standard, and that the audited accounts complied with relevant SSAPs. In particular, the auditor's acceptance of the company's treatment of SSAP 2 *Disclosure of accounting policies*, SSAP 18 *Accounting for contingencies* and SSAP 21 *Accounting for leases and hire purchase contracts* was called into question. The full details of the case are outside the scope of this book, but it is important as, for the first time, the judge based his conclusions on the precise wording of the standards. His judgement stated, *inter alia*, that accounting standards 'are very strong evidence as to what is the proper standard which should be adopted and, unless there is some justification, a departure from this will be regarded as constituting a breach of duty.'

The *Foreword to Accounting Standards* contains an appendix entitled 'The true and fair requirement' which gives a barrister's opinion on the relationship between accounting standards and the Companies Act requirement to give a true and fair view.

Paragraph 7 of the appendix states:

'The changes brought about by the Companies Act 1989* will in my view affect the way in which the Court approaches the question whether compliance with an accounting standard is necessary to satisfy the true and fair view requirement. The Court will infer from section 256 that statutory policy favours both the issue of accounting standards . . . and compliance with them . . . The Court will also in my view infer . . . that (since the requirement is to disclose particulars of non-compliance rather than compliance) accounts which meet the true and fair requirement will in general follow rather than depart from standards and that departure is sufficiently abnormal to require to be justified. These factors increase the likelihood . . . that the Courts will hold that in general compliance with accounting standards is necessary to meet the true and fair requirement.'

UK STANDARDS AND THE EUROPEAN UNION

The spectre of accounting standards being imposed upon the UK from Brussels was raised in a speech given in late 1994 to the European Accounting Association by Karel Van Hulle, the head of the European Commission's Accounting Unit. He said that a framework would be unveiled in the autumn of 1995 which would allow Europe to 'develop those standards which we believe are the best for us and for our companies'. However, there was a U-turn when European Financial Services Regulator Mario Monti told an IOSCO conference in July 1996 that he was *not* planning to set European standards in addition to existing national and international standards. In February 1999, it was reported that the European Commission had told EU finance ministers that 7,000 listed companies should be 'obliged' to follow international standards (*see below*) rather than national standards, e.g. SSAPs and FRSs. In February 2001 it was announced that 2005 is the latest year for its implementation.

---

* i.e. section 256 referring to accounting standards.

UK STANDARDS AND INTERNATIONAL STANDARDS

In addition to the accounting standards produced by the UK profession, many other countries have their own 'national' standards. In 1973, an organisation, the International Accounting Standards Committee (IASC), was established with the object of harmonising standards on a worldwide basis. It has representatives from over seventy countries, and the members seek to encourage compliance between their own national standards and those agreed by the IASC. In most cases, compliance with a Financial Reporting Standard will ensure automatic compliance with the relevant International Accounting Standard. One major problem that members face is that there is no internationally accepted conceptual framework within which the objectives of financial reporting can be agreed, due largely to the differing economic systems operating within the member countries.

Some countries have adopted IASC standards completely or developed their own versions based on the international approach. For example, the Hong Kong Stock Exchange issued new rules in 1993 requiring foreign incorporated companies to present reports in line with IASC standards. The Asian Development Bank and the United Nations Intergovernmental Working Group of Experts on International Standards of Accounting and Reporting have used IASC standards.

However, IASC standards have been criticised for the compromises necessary to build consensus between different countries' standards, and that they were devised in the developed world and may be far less appropriate without substantial modification in many of the emerging financial regions. The IASC has, for several years, been conducting a 'Comparability and Improvement' project which aims to update some of the existing standards and remove some of the choices which are available between accepted practices.

A survey conducted in 1993 by the Centre for International Financial Analysis and Research (Cifar), based in New Jersey, USA, pointed out a number of difficulties in interpreting financial statements in emerging markets. It said that the information on companies in such markets is limited and often filed long after the year-end. Many subsidiaries conduct transactions with parent companies, adding to the awkwardness of extracting relevant, timely data.

English translations of annual reports and other financial information are often unavailable or unreliable. Converting figures expressed in local currencies may prove problematic. Varying year-ends make comparisons difficult and auditing standards differ.

Regarding accounting standards, Cifar cited eight particular issues treated in different ways in different countries: depreciation, inventory methods, deferred taxes, consolidation principles, discretionary reserves, inflation adjustments, foreign currency translation, and the valuation of fixed income and equity securities.

An important announcement was made in July 1995 that an agreement had been reached between the IASC and the international securities body IOSCO that by 1999 companies preparing their accounts according to IASC rules would be able to list their shares on any of the world's capital markets, including the

US. Currently the US (the world's largest capital market) insists that foreign companies comply with US standards, which tend to be ultra prudent. To date, only a very few mainland European companies, including Daimler-Benz in Germany, have a US listing. In May 2000, Iosco announced that it had finalised its review of a core set of 30 IASs and that it would be recommending their use to its members (including the US).

A detailed analysis of International Accounting Standards (IASs) is outside the scope of this book, but there is an excellent website available (including a students' section) at http://www.iasc.org.uk. In May 2001 it was announced that in future, all new standards would be referred to as 'International Financial Reporting Standards' (IFRSs), whilst existing ones would remain as IASs. The following represents a list of all IASs in issue on 31 March 2001.

International Accounting Standards

IAS 1   Presentation of financial statements

IAS 2   Inventories

IAS 7   Cash flow statements

IAS 8   Profit or loss for the period, fundamental errors and changes in accounting policies

IAS 10   Events after the balance sheet date

IAS 11   Construction contracts

IAS 12   Income taxes

IAS 14   Segment reporting

IAS 15   Information reflecting the effects of changing prices

IAS 16   Property, plant and equipment

IAS 17   Leases

IAS 18   Revenue

IAS 19   Employee benefits

IAS 20   Accounting for government grants and disclosure of government assistance

IAS 21   The effects of changes in foreign exchange rates

IAS 22   Business combinations

IAS 23   Borrowing costs

IAS 24   Related party disclosures

IAS 26   Accounting and reporting by retirement benefit plans

IAS 27   Consolidated financial statements and accounting for investments in subsidiaries

IAS 28   Accounting for investments in associates

IAS 29   Financial reporting in hyperinflationary economies

IAS 30   Disclosures in the financial statements of banks and similar financial institutions

IAS 31   Financial reporting of interests in joint ventures

IAS 32   Financial instruments: disclosures and presentation

IAS 33   Earnings per share

IAS 34   Interim financial reporting

IAS 35   Discontinuing operations

IAS 36   Impairment of assets

IAS 37   Provisions, contingent liabilities and contingent assets

IAS 38   Intangible assets

IAS 39   Financial instruments: recognition and measurement

IAS 40   Investment property

IAS 41   Agriculture

SUMMARY OF SSAPs AND FRSs ISSUED TO DATE

FRS	Title	Chapter
1	Cash flow statements	12
2	Accounting for subsidiary undertakings	13
3	Reporting financial performance	8
4	Capital instruments	6
5	Reporting the substance of transactions	9
6	Acquisitions and mergers	13
7	Fair values in acquisition accounting	13
8	Related party disclosures	9
9	Associates and joint ventures	13
10	Goodwill and intangible assets	4
11	Impairment of fixed assets and goodwill	4
12	Provisions, contingent liabilities and contingent assets	11
13	Derivatives and other financial instruments: disclosures	6
14	Earnings per share	8
15	Tangible fixed assets	3
16	Current tax	7
17	Retirement benefits	15
18	Accounting policies	2
19	Deferred tax	7

SSAP		Chapter
1	(superseded by FRS 9)	–
2	(superseded by FRS 18)	Appx 2
3	(superseded by FRS 14)	–
4	Accounting treatment of government grants	3
5	Accounting for value added tax	7
6	(superseded by FRS 3)	–
7	(withdrawn)	–
8	(superseded by FRS 16)	–
9	Stocks and long term contracts	5
10	(superseded by FRS 1)	–
11	(withdrawn)	–
12	(superseded by FRS 15)	–
13	Accounting for research and development	4
14	(superseded by FRS 2)	–
15	(superseded by FRS 19)	Appx 2
16	(withdrawn)	–
17	Accounting for post balance sheet events	11
18	(superseded by FRS 12)	–
19	Accounting for investment properties	3
20	Foreign currency translation	14
21	Accounting for leases and hire purchase contracts	4
22	(superseded by FRS 10)	–
23	(superseded by FRS 6)	–
24	(superseded by FRS 17)	Appx 2
25	Segmental reporting	10

Summary of abbreviations

ASB	Accounting Standards Board
ASC	Accounting Standards Committee (now defunct)
CCAB	Consultative Committee of Accountancy Bodies
FRC	Financial Reporting Council
FRED	Financial Reporting Exposure Draft
FRS	Financial Reporting Standard
FRSSE	Financial Reporting Standard for Smaller Enterprises

IASC	International Accounting Standards Committee
IAS	International Accounting Standard
ICAEW	Institute of Chartered Accountants in England & Wales
SORP	Statement of Recommended Practice
SSAP	Statement of Standard Accounting Practice
UITF	Urgent Issues Task Force

APPLICATION IN PRACTICE

An auditor's report must make reference to any significant departures from standard accounting practice. It is unusual for listed companies to have a qualified audit report, but Figure 1.3 is an example.

CHAPTER SUMMARY

- First UK accounting standard 1970.
- Financial Reporting Council operates the whole process in UK.
- ASB actually issues standards.
- Review Panel acts on allegations of non-compliance by large companies.
- UITF issues Abstracts to plug gaps in standards or advise on best practice in areas where no standard exists.
- Small entities have their own standard (FRSSE) which exempts them from most requirements of standards.
- Departure from standards may be seen as a breach of duty (Lloyd Cheyham case).
- UK standards becoming harmonised with international standards – but differences still exist.

DISCUSSION QUESTIONS

1. Do you think that the exemption from most requirements of accounting standards is fair to the shareholders of 'smaller' entities?

2. 'Harmonisation of international accounting practice may ultimately mean the end of national accounting standards.' Discuss.

3. 'Every case which the Review Panel has pursued has been settled out of court. There is therefore no need for the Panel to have any statutory powers.' Discuss.

(*See Appendix 3* for outline responses.)

Fig. 1.3 Example of a qualified audit report

Audit report to the members of XYZ plc

We have audited the financial statements on pages . . . to . . . which have been prepared under the historical cost convention (as modified by the revaluation of certain fixed assets) and the accounting policies set out on page . . .

Respective responsibilities of directors and auditors

As described on page . . . the company's directors are responsible for the preparation of financial statements. It is our responsibility to form an independent opinion, based on our audit, on those statements and to report our opinion to you.

Basis of opinion

We conducted our audit in accordance with Auditing Standards issued by the Auditing Practices Board. An audit includes examination, on a test basis, of evidence relevant to the amounts and disclosures in the financial statements. It also includes an assessment of the significant estimates and judgements made by the directors in the preparation of the financial statements, and of whether the accounting policies are appropriate to the company's circumstances, consistently applied and adequately disclosed.

We planned and performed our audit so as to obtain all the information and explanations which we considered necessary in order to provide us with sufficient evidence to give reasonable assurance as to whether the financial statements are free from material misstatement, whether caused by fraud or error. In forming our opinion we also evaluated the overall adequacy of the presentation of information in the financial statements.

Qualified opinion arising from disagreement about accounting treatment

The company leases plant and equipment which have been accounted for in the financial statements as operating leases. In our opinion, these leases should be accounted for as finance leases as required by Statement of Standard Accounting Practice 21. If this accounting treatment were followed, the finance leases would be reflected in the company's balance sheet at £X and the profit for the year would have been reduced by £Y. The financial statements do not include an explanation for this departure from an applicable accounting standard as required by the Companies Act 1985.

Except for the failure to account for the leases referred to above as required by SSAP 21, in our opinion the financial statements give a true and fair view of the state of the company's affairs as at 31 December 20.. and of its profit for the year then ended and have been properly prepared in accordance with the Companies Act 1985.

Andrew Arthurson & Co.   The Red House

Registered auditors   London

10 November 20..

(*Source*: SAS 600 – Auditors' Reports on Financial Statements)

EXAMINATION QUESTIONS

1. You are required to discuss the influence on the published financial statements of British companies of the International Accounting Standards Committee and the European Union.

(20 marks)

CIMA

2. Your managing director has approached you saying that he is 'confused at all the different accounting bodies that have replaced the old Accounting Standards Committee'.

   You are required to draft a memorandum to your managing director explaining the purpose, a description of the type of work and, where applicable, examples of the work to date of the following:

   a) Financial Reporting Council

   (3 marks)

   b) Accounting Standards Board

   (4 marks)

   c) Financial Reporting Review Panel

   (5 marks)

   d) Urgent Issues Task Force

   (3 marks)
   (Total: 15 marks)

   (*See Appendix 4* for suggested answers.)

   CIMA

Chapter 2

Principles and policies: The Statement of Principles and FRS 18

Accounting policies

INTRODUCTION

When the ASB was formed in 1990, it set up a project to produce a statement of principles. Its aim was to assist preparers and users of financial statements, as well as auditors and others, to understand the Board's approach to formulating accounting standards and the nature and function of information reported in general purpose financial statements. It reported in 1995 as an Exposure Draft, and went through several further revisions before being released as a Statement (i.e. not a 'Standard') in 1999.

FRS 18, published in December 2000, replaced one of the earliest of all standards, SSAP 2, on the theme of the selection, application and disclosure of accounting policies. On the introduction of the new standard, the then chairman of the ASB, Sir David Tweedie, commented: 'SSAP2 has lasted well, but after 28 years without a service it isn't keeping up with the rest of accounting. After the Board published its draft Statement of Principles a number of respondents suggested that we should update SSAP2 . . .'

STATEMENT OF PRINCIPLES

In December 1999, the ASB published its *Statement of Principles*. It is not an Accounting Standard but sets out the concepts that underlie the preparation of financial statements for external users. Its main purpose is to assist the ASB in the development and review of accounting standards and to provide those interested in its work with an understanding of the Board's approach to the formulation of accounting standards.

The Statement comprises several chapters, each one having been published in draft form over a 5-year period. In 1995, they were combined into a draft '*Statement of Principles for Financial Reporting*'. This document caused much debate within the accounting profession, particularly regarding the extent to which current cost accounting (a system which, *inter alia*, requires companies to show the effect of replacing stocks and fixed assets at prices which differ from book values) was to be reintroduced. The ASB issued a booklet '*Some*

Questions Answered' in early 1999 to address such issues, and made it clear that its intentions were not as radical as some had feared.

The *Statement* as it now stands contains principles that are synonymous with those adopted by Australia, Canada, New Zealand, USA and the International Accounting Standards Committee.

The Statement has the following chapter headings:

1. The objective of financial statements
2. The reporting entity
3. The qualitative characteristics of financial information
4. The elements of financial statements
5. Recognition in financial statements
6. Measurement in financial statements
7. Presentation of financial information
8. Accounting for interests in other entities

Details of the chapters are given below.

Chapter 1: The objective of financial statements

Principles

- The objective of financial statements is to provide information about the financial performance and financial position of an enterprise that is useful to a wide range of users for assessing the stewardship of management and for making economic decisions.

- That objective can usually be met by focusing exclusively on the information needs of present and potential investors, the defining class of user.

- Present and potential investors need information about financial performance and position that is useful to them in evaluating the entity's ability to generate cash (including the timing and certainty of generation) and in assessing the entity's financial adaptability.

Users

A summary of the key users of financial statements, and their information needs, is shown below.

User group	Information needs
Investors (present and potential)	Investors need to assess the financial performance of the organisation they have invested in to consider the risk inherent in, and return provided by, their investments.
Lenders	Lenders need to be aware of the ability of the organisation to repay loans and interest. Potential lenders need to decide whether to lend, and on what terms.

Suppliers and other trade creditors	Should suppliers sell to the organisation? Will they be paid?
Employees	People will be interested in their employer's stability and profitability, in particular that part of the organisation (such as a branch) in which they work. They will also be interested in the ability of their employer to pay their wages and pensions.
Customers	Customers who are dependent on a particular supplier or are considering placing a long-term contract will need to know if the organisation will continue to exist.
Government and their agencies	Reliable financial data helps governments to assemble national economic statistics, which are used for a variety of purposes in controlling the economy. Specific financial information from an organisation also enables tax to be assessed.
The public	Financial statements often include information relevant to local communities and pressure groups such as attitudes to environmental matters, plans to expand or shut down factories, policies on employment of disabled persons, etc.

Limitations of financial statements

Financial statements do not seek to meet all the information needs of users, and other sources of information will usually be needed. The following 'inherent limitations' of financial statements are identified in the chapter:

- there is a substantial degree of classification and aggregation of transactions and other events, and the allocation of the effects of continuous operations to discrete reporting periods;
- they do not tend to focus on the significance of the non-financial effects of transactions or non-financial information in general;
- they provide information that is largely historical and therefore do not reflect future events or transactions that may enhance or impair the entity's operations, nor do they anticipate the impact of potential changes in the economic environment.

Information required by investors

- Financial performance: the return the entity obtains on the resources it controls, the components of that return and the characteristics of those components.
- Financial position: the economic resources an entity controls, its financial structure, its liquidity and solvency, its risk profile and risk management approach and its capacity to adapt to changes in the environment in which it operates.
- Generation and use of cash: the ways in which cash is generated and used in its operations, its investment activities and its financial activities.
- Financial adaptability: its ability to take effective action to alter the amount and timing of its cash flows so that it can respond to unexpected needs or uncertainties.

Chapter 2: The reporting entity

This sets out the conditions that determine in principle whether entities should prepare general purpose financial statements, both as individual entities and, by consolidation, as parents of groups. It also focuses on the circumstances in which one business interest controls another and on how to account for influence that is less than control but is still significant.

Principles

- An entity should prepare and publish financial statements if there is a legitimate demand for the information that its financial statements would provide and it is a cohesive economic unit.
- The boundary of the reporting entity is determined by the scope of its control. For this purpose, first direct control and, secondly, direct plus indirect control are taken into account. More information regarding this topic can be found in Chapter 13 of this book.

Chapter 3: The qualitative characteristics of financial information

This chapter identifies four principal qualitative characteristics, as follows:

Primary qualitative characteristics relating to content:

a) relevance

b) reliability

Primary qualitative characteristics relating to presentation:

a) comparability

b) understandability

Furthermore, there is the *threshold quality* of materiality. If information is not material, then it cannot be useful or have any of the four qualitative characteristics.

The Statement contains a diagrammatic representation of its main features (*see* Figure 2.1).

Chapter 4: The elements of financial statements

This sets out and discusses the definitions of the elements of financial statements, namely:

a) assets

b) liabilities

c) ownership interest

d) gains and losses

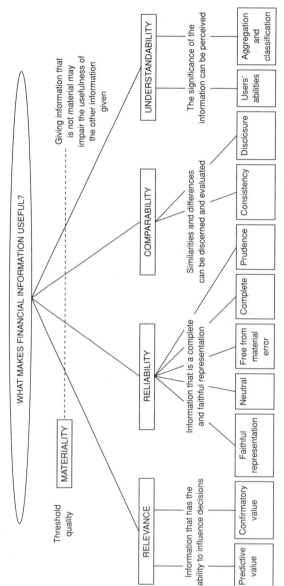

Fig. 2.1 Qualitative characteristics of financial information

e) contributions from owners

f) distributions to owners

Assets and liabilities

Assets are rights or other access to future economic benefits controlled by an entity as a result of past transactions or events.

Liabilities are obligations of an entity to transfer economic benefits as a result of past transactions or events.

Ownership interest

Ownership interest is the residual amount found by deducting all of the entity's liabilities from all of the entity's assets.

Gains and losses

Gains are increases in ownership interest not resulting from contributions from owners.

Losses are decreases in ownership interest not resulting from distributions to owners.

Contributions from owners and distributions to owners

Contributions from owners are increases in ownership interest resulting from transfers from owners in their capacity as owners.

Distributions to owners are decreases in ownership interest resulting from transfers to owners in their capacity as owners.

Chapter 5: Recognition in financial statements

This chapter identifies three stages of recognising elements for inclusion in financial statements, as follows.

Initial recognition, where an element should be recognised if there is sufficient evidence that the change in assets or liabilities inherent in the element has occurred (including evidence of future inflow or outflow of benefit), and it can be measured at a monetary amount with sufficient reliability.

Subsequent remeasurement, where a change in the recorded amount of an asset or liability should be recognised if there is sufficient evidence that the amount has changed and the new amount can be measured with sufficient reliability.

Derecognition, where an asset or liability should cease to be recognised if there is no longer any evidence of access to future economic benefits or obligations.

Chapter 6: Measurement in financial statements

This provides an overview of issues relevant to the measurement of assets and liabilities recognised in the financial statements and the significance of the associated gains and losses.

Principles

- In drawing up financial statements, a measurement basis – either historical cost or current value – needs to be selected for each category of assets or liabilities. The basis selected will be the one that best meets the objective of financial statements and the demands of the qualitative characteristics of financial information, bearing in mind the nature of the assets or liabilities concerned and the circumstances involved.

- An asset or liability being measured using the historical cost basis is recognised initially at transaction cost. An asset or liability being measured using the current value basis is recognised initially at its current value at the time it was acquired or assumed.

- Subsequent remeasurements will occur if it is necessary to ensure that:
  - assets measured at historical cost are carried at the lower of cost and recoverable amount;
  - monetary items denominated in foreign currency are carried at amounts based on up-to-date exchange rates; and
  - assets and liabilities measured on the current value basis are carried at up-to-date current values.

- Such remeasurements, however, will be recognised only if:
  - there is sufficient evidence that the monetary amount of the asset or liability has changed; and
  - the new amount of the asset or liability can be measured with sufficient reliability.

Chapter 7: Presentation of financial information

This analyses the way in which information should be presented in financial statements in order to meet the objectives as stated in chapter 1 of the Statement of Principles (*see above*).

Principles

- Financial statements comprise primary financial statements and supporting notes that amplify and explain the primary financial statements.

- The presentation of information on financial performance, financial position and cash flow focus, respectively, on:
  - components of the performance and on the characteristics of those components;

- the types and functions of assets and liabilities held and the relationships between them;
- the extent to which activities generate and use cash, distinguishing between those cash flows which result from operations and those which result from other activities.

- Disclosure of information in the notes to the financial statements is not a substitute for recognition and does not correct or justify any misrepresentation or omission in the primary financial statements.

Chapter 8: Accounting for interests in other entities

This chapter draws together various measurement and presentation issues which arise from one entity's interests in other entities. Several standards have been issued relating to these areas, which are summarised in Chapter 13 of this book.

FRS 18 ACCOUNTING POLICIES

(Issued December 2000)

Introduction

The accounting standard that FRS 18 replaced had been in existence for nearly 30 years and had proved to be relatively uncontroversial. However, with the Statement of Principles being issued in December 1999, the opportunity arose to update the standard on accounting policies, dealing with how such policies are selected, applied and disclosed.

Objectives

The objectives of the standard are illustrated in Figure 2.2.

Key definitions

Accounting policies – those principles, bases, conventions, rules and practices applied by an entity that specify how the effects of transactions and other events are to be reflected in its financial statements through:

- recognising
- selecting measurement bases for, and
- presenting

assets, liabilities, gains, losses and changes to shareholders' funds.

Accounting policies do *not* include *estimation techniques* such as depreciation methods or ways of evaluating bad debts.

Measurement bases – 'monetary attributes' of assets, liabilities, gains, losses and changes to shareholders' funds that may be reflected in financial statements.

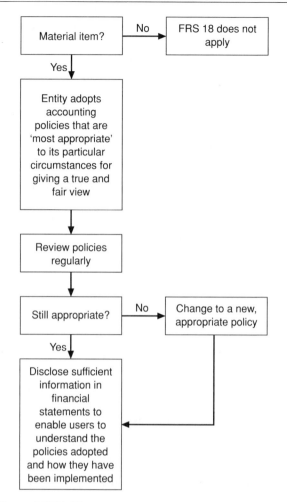

Fig. 2.2 Objectives of FRS 18

There are two broad categories of monetary attributes – those that reflect current values and those that reflect historical values.

The distinction between accounting policies and estimation techniques

Accounting policies determine which facts about a business are to be presented in the financial statements, and how those facts are to be presented; estimation techniques are used to establish what those facts are. It is important to appreciate the distinction between them, as changes in accounting policy must be reported in the financial statements, but not changes to estimation techniques. An Appendix to the Standard gives several examples, and advice as to whether they represent changes to accounting policy (*see* Table 2.1).

Table 2.1 Examples of changes to accounting policies and estimation techniques

Details	Recognition in Financial Statements	Presentation in Financial Statements	Measurement basis	Change to Accounting Policy?
1. Interest previously charged to P & L now to be added to asset, as allowed by FRS 15	Changed (part of an asset rather than an expense)	Changed (now to be shown on balance sheet)	Unchanged (interest calculation does not alter)	*Changed, so must be reported*
2. Indirect costs of a manufacturer allocated to production cost centres in different proportions to previous year	Unchanged (all costs are still allocated, but in different proportions)	Unchanged (there would be no change in the way that overheads are shown in the financial statements	Unchanged (only the proportions have changed, not the overall costing method)	*Unchanged – only the estimation technique is changed, so no need to report*
3. Overheads previously shown in 'cost of sales' are to be included in 'admin expenses'	Unchanged (costs are still debited to profit and loss account)	Changed (previously part of gross profit calculation, now omitted)	Unchanged (only the classification has changed, not the overall costing method)	*Changed, so must be reported*
4. Change from straight line to reducing balance depreciation method	Unchanged (only the amount of the expense is changed)	Unchanged (assets and depreciation shown as before)	Unchanged (historical cost measurement basis still used)	*Unchanged – only the estimation technique is changed, so no need to report*
5. Change of valuation of fungible stocks from weighted average historical cost to First In, First Out	Unchanged (only the *value* of stock is changed)	Unchanged (asset shown as before)	Changed (valuation method now differs from previous year)	*Changed, so must be reported*
6. Deferred taxation, previously reported on an undiscounted basis, is to be discounted (as allowed by FRS 19)	Unchanged (only the *amount* of the deferred tax is changed)	Unchanged (the deferred tax continues to be shown as a provision)	Changed (an alternative acceptable basis has been adopted)	*Changed, so must be reported*

Recognition and changes to presentation

As seen in Table 2.1, the decision as to whether an accounting policy is changed also requires consideration of 'recognition' and 'changes to presentation':

- Recognition: where accounting standards allow a choice of how a transaction is to be recognised (e.g. FRS 15 Tangible Fixed Assets allows directly attributable interest to be treated either as part of an asset or as an expense), that choice is a matter of accounting policy.
- Changes to presentation: when there is a change in the way in which a particular item is presented in the balance sheet or profit and loss account, this is a change of accounting policy. Simply giving more detailed analysis of the item is not a change in accounting policy.

The Appendix to the Standard previously referred to shows that consideration of both of these factors is essential when coming to a decision as to whether accounting policies have changed.

Which policies to be adopted?

Accounting policies should be adopted that enable an entity's financial statements to give a true and fair view. The standard refers to the 'pervasive role' of two concepts, going concern and accruals, in selecting policies.

- Going concern: one of the accounting principles enshrined within the 1985 Companies Act, the Standard's requirements are set out in Table 2.2 below.
- Accruals: again, one of the Companies Act's accounting principles. The Standard states that, with the exception of cash flow information, financial statements should be prepared on the accrual basis of accounting. This

Table 2.2 The going concern concept

Circumstances	Application of going concern
No significant doubts about ability to continue as going concern	Going concern basis will apply. This is the usual assumption, based on the hypothesis that the entity is considered to continue in operational existence for the foreseeable future
Significant doubts about ability to continue as going concern	If there are material uncertainties regarding the entity's going concern status, the directors must disclose those uncertainties
Entity is in liquidation or has ceased trading Directors have no realistic alternative but to liquidate or cease trading	Going concern basis will not apply; directors must consider alternative bases, including break-up values for assets

requires the non-cash effects of transactions and other events to be reflected, as far as possible, in the financial statements for the accounting period in which they occur, and not, for example, in the period in which any cash involved is received or paid.

In preparing the financial statements, only profits *realised* at the balance sheet date should be included in the profit and loss account, i.e. in the form of cash or of other assets, the ultimate cash realisation of which can be assessed with reasonable certainty.

Objectives and constraints in selecting accounting policies

The objectives used for judging the appropriateness of accounting policies are:

- Relevance: financial information is relevant if it has the ability to influence the economic decisions of users and is provided in time to influence those decisions.
- Reliability: financial information is reliable if it can be depended upon by users to represent faithfully what it either purports to represent or could reasonably be expected to represent, and therefore reflects the substance of the transactions and other events that have taken place. It should also be free from deliberate or systematic bias and material error, and complete within the bounds of materiality. Where there are conditions of uncertainty, it has been prudently prepared.
- Comparability: financial information should be capable of being compared with similar information about the entity for some other period or point in time, and with similar information about other entities.
- Understandability: financial statements need to be capable of being understood by users having a reasonable knowledge of business and economic activities and accounting and a willingness to study with reasonable diligence the information provided.

The constraints to be taken into account when judging the appropriateness of accounting policies are:

- the need to balance the four objectives listed above;
- the need to balance the cost of providing information with the likely benefit of such information to users.

Disclosures

The following information should be disclosed in the financial statements:

- A description of each of the accounting policies that are material in the context of the entity's financial statements.

- A description of those estimation techniques adopted that are significant.
- Details of any changes to the accounting policies that were followed in preparing financial statements for the preceding period, including:
  - a brief explanation of why each new accounting policy is thought more appropriate;
  - where practicable, the effect of a prior period adjustment on the results of the preceding period;
  - where practicable, an indication of the effect of a change in accounting policy on the current period's results.
- Any material change to an estimation technique should be described and, where practicable, the effect on the current period's results.
- Material uncertainties regarding the going concern status of the entity.
- Particulars, and reasons for, any material departures (referred to as a 'true and fair override') from the requirements of an accounting standard, UITF Abstract or companies legislation.

Comparisons with the predecessor standard: prudence and consistency

FRS 18 replaced SSAP 2, a standard which had remained unchanged for nearly 30 years. Details of this standard are given in Appendix 2. The old standard had included four 'fundamental accounting concepts': going concern, accruals, prudence and consistency. Although the first two are included in FRS 18 (being described as '. . . part of the bedrock of accounting, and hence critical to the selection of accounting policies'), the latter two have been reconsidered in the light of the 'Statement of Principles', as follows:

- Prudence is seen as one aspect of the overall objective of 'reliability', and the Statement reflects that since SSAP 2 was issued, 'the smoothing of reported profits has become as great a concern as their overstatement and, as a result, the deliberate understatement of assets and gains and the deliberate overstatement of liabilities are no longer seen as virtues'.
- Consistency, although important, should not be allowed to prevent improvements in accounting. Consequently, the FRS regards *comparability* as a more fundamental objective, which means that consistency can be abandoned if a new accounting policy is more appropriate than that used previously.

APPLICATION IN PRACTICE

Companies are required to disclose the principal accounting policies which have been followed in preparation of the financial statements. Figure 2.3 is an extract from the annual report of Kingfisher plc:

Fig. 2.3 Accounting policies of Kingfisher plc

Accounting policies

Accounting conventions

The financial statements of the Company and its subsidiaries are made up to the Saturday nearest to 31 January each year. The financial statements of the Company and its subsidiaries are prepared under the historical cost convention, except for certain land and buildings that are included in the financial statements at valuation, and are prepared in accordance with applicable accounting standards in the United Kingdom. However, compliance with SSAP 19 'Accounting for Investment Properties' relating to depreciation on investment properties and FRS 10 'Goodwill and Intangible Assets' relating to the capitalisation and amortisation of goodwill both require a departure from the requirements of the Companies Act 1985 as explained below. Accounting policies have been consistently applied.

Basis for consolidation

The consolidated financial statements incorporate the financial statements of the Company, its subsidiary undertakings, joint ventures and associated undertakings. Subsidiary undertakings acquired during the year are recorded under the acquisition method and their results are included from the date of acquisition.

Associated undertakings are accounted for using the equity method and joint ventures are accounted for using the gross equity method. Kingfisher plc has not presented its own profit and loss account as permitted by Section 230 of the Companies Act 1985.

Foreign currencies

Transactions denominated in foreign currencies are translated into sterling at contracted rates or, where no contract exists, at average monthly rates.

Monetary assets and liabilities denominated in foreign currencies which are held at the year end are translated into sterling at year end exchange rates. Exchange differences on monetary items are taken to the profit and loss account.

The balance sheets of overseas subsidiary undertakings are expressed in sterling at year end exchange rates. Profits and losses of overseas subsidiary undertakings are expressed in sterling at average exchange rates for the year. Exchange differences arising on the translation of opening shareholders' funds are recorded as a movement on reserves.

The Group's share of net assets or liabilities of associated undertakings and joint ventures are expressed in sterling at year end exchange rates. The share of profits or losses for the year are expressed in sterling at average exchange rates for the year. Exchange differences arising on the translation of opening net equity are recorded as a movement on reserves.

Exchange differences arising on borrowings used to finance, or provide a hedge against, Group equity investments in foreign subsidiaries are recorded as movements on reserves.

Principal rates of exchange

	2000	1999
French franc		
Year end rate	**10.841**	9.489
Average rate (weighted in proportion to the turnover of the French subsidiaries)	**10.083**	9.622
German Deutschmark	**2000**	1999
Year end rate	**3.145**	2.829
Average rate (weighted in proportion to the turnover of the German subsidiaries)	**2.990**	2.844

Fig. 2.3 continued

The German Deutschmark is used for translation of the Group's German subsidiaries which have a 31 December accounting reference date.

Goodwill and intangible assets
Intangible assets, which comprise goodwill arising on acquisitions and acquired licences and copyrights, are stated at cost less amortisation.

Goodwill arising on all acquisitions prior to 31 January 1998 remains eliminated against reserves. This goodwill will be charged in the profit and loss account on subsequent disposal of the business to which it relates. Purchased goodwill arising on acquisitions after 31 January 1998 is treated as an asset on the balance sheet. Where goodwill is regarded as having a limited estimated useful economic life it is amortised on a systematic basis over its life. Where goodwill is regarded as having an indefinite life it is not amortised. The estimated useful economic life is regarded as indefinite where goodwill is capable of continued measurement and the durability of the acquired business can be demonstrated. Where goodwill is not amortised an annual impairment review is performed and any impairment will be charged to the profit and loss account.

In estimating the useful economic life of goodwill arising, account has been taken of the nature of the business acquired, the stability of the industry, the extent of continuing barriers to market entry and expected future impact of competition. With the exception of BUT S.A. all acquisitions since 31 January 1998 are considered by the directors to have an estimated useful economic life of 20 years.

Goodwill arising on the acquisition of shares in BUT S.A. is £135.4 million. The directors consider that BUT S.A. has a proven ability to maintain its market leading position over a long period and will adapt successfully to any foreseeable technological or customer-led changes and that barriers to entry into its market place exist, such that the business will prove to be durable. BUT S.A.'s record since 1972, when it commenced trading, has been one of consistent growth in both turnover and operating profits. Accordingly, the goodwill is not amortised and, in order to give a true and fair view, the financial statements depart from the requirement of amortising goodwill over a finite period, as required by the Companies Act. Instead an annual impairment test is undertaken and any impairment that is identified will be charged to the profit and loss account. It is not possible to quantify the effect of the departure from the Companies Act, because no finite life for goodwill can be identified.

Goodwill arising on purchase of pharmacy businesses is amortised over a useful economic life of 20 years. Acquired licences and copyrights are amortised over the period of the underlying legal agreement, which do not exceed 20 years.

Depreciation
Depreciation of tangible fixed assets is provided where it is necessary to reflect a reduction from book value to estimated residual value over the estimated useful life of the asset to the Group. It is the Group's policy to maintain its properties in a state of good repair to prolong their estimated useful lives.

The directors consider that, in the case of freehold and long leasehold properties occupied by the Group, the estimated residual values at the end of their useful economic lives, based on the prices prevailing at the time of acquisition or subsequent valuation, are not materially different from their current carrying values. The lives of these properties and their residual values are such that no provision for depreciation is considered necessary. Any permanent diminution is charged to the profit and loss account.

Fig. 2.3 continued

Depreciation of other tangible fixed assets is calculated by the straight line method and the annual rates applicable to the principal categories are:

Short leaseholds	– over remaining period of the lease
Tenants' improvements	– over estimated useful life
Tenants' fixtures	– between 10% and 15%
Computers and electronic equipment	– between 25% and 50%
Motor cars	– 25%
Commercial vehicles	– $33^1/3$%

Impairment of fixed assets and goodwill

The need for any fixed asset or goodwill impairment write-down is assessed by comparison of the carrying value of the asset against the higher of net realisable value or value in use. The value in use is determined from estimated discounted future cash flows. Discount rates used are based on the circumstances of the individual businesses.

Disposal of land and buildings

Profits and losses on disposal of land and buildings represent the difference between the net proceeds and the net carrying value at the date of sale. Sales are accounted for when there is an unconditional exchange of contracts.

Leased assets

All operating lease payments are charged to the profit and loss account in the financial year to which the payments relate.

The cost of assets held under finance leases is included within tangible fixed assets and depreciation is provided in accordance with the policy for the class of asset concerned. The corresponding obligations under these leases are shown as creditors. The finance charge element of rentals is charged to the profit and loss account as incurred.

Properties

Group occupied properties are revalued annually and included in the balance sheet at existing use value.

Investment properties are revalued annually and included in the balance sheet at their open market value.

In accordance with SSAP 19, no depreciation is provided in respect of investment properties. This represents a departure from the Companies Act 1985 requirements to provide for the systematic annual depreciation of fixed assets. However, these properties are held for investment and the directors consider that the adoption of the above policy is necessary in order to give a true and fair view. It is not possible to quantify the effect of the departure from the Companies Act, because no useful economic life is deemed appropriate.

Capitalisation of interest

Interest on borrowings to finance property development is capitalised. Interest is capitalised from the date work starts on the development to practical completion.

Interest on borrowings to finance the construction of properties held as tangible fixed assets is capitalised. Interest is capitalised from the date work starts on the property to the date when substantially all the activities that are necessary to get the property ready for use are complete. Where construction is completed in parts each part is considered separately when capitalising interest.

Interest is capitalised before any allowance for tax relief.

▶

Fig. 2.3 continued

Property developments
Property developments are stated at the lower of cost and net realisable value. Development profits are taken when developments are sold. Sales are accounted for when there is an unconditional exchange of contracts or where the conditions of a sales contract are substantially satisfied.

Stocks
Stocks are stated at the lower of cost and net realisable value. Cost includes appropriate attributable overheads.

Rebates receivable from suppliers
Volume related rebates receivable from suppliers are credited to the carrying value of the stock to which they relate. Where a rebate agreement with a supplier covers more than one year the rebates are recognised in the accounts in the period in which they are earned.

CHAPTER SUMMARY

Statement of Principles

- Is not an accounting standard.
- Eight chapters: 'ORQERMPA':
  - objective of financial statements;
  - reporting entity;
  - qualitative characteristics of financial information;
  - elements of financial statements;
  - recognition in financial statements;
  - measurement in financial statements;
  - presentation of financial information;
  - accounting for interests in other entities.

FRS 18 Accounting Policies

- Contrasts accounting policies with estimation techniques.
- Two concepts have 'pervasive role': going concern and accruals.
- Relevance, reliability, comparability and understanding are objectives for judging appropriateness of policies.

DISCUSSION QUESTIONS

1. The Statement of Principles refers to four qualitative Characteristics of Financial Information. One of these is 'Understandability'. Discuss this quality in the context of the other three (Relevance, Reliability and Comparability).

2. With reference to FRS 18, contrast *accounting policies* with *estimation techniques*.

3. In the Companies Act and SSAP 2 (the predecessor standard to FRS 18), two accounting concepts, prudence and consistency were included. However, they are omitted from the new standard. Discuss this omission.

(*See Appendix 3* for outline responses.)

EXAMINATION QUESTIONS

1. The Statement of Principles is not an accounting standard, but will have a significant impact on future standards. Explain the *qualitative characteristics of financial information* contained within the statement and, for each one, explain briefly how it will affect the way user groups may benefit from their application.

(20 marks)

2. FRS 18 *Accounting policies* refers to the 'pervasive role' of two concepts, going concern and accruals, in selecting policies. Explain the meaning and importance of each of these concepts.

(20 marks)

(*See Appendix 4* for suggested answers.)

Chapter 3

Asset valuation (1):
SSAPs 4 & 19 and FRS 15

Government grants; Investment properties; Tangible fixed assets

INTRODUCTION

Although most readers should be familiar with the various *methods* of charging depreciation, they may be less certain about the reasons *why* it is charged. Two standards relate to the subject of fixed assets and their valuation, while a third looks at the problems involved when government grants are received, either towards the cost of fixed assets, or against revenue expenditure.

SSAP 4 ACCOUNTING TREATMENT OF GOVERNMENT GRANTS
(Issued April 1974, revised July 1990)

Many businesses receive grants from local and national government, government agencies, the European Union and other international bodies. This financial assistance is given for various purposes, including the establishment of companies in areas of high unemployment and the provision of training schemes for young people. Most grants can be classified into either those which relate to *revenue expenditure* (e.g. refunds of wages paid to trainees) or those relating to *capital expenditure* (e.g. financial assistance given towards purchasing machinery).

Some grants, however, do not fit easily into either category, being given for an unspecific purpose such as 'to encourage job creation' or simply 'to assist with a project'. Such cases need to be looked at individually, and it may be that in some circumstances the grant is paid on the production of specific invoices (perhaps some being for fixed assets, others for revenue items) and the allocation can be made accordingly. In other cases, the grant may be paid on the achievement of a general objective such as an increase in the numbers employed by the enterprise. Where this happens, the grant should be matched with identifiable costs incurred in achieving the objective, for example the cost of job advertisements, training and other staff costs etc.

Revenue and profits should not be anticipated, so there must be reasonable assurance that a grant will be received before bringing it into the accounts, and any conditions attaching to the payment of the grant complied with.

Under some circumstances, a grant may have to be repaid by the recipient at some future date if certain conditions made at the time of the award of the grant are not met. Provided that the grantee is a going concern, no special provision need be made in respect of any potential repayment, but if a breach of the conditions has occurred or is likely to occur, then provision should be made for the liability. When it becomes repayable, it should be charged to profit and loss account immediately, and treated in accordance with FRS 3 *Reporting financial performance* (*see* p. 120).

The accounting treatment is different for each type of grant, 'revenue based' grants being credited (under the 'accruals' concept – *see* p. 28) against related expenditure in the same period, whilst 'capital-based' grants can be treated in either of two ways:

1. by reducing the cost of the fixed asset by the amount of the grant; or
2. by treating the amount of the grant as a 'deferred credit', a portion of which is transferred to revenue annually.

Whilst the standard considers both treatments are 'capable of giving a true and fair view', it also points out that Counsel's opinion states that the first option is *not acceptable* under the Companies Act 1985.

The arguments in favour of each method are:

First alternative:

Simplicity, as the reduced depreciation charge automatically credits the amount of the grant to revenue over the life of the asset.

Second alternative:

a) Assets acquired at different times and locations (i.e. some eligible, others ineligible) are recorded on a uniform basis, regardless of changes in government policy.
b) Control over the ordering, construction and maintenance of assets is based on the gross value.
c) As capital allowances for tax purposes are normally calculated on the cost of an asset before deduction of a grant, adjustments to the depreciation charge shown in the profit and loss account are avoided when computing the amount of deferred taxation (*see* Chapter 7).

Note that two other possibilities were considered by the ASC when the standard was first drafted in the early 1970s: crediting the total grant immediately to profit and loss account, or crediting the grant to a non-distributable (i.e. not available for dividends) reserve. These were rejected on the grounds that the methods provided no correlation between the accounting treatment of the grant and the accounting treatment of the expenditure to which the grant relates.

The two methods allowed by SSAP 4 can be explained using an example of a machine costing £10,200 on which a grant of £1,800 is received. The machine is to be depreciated on the straight line basis over three years.

Method 1: Reducing the cost of the asset

Machine account

Year 1 Cost	10,200	Year 1 Grant received	1,800

Depreciation account

Year 1 Balance c/d	2,800	Year 1 P&L	2,800
		Year 2 Balance b/d	2,800
Year 2 Balance c/d	5,600	P&L	2,800
	5,600		5,600
		Year 3 Balance b/d	5,600
Year 3 Balance c/d	8,400	P&L	2,800
	8,400		8,400
		Year 4 Balance b/d	8,400

Profit and loss account

Year 1	Depreciation	2,800
Year 2	Depreciation	2,800
Year 3	Depreciation	2,800

Balance sheet

Year 1	Cost 8,400	Less Depreciation	2,800	=	5,600
Year 2	Cost 8,400	Less Depreciation	5,600	=	2,800
Year 3	Cost 8,400	Less Depreciation	8,400	=	Nil

(Reminder: this method is considered *unacceptable* under the 1985 Companies Act.)

Method 2: Crediting the grant to a deferred credit account

Machine account

Year 1	Cost	10,200

Government Grant account

Year 1	P&L	600	Year 1 Grant received	1,800
	Balance c/d	1,200		
		1,800		1,800
Year 2	P&L	600	Year 2 Balance b/d	1,200
	Balance c/d	600		
		1,200		1,200
Year 3	P&L	600	Year 3 Balance b/d	600

Depreciation account

		Year 1	P&L	3,400
		Year 2	P&L	3,400
		Year 3	P&L	3,400

Profit and loss account (year 1) (repeated for years 2 and 3)

Debit		Credit	
		Deferred income	
Depreciation	3,400	Transfer from Government Grant a/c	600

Balance sheet

Fixed Assets

(Year 1)	Cost 10,200	Depreciation	3,400	=	6,800
(Year 2)	Cost 10,200	Depreciation	6,800	=	3,400
(Year 3)	Cost 10,200	Depreciation	10,200	=	Nil

Accruals and deferred income*

Government grant:	Year 1	1,200
	Year 2	600

*A separate heading in the Companies Act balance sheet format, part of shareholders' funds.

Disclosure in financial statements

Disclosure should be made of:

a) the accounting policy adopted for government grants;

b) the effects of grants on the results for the period and/or the financial position of the business;

c) the nature of government assistance received other than in the form of grants, with an estimate of the effects, where the results are materially affected by such assistance.

Summary of SSAP 4

A summary of SSAP 4 is provided in Figure 3.1.

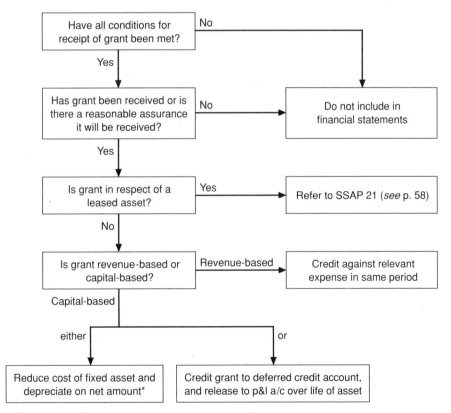

* Although permitted by the standard, legal opinion is that such treatment is contrary to the Companies Act 1985.

Fig. 3.1 SSAP 4

FRS 15 TANGIBLE FIXED ASSETS
(Issued February 1999)

This standard came into force for accounting periods ending on or after 23 March 2000, and replaced SSAP 12 Accounting for Depreciation. On its introduction, the chairman of the ASB stated:

'. . . the FRS addresses a number of discrepancies and loopholes in existing practices and will, I believe, improve the consistency of reporting in this area. Importantly, it will put to an end the present absurd practice of revaluing only when convenient and carrying assets in the accounts for years at revaluations that fail to reflect significant falls in the market value of the asset in the hope that the fall will not prove to be permanent. Wishful thinking is not an acceptable accounting concept – we have to show what has actually happened.'

It applies to all tangible fixed assets, with the exception of investment properties (*see* SSAP 19, p. 47).

Objectives

The objectives of the standard are to ensure that:

- consistent principles are applied to the initial measurement of tangible fixed assets;
- where an entity chooses to revalue tangible fixed assets the valuation is performed on a consistent basis and kept up-to-date, and gains and losses on revaluation are recognised on a consistent basis;
- depreciation of tangible fixed assets is calculated in a consistent manner and recognised as the economic benefits are consumed over the assets' useful economic lives;
- sufficient information is disclosed in the financial statements to enable users to understand the impact of the entity's accounting policies regarding initial measurement, valuation and depreciation of tangible fixed assets on the financial position and performance of the entity.

Definitions

Key definitions within the standard include:

Current value – the current value of a tangible fixed asset to the business is the lower of replacement cost and recoverable amount.

Depreciable amount – the cost of a tangible fixed asset (or, where an asset is revalued, the revalued amount) less its residual value.

Depreciation – the measure of the cost or revalued amount of the economic benefits of the tangible fixed asset that have been consumed during the period. Consumption includes the wearing out, using up or other reduction in the useful economic life of a tangible fixed asset whether arising from use, effluxion of time or obsolescence through either changes in technology or demand for the goods and services produced by the asset.

Impairment – a reduction in the recoverable amount of a tangible fixed asset below its carrying amount.

Recoverable amount – the higher of net realisable value and value in use (*see* FRS 11, p. 66).

Tangible fixed assets – assets that have physical substance and are held for use in the production or supply of goods or services, for rental to others, or for administrative purposes on a continuing basis in the reporting entity's activities.

Useful economic life – the period over which the entity expects to derive economic benefit from the asset.

Structure of the standard

The standard's contents are structured into the following main areas:
Initial measurement:

- cost;
- finance costs;
- recoverable amount;
- subsequent expenditure;
- valuation;
- frequency;
- valuation basis;
- class of assets;
- reporting gains and losses on revaluation;
- reporting gains and losses on disposal;
- disclosures.

Depreciation:

- depreciable amount;
- review of useful economic life and residual value;
- renewals accounting;
- disclosures.

Initial measurement

Cost

The way in which the cost of a tangible fixed asset is established is explained in Figure 3.2.

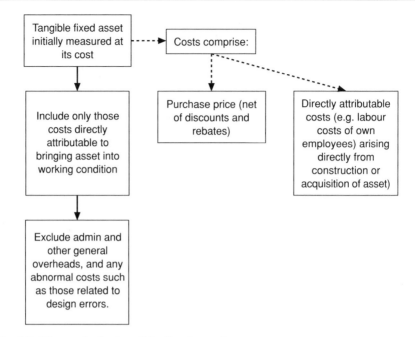

Fig. 3.2 The cost of a tangible fixed asset

Finance costs

These include interest on bank overdrafts and short-term and long-term debt. An entity can choose whether to capitalise such costs, but only if they are directly attributable to the construction of a tangible fixed asset, or the financing of progress payments on its construction. Once a policy of capitalisation has been adopted, it should be consistently applied to all tangible fixed assets. Full disclosure of the accounting policy adopted must be made, including the aggregate amount of the finance costs included in the cost of tangible fixed assets.

Recoverable amount

If the amount recognised when a tangible fixed asset is acquired or constructed exceeds its recoverable amount (see definition above), it should be written down to its recoverable amount.

Subsequent expenditure

'Repairs and maintenance expenditure' should be recognised in the profit and loss account as it is incurred. Other subsequent expenditure can be capitalised in the circumstances shown in Figure 3.3.

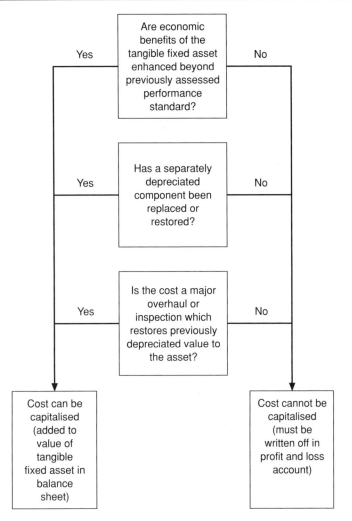

Fig. 3.3 Capitalisation of subsequent expenditure

Valuation

Individual classes of tangible fixed assets should be revalued where the entity adopts such a policy, but this policy need not apply to *all* classes of tangible fixed assets.

Frequency

Where a tangible fixed asset is revalued as policy, its carrying amount should be its current value as at the balance sheet date. An annual valuation is not required, but for properties a full valuation is needed (which must involve a qualified external valuer) at least every 5 years and an interim valuation (which might involve either an external or internal valuer) in year 3. Interim valuations should also be carried out in years 1, 2 and 4 if it is likely that there has been a material change in value.

Valuation basis

Revalued properties that are not impaired should be valued as follows:

- Non-specialised properties at existing use value. If open-market value was materially different from the existing use value, the open-market value and reasons for the difference should be disclosed.
- Specialised properties at depreciated replacement cost.
- Properties surplus to requirements at open-market value, with expected directly attributable selling costs deducted where material.

Tangible fixed assets other than properties should be valued using market value where possible or, if unobtainable, at depreciated replacement cost.

Class of assets

Where a tangible fixed asset is revalued, all tangible fixed assets of the same class should be revalued.

Reporting gains and losses on revaluation

This is explained in Figure 3.4.

Reporting gains and losses on disposal

The profit or loss on the disposal of a tangible fixed asset should be accounted for in the profit and loss account of the period in which the disposal occurs as the difference between the net sale proceeds and the carrying amount, whether carried at historical cost (less any provisions made) or at a valuation.

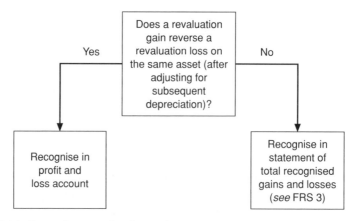

Fig. 3.4 (a) Reporting revaluation gains

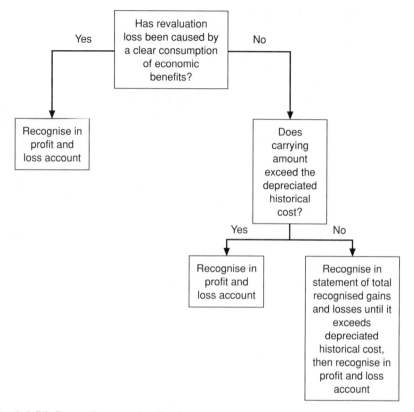

Fig. 3.4 (b) Reporting revaluation losses

Disclosures

These include the names and qualifications of valuers and the basis, dates and amounts of valuations.

Depreciation

Depreciable amount

The key requirements are summarised in Table 3.1.

Factors other than the use of an asset result in a consumption of the economic benefits and must be considered when calculating the depreciation charge, including:

- physical deterioration through use or effluxion of time;
- economic or technological obsolescence, e.g. arising from changes in market demand;
- legal or similar limits on the use of an asset, e.g. expiry dates of related leases.

Table 3.1 Depreciable amount

Allocation	Method used	Recognition
Systematic basis over asset's useful economic life	Should reflect as fairly as possible the pattern in which the asset's economic benefits are consumed by the entity	Each period's charge should be recognised as an expense in the profit and loss account

No specific depreciation method is recommended by the standard, though both the straight line and reducing balance methods are explained. The method chosen 'should result in a depreciation charge throughout the asset's useful economic life and not just towards the end of its useful economic life or when the asset is falling in value'. However, where the pattern of consumption of an asset's economic benefits is uncertain, '. . . a straight line method is usually adopted'.

A change from one method to another is permitted only if the new method will give a fairer presentation of the results. This would not be considered a change of accounting policy (*see* FRS 18).

Subsequent expenditure

Subsequent expenditure that has been capitalised (*see* above) does not negate the need to charge depreciation.

Impairment

Tangible fixed assets, other than non-depreciable land, should be reviewed for impairment (*see* FRS 11) at the end of each reporting period, when either:

- no depreciation is charged on the grounds of immateriality; or
- the estimated useful economic life of the tangible fixed asset exceeds 50 years.

Grounds for non-depreciation

Other than for non-depreciable land, the only grounds for non-depreciation are that the depreciation charge and accumulated depreciation are immaterial (i.e. they would 'not reasonably influence the decisions of a user of the accounts').

Review of useful economic life and residual value

The useful economic life of a tangible fixed asset should be reviewed at the end of each reporting period and revised if expectations are significantly different from previous estimates. If it is revised, the asset should be depreciated over the revised remaining economic life.

Disclosures

The following information should be disclosed separately for each class of tangible fixed assets:

- the depreciation methods used;
- the useful economic lives or the depreciation rates used;
- total depreciation charged for the period;
- where material, the financial effect in either the estimate of useful economic lives or the estimate of residual values;
- the cost or revalued amount at the beginning of the financial period and at the balance sheet date;
- the cumulative amount of provisions for depreciation or impairment at the beginning of the financial period and at the balance sheet date;
- a reconciliation of the movements, separately disclosing additions, disposals, revaluations, transfers, depreciation, impairment losses and reversals of past impairment losses written back in the financial period;
- the net carrying amount at the beginning of the financial period and at the balance sheet date.

Where there has been a change in the depreciation method used, the effect, if material, should be disclosed in the period of change, and the reason for the change should be given.

SSAP 19 ACCOUNTING FOR INVESTMENT PROPERTIES
(Issued January 1975, amended July 1994)

Where a significant proportion of the fixed assets of an enterprise is held not for consumption in the business but as investments, the *current value* of such investments and changes in that current value are of prime importance for the proper appreciation of the financial position, rather than the *depreciated* value.
Investment properties are defined as:

'an interest in land and/or buildings:

a) in respect of which construction work and development have been completed; and

b) which is held for its investment potential, any rental income being negotiated at arm's length.

The following are exceptions from the definition:

a) A property which is owned and occupied by a company for its own purposes is not an investment property.

b) A property let to and occupied by another group company is not an investment property for the purposes of its own accounts or the group accounts.'

The standard (which does *not* apply to charities) states that investment properties should not be depreciated but included in the balance sheet at their *open market value*. In the case of those held on short leases (i.e. 20 years or less) they should be depreciated in accordance with FRS 15 (*see* p. 40).

Open market value

'Open market value' does not have to be determined by qualified or independent valuers, but the standard requires disclosure of the names or qualifications of the valuers, the bases used by them and whether the valuer is an employee or officer of the company. However, where investment properties represent a substantial proportion of the total assets of a major enterprise (e.g. a listed company) their valuation would normally be carried out:

a) annually by a qualified person having recent experience of valuing similar properties; and

b) at least every five years by an external valuer.

Accounting treatment of revaluations

Changes in the value of investment properties should not be taken to the profit and loss account, but should be disclosed as a movement on an *investment revaluation reserve*. If a deficit on revaluation exceeds the balance on the reserve then the difference shall be taken directly to the profit and loss account (an exception to this rule is made for investment trust companies and property unit trusts).

The balances of both the investment properties and the investment revaluation reserve should be displayed prominently in the financial statements.

SSAP 19 and FRS 3

In April 1994, the ASB issued FRED 9 *Proposed amendment to SSAP 19 'Accounting for investment properties'*. This proposed that movements in the valuation of investment properties should be shown in the statement of total recognised gains and losses (*see* FRS 3, p. 120), with the exception that deficits on individual investment properties that are expected to be permanent should be charged in the profit and loss account. The FRED subsequently became an amendment to SSAP 19 in July 1994.

Summary of SSAP 19

A flow chart summarising SSAP 19 is provided in Figure 3.5.

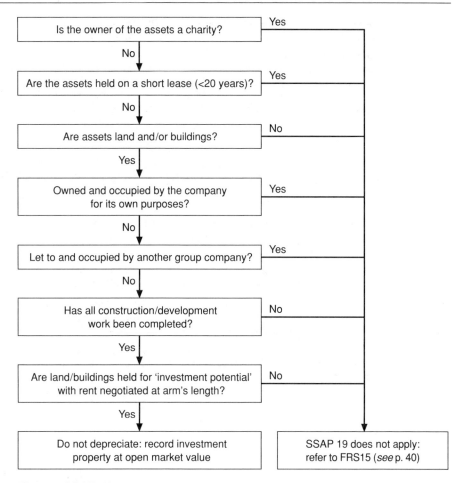

Fig. 3.5 SSAP 19

APPLICATION IN PRACTICE

Figure 3.6 shows the policy adopted for government grants by Gremlin Group plc while Figure 3.7 shows the accounting policy for depreciation adopted by J Sainsbury plc as disclosed in its 2000 accounts. George Wimpey plc is a development company with significant interests in investment properties. Figure 3.8, is an extract from its 2000 accounts showing the accounting policy adopted for these properties.

Fig. 3.6 Gremlin Group plc: treatment of government grants

Government grants

Government grants in respect of capital expenditure are treated as deferred credits, a proportion of which is transferred to revenue annually over the life of the asset. Government grants in respect of revenue expenditure are recognised in the profit and loss account so as to match them with the expenditure towards which they are intended to contribute.

Fig. 3.7 J Sainsbury plc: 2000 accounts – fixed assets and depreciation

Fixed assets

Freehold land is not depreciated. Freehold buildings, and leasehold buildings with more than 50 years unexpired, are depreciated in equal annual instalments at the rate of 2 per cent per annum.

Leasehold properties with less than 50 years unexpired are depreciated to write off their book value in equal annual instalments over the unexpired period of the lease.

Fixtures, equipment (including computer software) and vehicles are depreciated in equal annual instalments to write off their cost over their estimated useful lives, which range from 3 to 15 years, commencing when they are brought into use.

Acquired pharmacy licences are included in intangible assets and are stated at cost less amortisation. These are amortised on a straight line basis over a useful economic life of 15 years.

Fixed assets are subject to review of impairment in accordance with FRS11, Impairment of Fixed Assets and Goodwill. Any impairment in the value of such fixed assets is charged to the profit and loss account as it arises.

Fig. 3.8 George Wimpey plc: 2000 accounts – treatment of investment properties

Investment properties

In accordance with SSAP 19, (i) investment properties are revalued annually and the aggregate surplus or deficit is transferred to a revaluation reserve, and (ii) no depreciation or amortisation is provided in respect of freehold investment properties and leasehold properties with over 20 years to run. The requirement of the Companies Act 1985 is to depreciate all properties, but that requirement conflicts with the generally accepted accounting principle set out in SSAP 19. The Directors consider that this accounting policy results in the accounts giving a true and fair view. Depreciation or amortisation is only one of many factors reflected in the annual valuation and the amount which might otherwise have been shown cannot be separately identified or quantified. Where in the opinion of the Directors there has been a permanent diminution in value, the shortfall against original cost is provided for in the profit and loss account.

CHAPTER SUMMARY

SSAP 4 Accounting for Government Grants

- Revenue-based grants are credited against expense in same period.
- Capital-based grants reduce fixed asset cost: net amount is depreciated.

FRS 15 Tangible Fixed Assets

- Cost of a tangible fixed asset is purchase cost plus directly attributable costs.
- Administration and general overheads excluded from cost.
- Finance costs can be included if entity chooses.
- Revaluations only if entity adopts such a policy, in which case full valuation on properties every 5 years, interim in year 3.
- Allocate depreciation on a systematic basis over asset's useful economic life.

SSAP 19 Accounting for Investment Properties

Investment properties are:
- land or completed buildings;
- have more than 20 years lease life;
- not owned or occupied by the entity for its own purposes;
- not let to and occupied by another group company;
- rented out at arm's length;
- not depreciated.

DISCUSSION QUESTIONS

1. SSAP 4 is the oldest of the UK's accounting standards. Does it need replacing because of its age?

2. Do you agree that individual entities should be given the right to choose whether to revalue their tangible fixed assets?

3. Explain why investment properties are exempt from depreciation when all 'non-investment properties' are usually depreciated.

(*See Appendix 3* for outline responses.)

EXAMINATION QUESTIONS

1. SSAP 4 *The accounting treatment of government grants* permits a choice between two accounting methods for capital-based grants.

a) What two methods are allowed?

(7 marks)

b) What are the main arguments in favour of each method?

(8 marks)

ACCA

2. A property costs £3m and is depreciated over 10 years on a straight-line basis with no residual value. It is revalued annually. At the end of Years 1 and 2 it has an estimated sale value of £3,024,000 and £2,100,000 respectively. At the end of Year 2, the recoverable amount of the asset is £2,280,000. Explain the accounting treatment of the asset at the end of Years 1 and 2.

(20 marks)

3. The managing director of your company has always been unhappy at depreciating the company's properties because he argues that these properties are in fact appreciating in value.

Recently he heard of another company which has investment properties and does not depreciate those properties.

You are required to write a report to your managing director explaining

a) the consequence of not depreciating the company's existing properties;

(2 marks)

b) the meaning of investment properties;

(5 marks)

c) the accounting treatment of investment properties in published financial statements.

(8 marks)

CIMA

4. Toumey Enterprises plc owns three identical properties, North, South and East. North is used as the head office of Toumey Enterprises plc. South is let to, and is occupied by, a subsidiary. East is let to, and is occupied by, an associated company. A fourth property, West is leased by Toumey Enterprises plc and the unexpired term on the lease is 15 years. West is let to, and is occupied by, a company outside the group.

Required:

a) Which, if any, of these properties is likely to be an investment property of Toumey Enterprises plc and what additional information may be necessary for a final decision? State your reasons.

(10 marks)

b) Identify and justify the appropriate depreciation policy for each of the properties.

(10 marks)

ACCA

(*See Appendix 4* for suggested answers.)

Chapter 4

Asset valuation (2):
SSAPs 13 & 21 and FRSs 10 & 11

Research and development; Hire purchase and leasing; Goodwill and Intangible assets; Impairment of fixed assets and goodwill

INTRODUCTION

In this chapter, we continue the theme of fixed assets into several areas which have caused accounting problems over time, particularly the treatment of goodwill which, until the issue of FRS 10, saw Britain out of step with the rest of the world. SSAP 13, the standard on research and development, allows a certain amount of choice to companies regarding treatment of costs incurred in the development of projects which may be several years away from commercial exploitation. The leasing standard, SSAP 21, introduced the concept of *substance over form*, where we see that legal ownership of an asset does not necessarily lead to that asset's inclusion on the owner's balance sheet. Finally, FRS 11 explores the appropriate accounting treatment where assets suffer a decline in value (impairment) for various reasons.

SSAP 13 ACCOUNTING FOR RESEARCH AND DEVELOPMENT
(Issued December 1977, revised January 1989)

Companies wishing to maintain or improve profitability often have to spend material amounts on research into new or improved products, or new applications for existing products. There are two types of research identified within the standard: *pure* research, which is work directed primarily to the advancement of knowledge, and *applied* which is work directed primarily towards exploiting pure research, other than work defined as *development* expenditure (work directed towards the introduction or improvement of specific products or processes).

Such expenditure is often highly speculative in nature, with uncertainty being attached to the likely level of future revenues. Application of the prudence concept would result normally in it being written off against revenue in the year in which it is incurred. However, the standard recognises that, in certain closely defined circumstances, development expenditure can, following the *accruals* concept, be deferred to be matched against future revenues (i.e. shown as a 'deferred asset' on the balance sheet).

Definitions

The standard, which does not apply to expenditure incurred in locating and extracting mineral deposits, contains the following definitions:

Pure (or basic) research: experimental or theoretical work undertaken primarily to acquire new scientific or technical knowledge for its own sake rather than directed towards any specific aim or application.

Applied research: original or critical investigation undertaken in order to gain new scientific or technical knowledge and directed towards a specific practical aim.

Development: use of scientific or technical knowledge in order to produce new or substantially improved materials, devices, products or services, to install new processes or systems prior to the commencement of commercial production or commercial applications, or to improve substantially those already produced or installed.

The 'explanatory note' to the standard recognises that the dividing line between the three categories is often indistinct and particular expenditure may have the characteristics of more than one category. However, the decision as to whether or not to include a particular activity as being research and development based depends upon the presence or absence of *innovation*. If the activity is merely 'routine' then it should be excluded; if it breaks new ground it can be included.

The definitions given in the standard are based on those devised by the Organisation for Economic Co-operation and Development in 1980, which were intended to be suitable for use in different operating sectors. However, companies are able to apply a large degree of subjectivity in compiling their R&D figures, which has led to calls for a tightening up of the definitions.

The explanatory note to the standard gives several examples of activities which would either be included within or excluded from research and development.

Included:

a) experimental, theoretical or other work aimed at the discovery of new knowledge, or the advancement of existing knowledge;

b) searching for applications of that knowledge;

c) formulation and design of possible applications for such work;

d) testing in search for, or evaluation of, product, service or process alternatives;

e) design, construction and testing of pre-production prototypes and models and development batches;

f) design of products, services, processes or systems involving new technology or substantially improving those already produced or installed;

g) construction and operation of pilot plants.

Excluded:

a) testing and analysis of either equipment or product for purposes of quality or quantity control;

b) periodic alterations to existing products, services or processes even though these may represent some improvement;

c) operational research not tied to a specific research and development activity;

d) cost of corrective action in connection with breakdowns during commercial production;

e) legal and administrative work in connection with patent applications, records and litigation and the sale or licensing of patents;

f) activity, including design and construction engineering, relating to the construction, relocation, rearrangement or start-up of facilities or equipment other than facilities or equipment whose sole use is for a particular development project;

g) market research.

Accounting treatment

1. The cost of fixed assets acquired or constructed to provide R&D facilities is capitalised and written off over the useful life in the usual way (*see* FRS 15, p. 40).

2. All expenditure (other than on fixed assets) incurred on *pure and applied research* should be written off in the year of expenditure.

3. Development expenditure should be written off in the year of expenditure except in the following circumstances, when it may be deferred to future periods to the extent that its recovery can reasonably be assured:

a) there is a clearly defined project; and

b) the related expenditure is separately identifiable; and

c) the outcome of such a project has been assessed with reasonable certainty as to

    i) its technical feasibility; and

    ii) its ultimate commercial viability considered in the light of factors such as likely market conditions (including competing products), public opinion, consumer and environmental legislation; and

d) the aggregate of the deferred development costs, any further development costs and related production, selling and administration costs is reasonably expected to be exceeded by related future sales or other revenues;

e) adequate resources exist, or are reasonably expected to be available, to enable the project to be completed and to provide any consequential increases in working capital.

Note that the criteria for determining whether development expenditure may be deferred should be applied consistently.

The following mnemonic *decorate* may help you to remember the above criteria:

Defined project.

Environmentally acceptable and commercially viable.

Criteria to be applied consistently.

Only defer as long as recovery can be assured.

Revenues of future to more than cover further costs.

Adequate resources exist for completion and working capital.

Technically feasible.

Expenditure separately identifiable.

Write off or defer?

A company's decision whether to defer development expenditure may be influenced by a number of factors.

1. A 'write-off' policy for all R&D will reduce profits in the year of expenditure and boost profits when the project starts yielding a commercial return. However, this goes against the accruals concept of matching income to related expenditure.

2. Capitalising development expenditure may give a false impression of a company's profitability, leading to payment of dividends which are unjustified. The danger of capitalising development expenditure was clearly shown in the case of Rolls Royce Limited in the early 1970s, where substantial expenditure on the research and development of a new aero engine was taken to the balance sheet as a deferred asset, but the hoped-for returns from the project failed to materialise.

3. The subjective nature of allocation between the three categories of R&D may cause distortions if the deferral policy is followed, but has no such implications if all R&D is written off.

4. The policy adopted by other companies in the same industry may influence the decision, as the company may come under greater scrutiny from analysts if it adopts a different policy to that used by similar companies.

5. The difficulty of satisfying the company's auditors regarding the criteria for deferral may prove the prime determining factor. For example, a project's 'ultimate commercial viability' may be difficult both to predict and justify.

Amortisation

If a decision is taken to defer development costs to future periods, their amortisation* should commence with the commercial production or application

---

* From a medieval French verb *amortir*, to reduce to the point of death.

of the product, service, process or system. It should also be allocated on a systematic basis to each accounting period, by reference to either the sale or use of the product, service, process or system or the period over which these are expected to be sold or used.

A review of deferred development expenditure should take place at the end of each accounting period. Where the circumstances which originally justified the decision to defer no longer apply, or are considered doubtful, that proportion of the expenditure which is considered to be irrecoverable should be written off immediately project by project.

Disclosure in accounts

The accounting policy followed should be clearly stated and explained.

The *total* amount of R&D expenditure charged in the profit and loss account should be disclosed, analysed between the current year's expenditure and amounts amortised from deferred expenditure.†

Deferred development expenditure should be separately disclosed, with movements in the period and the balances at the start and end of the period being shown.

Exceptions

Apart from the exception relating to 'mineral deposits' mentioned earlier, the only other exception relates to companies which enter into firm contracts to carry out development work for third parties on such terms that the related expenditure is to be fully reimbursed, or to develop and manufacture at an agreed price which has been calculated to reimburse expenditure on development as well as manufacture. In such cases, any such expenditure not reimbursed at the balance sheet date should be included in *work in progress*.

Summary of SSAP 13

A summary of SSAP 13 is provided in Figure 4.1.

Criticism of SSAP 13

In January 1996, The ASB rejected calls from a leading UK software house, Coda plc, that more guidance should be given as to how software developers should account for R&D costs. At present, several companies capitalise development costs, while others write them off. In Coda's case, it had to write off £6.3m against its 1995 profits.

---

† Does not apply to a company which is not a plc, a 'special category company' (as defined in the Companies Act 1985) or a holding company with a plc or special category company as a subsidiary, and satisfies the CA 85 criteria (multiplied by 10) for definition as a middle-sized company.

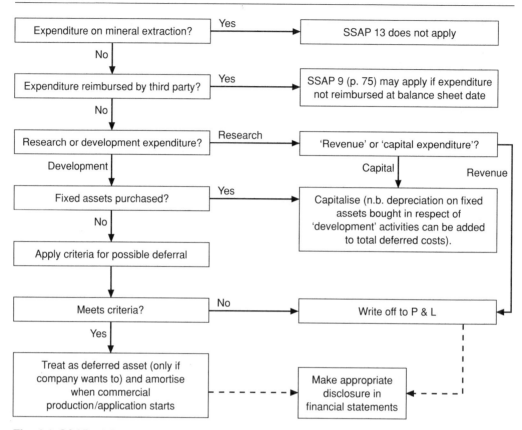

Fig. 4.1 SSAP 13 Research and development

SSAP 21 ACCOUNTING FOR LEASES AND HIRE PURCHASE CONTRACTS

(Issued August 1984, amended February 1997)

Leases and hire purchase contracts are means by which companies obtain the right to use or purchase assets. In the case of leasing, the ownership of the asset remains with the *lessor* (i.e. the original purchaser of the asset) and never passes to the *lessee* (i.e. the 'user' of the asset). With hire purchase contracts, however, the hirer of the asset may exercise an option to purchase the asset after certain conditions contained within the agreement have been met (e.g. the payment of an agreed number of instalments).

Until the implementation of this standard, companies which leased the majority of their equipment, vehicles, etc., did not show such items on their balance sheets. Only the rental payments were disclosed in the profit and loss account. This treatment was felt to be misleading to users of the financial statements, and SSAP 21 requires a company to include certain leased assets in its balance sheet, despite the fact that the company does not enjoy legal ownership of those assets (*see also* FRS 5, p. 142).

The standard accounting practice is the same for both hire purchase and leasing contracts, and in the following text the word 'lease' is used to describe both types of transaction.

Operating lease or finance lease?

The accounting treatment depends upon the classification of the leases between those which are 'operating leases' and those which are 'finance leases'. The explanatory note to the standard gives the following definitions.

An operating lease involves the lessee paying a rental for the hire of an asset for a period of time which is normally substantially less than its useful economic life. The lessor retains most of the risks and rewards of ownership of an asset in the case of an operating lease.

A finance lease usually involves payment by a lessee to a lessor of the full cost of the asset together with a return on the finance provided by the lessor. The lessee has substantially all the risks and rewards associated with the ownership of an asset*, other than its legal title.

In practice all leases transfer some of the risks and rewards of ownership to the lessee, and the distinction between a finance lease and an operating lease is essentially one of degree.

Lessee's books

The standard requires that a *finance lease* be capitalised (i.e. shown as a fixed asset under the subheading 'leased assets') in the lessee's accounts, despite the fact that the lessee is not the legal owner of the asset. This treatment recognises that, on occasions, the *substance* of a transaction should take precedence over its *legal form*, to ensure that the financial statements show as fair a picture as possible for the user. The explanatory note to the standard argues that it is not the asset itself, but the lessee's *rights in the asset* which are being capitalised. Note that, in addition to capitalising the asset, the obligation of the lessee to make future payments will be shown as a liability.

Rentals payable should be apportioned between the finance charge and a reduction of the outstanding obligation for future amounts payable. The finance charge is then apportioned to accounting periods so as to produce a constant

---

* The standard states that it should be presumed that such a transfer of risks and rewards occurs if at the inception of a lease the present value of the minimum lease payments, including any initial payment, amounts to substantially all (normally 90 per cent or more) of the fair value of the leased asset. The present value should be calculated using the interest implicit in the lease. If the fair value of the asset is not determinable, an estimate should be used.

periodic rate of charge on the remaining balance of the obligation for each accounting period (or a reasonable approximation thereof).

With an *operating lease* the lessee need only show the rental as an expense in the profit and loss account, charged usually on a straight line basis over the lease term.

Lessor's books

The accounting treatment in the lessor's books is, in essence, the opposite of that applied to the lessee, with the amounts due from hiring out assets under *finance leases* being shown under 'debtors', the assets themselves being excluded from the fixed assets section of the balance sheet. Assets hired out under *operating leases* are capitalised, with rental income (excluding any service charges, e.g. for insurance and maintenance) being credited to profit and loss account.

Any initial direct costs incurred by a lessor in arranging a lease may be apportioned over the period of the lease on a systematic and rational basis.

Note that disclosure should be made of the accounting policies adopted for operating and finance leases in the financial statements of both the lessees and the lessors.

Exceptions

a) A manufacturer or dealer lessor (i.e. where leasing is used as a means of marketing products, which may involve leasing a product to one customer or to several customers) should not recognise a selling profit under an operating lease. The selling profit under a finance lease should be restricted to the excess of the fair value of the asset over the manufacturer's or dealer's costs less any grants receivable by them towards the purchase, construction or use of the asset.

b) Any profit or loss arising from a *sale and leaseback* transaction which results in a finance lease should be deferred and amortised in the financial statements of the seller/lessee over the shorter of the lease term and the useful life of the asset.

If the leaseback is an operating lease, any profit or loss should be recognised immediately, provided it is clear that the transaction is established at fair value. The standard contains provisions dealing with the situation where the price is above or below 'fair value'.

Definitions

Part two of the standard contains 17 definitions of various terms relevant to hire purchase and leasing transactions. Some, including the basic definitions of operating and finance leases, have already been referred to, but the others are of some complexity and are outside the scope of this book.

Summary of SSAP 21

Accounting by lessees (main provisions only)

A summary of the main provisions of SSAP 21 relating to accounting by lessees is provided in Figure 4.2.

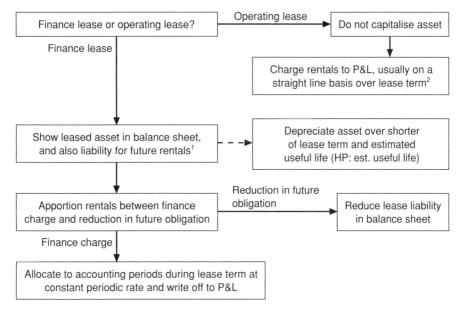

Notes:
1. To be divided between those payable in the next year, and amounts payable in the 2nd to 5th years inclusive from the balance sheet date.
2. Analysed between amounts payable in respect of hire of plant and machinery, and in respect of other operating leases.

Fig. 4.2 SSAP 21 Accounting by lessees (main provisions)

Accounting by lessors (main provisions only)

A summary of the main provisions of SSAP 21 relating to accounting by lessors is provided in Figure 4.3.

Current position of SSAP 21

In December 1999 the Accounting Standards Board issued a discussion paper on lease accounting entitled '*Leases: Implementation of a New Approach*'. This proposes removing the distinction between finance and operating leases. For lessees, this would require the recognition of a liability for non-cancellable

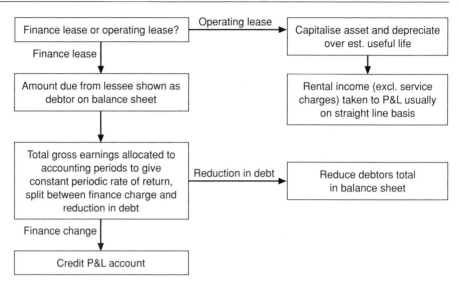

Fig. 4.3 SSAP 21 Accounting by lessors (main provisions)

lease payments, together with a corresponding asset. The proposals could have a dramatic effect on lessees' balance sheets – for example, it has been suggested that British Airways' debts would increase by 30%, and that UK car fleet companies such as Lex Vehicle Leasing may have to add £18bn of lease liabilities onto their balance sheets (currently omitted due to their being classified as operating leases). The proposals are currently under discussion.

FRS 10 GOODWILL AND INTANGIBLE ASSETS
(Issued December 1997)

Objectives

The standard has two objectives:

1. to ensure that capitalised goodwill and intangible assets are charged in the profit and loss account in the periods in which they are depleted; and
2. to ensure that sufficient information is disclosed in the financial statements to enable users to determine the impact of goodwill and intangible assets on the financial position and performance of the reporting entity.

Recognition within financial statements

1. Positive purchased goodwill should be capitalised and classified as an asset on the balance sheet.
2. Internally generated goodwill should not be capitalised.

3. Intangible assets purchased separately from a business should be capitalised as assets.

4. Intangible assets acquired as part of the acquisition of a business should be capitalised separately from goodwill if the value of goodwill cannot be measured reliably on initial recognition. If its value cannot be measured reliably, it should be subsumed within the amount of the purchase price attributed to goodwill.

5. Internally developed intangible assets should be capitalised only where they have a readily ascertainable market value.

Key definitions (1)

Purchased goodwill: the difference between the cost of an acquired entity and the aggregate of the fair values of the entity's identifiable assets and liabilities.
Positive goodwill arises when:

Acquisition cost > Aggregate fair values of the identifiable assets and liabilities

Negative goodwill arises when:

Aggregate fair values of the identifiable assets and liabilities > Acquisition cost

Intangible assets: non-financial fixed assets that do not have physical substance but are identifiable and are controlled by the entity through custody or legal rights. An identifiable asset is one that can be disposed of separately without disposing of a business of the entity.

Readily ascertainable market value: the value of an intangible asset that is established by reference to a market where:

a) the asset belongs to a homogenous population of assets that are equivalent in all material respects, and

b) an active market, evidenced by frequent transactions, exists for that population of assets.

(Examples of intangible assets meeting these conditions include certain operating licences, franchises and quotas. Brands, publishing titles, patented drugs and engineering design patents are unique in nature so do not have a readily ascertainable market value.)

Amortisation of positive goodwill and intangible assets

Where goodwill and intangible assets are regarded as *having limited useful economic lives*, they should be amortised on a systematic basis over those lives. (The straight line method is usually chosen.)

If they are regarded as having *indefinite useful economic lives*, they should not be amortised. There is a rebuttable presumption that the useful economic lives of purchased goodwill and intangible assets are limited to periods of 20 years or less. The presumption may be rebutted where:

a) the durability of the acquired business or intangible asset can be demonstrated and justifies estimating the useful economic life to exceed 20 years; and

b) the goodwill or intangible asset is capable of continued measurement (so that annual impairment reviews will be feasible).

Useful economic lives should be reviewed at the end of each reporting period and revised if necessary.

In amortising an intangible asset (other than goodwill) a residual value can be assigned to that asset only if such residual value can be measured reliably.

Key definitions (2)

Useful economic life: the period over which the entity expects to derive economic benefit from that asset. The useful economic life of purchased goodwill is the period over which the value of the underlying business acquired is expected to exceed the values of its identifiable net assets.

Impairment: a reduction in the recoverable amount of a fixed asset or goodwill below its carrying value.

Residual value: the net realisable value at the end of its useful economic life.

Impairment

Amortisation period not exceeding 20 years

Goodwill and intangible assets should be reviewed for impairment at the end of the first full financial year following the acquisition and in other periods if events or changes in circumstances indicate that the carrying values may not be recoverable.

Amortisation period exceeding 20 years or no amortisation

Goodwill and intangible assets should be reviewed for impairment at the end of each reporting period.

After the first period, the reviews need only be updated. *See* FRS 11, p. 66 for a detailed review of the standard on impairment of fixed assets and goodwill.

If an impairment loss is recognised, the revised carrying value, if being amortised, should be amortised over the current estimate of the remaining useful economic life.

Revaluation

Where one or more capitalised intangible assets of the same class have a readily ascertainable market value, they can be revalued to market value, with further revaluations taking place sufficiently often to ensure that the carrying value does not differ materially from the market value at the balance sheet date.

Where an impairment loss is subsequently reversed due to events unforeseen when making the impairment calculations, and the reversal takes the recoverable amount above its current carrying value, it should be recognised in the current period.

Negative goodwill

After testing the values of acquired assets for impairment and ensuring that no acquired liabilities have been omitted or understated, negative goodwill should be disclosed on the balance sheet immediately below the goodwill heading, with a sub-total showing the net amount of positive and negative goodwill.

Disclosures

The financial statements should describe:

1. the method used to value intangible assets;
2. separately for positive goodwill, negative goodwill and each class of intangible asset capitalised on the balance sheet date:
   a) the cost or revalued amount at the start and end of the financial period;
   b) the cumulative amount of provisions for amortisation or impairment at the start and end of the financial period;
   c) a reconciliation of the movements, separately disclosing additions, disposals, revaluations, transfers, amortisation, impairment losses, reversals of past impairment losses and amounts of negative goodwill written back in the financial period; and
   d) the net carrying amount at the balance sheet date;
3. the profit or loss on each material disposal of a previously acquired business or business segment;
4. the methods and periods of amortisation and the reasons for choosing them;
5. reasons and effect of changing amortisation methods;
6. justification for exceeding a 20-year life;
7. reasons for not amortising goodwill;
8. where a class of assets has been revalued, the value, the year and basis of valuation and the original cost or fair value and the amortisation which would have been charged if the assets had been valued at their original cost or fair value;
9. if any asset has been revalued during the year, the name and qualification of the valuer;
10. the periods over which negative goodwill is being written back in the profit and loss account;
11. where negative goodwill exceeds the fair values of the non-monetary assets, the amount and source of the excess negative goodwill and the period over which it is being written back.

Summary of FRS 10

A summary of FRS 10 is provided in Figure 4.4.

FRS 11 IMPAIRMENT OF FIXED ASSETS AND GOODWILL
(Issued July 1998)

Objectives

The standard's objectives are to ensure that:

1. fixed assets and goodwill are recorded in the financial statements at no more than their recoverable amount;

2. any resulting impairment loss is measured and recognised on a consistent basis; and

3. sufficient information is disclosed in the financial statements to enable users to understand the impact of the impairment on the financial position and performance of the reporting entity.

Investment properties (*see* SSAP 19, p. 47) are not covered by the requirements of the standard.

Key definitions (1)

Impairment: a reduction in the recoverable amount of a fixed asset or goodwill below its carrying amount.

Recoverable amount: the higher of net realisable value and value in use.

Net realisable value: the amount at which an asset could be disposed of, less any direct selling costs.

Value in use: the present value of the future cash flows obtainable as a result of an asset's continued use, including those resulting from its ultimate disposal.

(*Note*: The standard allows a group of assets ('income generating units') to be considered for identification of material impairment, rather than individual assets, where appropriate.)

Indications of impairment

An impairment review of a fixed asset or goodwill is undertaken if events or changes in circumstances indicate that the carrying amount of the asset may not be recoverable. Examples of events or changes in circumstances that indicate an impairment include:

1. operating losses;

2. net cash outflows;

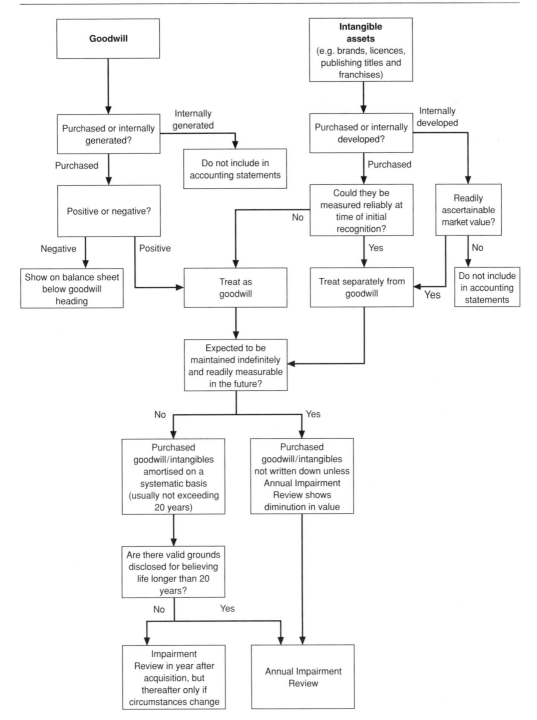

Fig. 4.4 Accounting for goodwill and intangible assets

3. significant decline in a fixed asset's market value during the period;

4. evidence of obsolescence or physical damage to the fixed asset;

5. significant adverse changes, e.g. major new competitor, harsher statutory or regulatory environment, decline in an 'indicator of value' such as turnover used to measure the fair value of a fixed asset on acquisition;

6. major loss of key employees;

7. significant increase in interest rates likely to affect the fixed asset's recoverable amount.

Even if fixed assets and goodwill are not considered impaired following a review triggered by any of the above events or changes in circumstances, their remaining useful economic lives and residual values may have changed.

There is no requirement for an impairment review if no such events or changes in circumstances have been identified. The standard states that 'For tangible fixed assets, impairments will therefore be a relatively infrequent addition to depreciation'.

Measurement of impairment losses

The impairment review should comprise a comparison of the carrying amount of the fixed asset or goodwill with its recoverable amount (the higher of net realisable value and value in use).

If: Carrying amount > Recoverable amount

Fixed asset or Goodwill is impaired and should be written down to recoverable amount.

If: Net realisable value or Value in use > Carrying amount

Fixed asset or Goodwill is not impaired.

Recognition of impairment losses

The impairment loss should be recognised in the profit and loss account (unless it arises on a previously revalued fixed asset – *see below*), and the remaining useful economic life and residual value reviewed and revised where necessary. The revised carrying amount should be depreciated over the revised estimate of the remaining useful economic life.

Reversal of past impairments

Tangible fixed assets and investments in subsidiaries, associates and joint ventures

A reversal in a past impairment should be recognised in the profit and loss account of the current period (unless it arises on a previously revalued fixed asset – *see below*). This is to the extent that it increases the carrying amount of the fixed asset up to the amount that it would have been if the original impairment had not occurred.

Increases in recoverable value could be indicated by the reverse of the 'indications of impairment' listed above.

Goodwill and intangible assets

A reversal in a past impairment should be recognised in the current period, if and only if:

1. an external event which caused the impairment loss is clearly and demostrably reversed in a way that was not foreseen in the original impairment calculations;

2. the impairment loss arose on an intangible asset with a readily ascertainable market value (*see* FRS 10, p. 62) and the net realisable value based on that market value has increased above the intangible asset's impaired carrying value.

The reversal of the impairment should be recognised to the extent that it increases the carrying amount of the goodwill or intangible asset up to the amount that it would have been if the original impairment had not occurred.

Revalued fixed assets

If an impairment loss on a revalued fixed asset has been caused by a clear consumption of economic benefits, it should be recognised in the profit and loss account. Other impairments of revalued fixed assets should be recognised in the statement of total recognised gains and losses (*see* FRS 3, p. 120) until the carrying amount of the asset reaches its depreciated historical cost and thereafter in the profit and loss account.

A reversal of an impairment loss should be recognised in the profit and loss account to the extent that the original impairment loss (adjusted for subsequent depreciation) was recognised in the profit and loss account. Any remaining balance of the reversal of an impairment should be recognised in the statement of total recognised gains and losses.

Disclosure

Impairment losses should be disclosed as follows:

1. If recognised in the profit and loss account, include within operating profit under the appropriate statutory heading, and disclose as an exceptional item if appropriate.

2. If recognised in the statement of total recognised gains and losses, disclose separately on the face of the statement.

APPLICATION IN PRACTICE

Figure 4.5 provides extracts from the accounts of a number of plcs showing their treatment of research and development, leased assets and goodwill.

Fig. 4.5 Extracts from selected accounts showing treatment of R&D, leased assets and goodwill

Oxford Instruments plc: Research and development and grants

Research and development expenditure, net of the relevant proportion of grants receivable, is charged to the profit and loss account in the year in which it is incurred, unless it is recoverable under a customer contract when it is carried forward as work in progress at the lower of cost and net realisable value.

J Sainsbury plc: Leased assets

Leased assets

Assets used by the Group which have been funded through finance leases are capitalised and the resulting lease obligations are included in creditors net of finance charges. Interest costs on finance leases are charged direct to the profit and loss account. Rentals under operating leases are charged on a straight line basis up to the date of the next rental review.

Tate & Lyle plc: Financial commitments

Financial Commitments

The Group leases railway wagons, vehicles, plant and equipment and office buildings through non-cancellable operating leases. Certain of these leases contain escalation clauses, renewal options and purchase options.

	2000 Group £ million	1998 Group £ million	2000 Tate & Lyle PLC £ million	1998 Tate & Lyle PLC £ million
(a) Commitments under operating leases to pay rentals for the next year				
Annual commitments in respect of plant and machinery operating leases which expire:				
– within one year	2	3	–	–
– between second and fifth years	7	12	–	–
– over five years	12	10	–	–
	21	25	–	–
Annual commitments in respect of land and building operating leases which expire:				
– within one year	–	–	–	–
– between second and fifth years	1	1	–	–
– over five years	3	4	2	1
	4	5	2	1
(b) Commitments under operating leases to pay rentals in future years				
within one year	25	30		
in second year	22	24		
in third year	21	19		
in fourth year	19	17		
in fifth year	17	14		
more than five years	119	81		
	223	185		

Fig. 4.5 continued

Pace Micro Technology plc: Goodwill

Acquisitions

On 3rd June 1999, the assets and liabilities of the multi media terminals division of Acorn Group PLC were acquired for £209,000. No goodwill arose on the purchase.

On 7 March 2000, the whole of the issued share capital of Vegastream Limited was acquired. The initial consideration totalled £19,847,000 and deferred consideration has been estimated at £4,593,000. Total consideration is capped at £40,000,000. Goodwill of £23,976,000 is estimated to have arisen on the acquisition, of which £300,000 has been amortised in the current year. The goodwill is being amortised over a period of 20 years, being the estimated economic useful life. The Group results include a post-acquisition loss of £151,000.

The following table explains the adjustments made to the book value of the assets and liabilities acquired to arrive at fair values included in the consolidated financial statements at the date of acquisition. The cash flow effects of the acquisition are stated in note 27.

	Book Amount £000	Revaluation £000	Alignment of Accounting Policies £000	Fair Value to the Group £000
Intangible fixed assets	133	–	(133)	0
Tangible fixed assets	529	–	–	529
Current assets	1,985	(66)	–	1,919
Creditors and provisions	(1,760)	(14)	–	(1,774)
	887	(80)	(133)	674
Goodwill				23,976
				24,650

Satisfied by:	
Cash	352
Issue of ordinary share capital	19,705
Deferred contingent issue of ordinary share capital	4,593
	24,650

It has been necessary to revalue certain of the assets and liabilities acquired to recognise a potential shortfall in their realisable value. Furthermore it is the accounting policy of the Group to expense the cost of licences as incurred, not to capitalise as an intangible fixed asset.

CHAPTER SUMMARY

SSAP 13 Accounting for Research and Development

- Research always written off to profit and loss account, unless relating to fixed assets which would be capitalised.
- Development expenditure must meet 'DECORATE' criteria (see p. 56) to be carried forward as deferred asset – otherwise write off.

- Entity can choose whether to treat development expenditure as a deferred asset or to write it off.

- Amortise when commercial production starts.

SSAP 21 Accounting for Leases and Hire Purchase Contracts

- Treatment depends on whether operating or finance lease.

- Operating lease: period of time substantially less than useful economic life, lessor retains most risk and rewards.

- Finance lease: lessee pays full cost to lessor, plus finance charge. Lessee has most risk and rewards.

- Operating lease – lessee's books: rentals charged to profit and loss account. Lessor's books: asset capitalised and depreciated, rental income shown in profit and loss account.

- Finance lease – lessee's books: asset capitalised and depreciated. Liability to lessor also shown. Lessor's books: debtor (due from lessee) shown as asset, gradually reducing over lease life. Profit and loss account shows finance charge.

FRS 10 Goodwill and Intangible Assets

- Internally generated goodwill not included in accounting statements.

- Positive purchased goodwill amortised if not expected to be maintained indefinitely – usually not exceeding 20 years.

- No amortisation if goodwill is expected to be maintained indefinitely.

- Annual impairment review for non-amortised goodwill, otherwise only in year after acquisition.

FRS 11 Impairment of Fixed Assets and Goodwill

- Impairment = reduction in the recoverable amount of a fixed asset or goodwill below its carrying amount.

- Various reasons for potential impairment, e.g. losses, cash outflows, obsolescence, damage to asset, etc.

- Impairment losses (and reversals of impairments) recognised in profit and loss account in the majority of cases.

DISCUSSION QUESTIONS

1. Most companies engaged in research and development will write off R&D expenditure, regardless of whether it meets the SSAP 13 criteria. Why is this?

2. The distinction between operating and finance leases is arbitrary and should be abandoned. Discuss.

3. Internally generated goodwill cannot appear on a company balance sheet. This gives rise to huge anomalies when comparisons are made between old established, profitable businesses that have grown organically, and companies which have grown big by takeovers. Discuss.

(*See Appendix 3* for outline responses.)

EXAMINATION QUESTIONS

1. In connection with SSAP 13 *Accounting for research and development*:

a) Define applied research and development.

(4 marks)

b) Why is it considered necessary to distinguish between applied research and development expenditure and how does this distinction affect the accounting treatment?

(8 marks)

c) State whether the following items are included within the SSAP 13 definition of research and development, and give your reasons.

i)   Market research

(2 marks)

ii) Testing of pre-production prototypes

(2 marks)

iii) Operational research

(2 marks)

iv) Testing in search of process alternatives

(2 marks)

ACCA

2. In connection with SSAP 21 *Accounting for leases and hire purchase contracts*:

a) What is the distinction between a finance lease and an operating lease? Why is this distinction important in financial reporting?

(8 marks)

b) You have been shown, by a non-financial director, this extract from a company's disclosure of accounting policies.

'Amounts receivable under finance leases are included in debtors at the amount of the net investment. Income from finance leases is credited to the profit and loss account using an actuarial method to give a constant periodic return on the net cash investment. The income includes amounts in respect of government grants grossed up at the average rate of corporation tax applicable to the lease period.'

You are required to explain to the director the meaning of the policy.

(12 marks)

ACCA

3. In relation to SSAP 21 *Accounting for leases and hire purchase payments*:

a) What is the difference between a finance lease and an operating lease?

(10 marks)

b) In preparing both the balance sheet and the profit and loss account of a finance company (the lessor) how should you treat

i) an asset subject to a finance lease?

(6 marks)

ii) an asset subject to an operating lease?

(4 marks)

ACCA

4. a) Define *purchased goodwill*.

(8 marks)

b) Explain the circumstances where positive goodwill and intangible assets would or would not be amortised.

(12 marks)

(*See Appendix 4* for suggested answers.)

Chapter 5

Asset valuation (3): SSAP 9

Stocks and long-term contracts

INTRODUCTION

Stock often represents a material amount in a business's balance sheet, over- or under-valuation resulting in distortions occurring in reported profit levels and net asset totals, whilst taxation may be under- or overpaid. In addition, an error in one year's stock figure has a 'knock-on' effect, in that the results of the succeeding year will also be distorted.

Public limited companies must appoint a *qualified* auditor, whose job it is, *inter alia*, to report whether the company's accounts show a *true and fair view*. One of the major problems which auditors have is that of ensuring that the stock figure is reasonable. It is normal practice for them to attend the stocktaking to confirm that the physical quantities of stock have been correctly recorded, but this can, on occasions, be a highly specialised and even dangerous operation (The author has unpleasant memories of scaling the outside of a 100 metre high grain silo to perform part of a stock audit!).

Once the quantities have been audited, the next stage will be to confirm the valuations. The auditors will check them to ensure compliance with SSAP 9, and have the option of 'qualifying' their report on the accounts (i.e. drawing attention to specific problems) if they are dissatisfied with the way in which the valuations have been made.

SSAP 9 STOCKS AND LONG-TERM CONTRACTS
(Issued May 1975, revised September 1988)

Stocks comprise:

a) goods or other assets purchased for resale;

b) consumable stores;

c) raw materials and components purchased for incorporation into products for sale;

d) products and services in intermediate stages of completion;

e) long-term contract balances; and

f) finished goods.

The fundamental concept underlying the need to arrive at a stock valuation is the *matching* of cost and revenue in the *year in which the revenue arises* rather than the *year in which the cost is incurred*. If the revenue anticipated to arise (i.e. the net realisable value) is expected to be less than the cost incurred (e.g. due to obsolescence, deterioration or change in demand) then the irrecoverable cost should be written off to revenue in the year under review.

Stock is to be stated at the total of the lower of cost and net realisable value of the separable items of stock or of groups of similar items.

Although we shall be considering in due course the detailed ways in which 'cost' is determined, it is useful at this stage to consider the following basic definitions.

Cost: '. . . that expenditure which has been incurred in the normal course of business in bringing the product or service to its present location and condition . . .'

Net realisable value: '. . . the estimated proceeds from the sale of items of stock less all further costs to completion and less all costs to be incurred in marketing, selling and distributing directly related to the items in question.'

The principal situations in which net realisable value is likely to be less than cost are where there has been:

a) an increase in costs or a fall in selling price;

b) physical deterioration of stocks;

c) obsolescence of products;

d) a decision as part of a company's marketing strategy to manufacture and sell products at a loss;

e) errors in production or purchasing.

Furthermore, when stocks are held which are unlikely to be sold within the turnover period normal in that company (i.e. excess stocks), the impending delay in realisation increases the risk that the situations outlined in (a) to (c) above may occur before the stocks are sold and needs to be taken into account in assessing net realisable value.

The comparison of cost and net realisable value needs to be made in respect of *each item of stock separately*. Where this is impossible, groups or categories of stock items which are similar (referred to as *fungible assets* by the Companies Act) will need to be taken together. If this were not the case, then material distortions could arise in the overall valuation as the following example shows.

Stock group	Cost £	Net realisable value £
A	50,000	90,000
B (damaged)	65,000	34,000
C	70,000	120,000
D (obsolete)	28,000	10,000
	213,000	254,000

If the 'lower of cost and net realisable value' rule were applied to the *total* stock, then this would give rise to a total of £213,000. However, this represents an overvaluation of £49,000 when we consider the results of applying the rule to the *individual* stock groups:

	£
A	50,000
B	34,000
C	70,000
D	10,000
	164,000

What is cost?

Although *net realisable value* is a relatively simple concept to grasp, the *cost* of stock is rather more complicated. The price paid for the asset *might* be easily ascertained, e.g. from a purchase invoice. However, in many cases, the price paid cannot be matched to actual goods, perhaps due to the physical nature of the stock. For example, petrol might be delivered to a garage on fifty separate occasions and at fifty separate prices during an accounting year. The stock of petrol at the end of the year may be 'cheap' petrol, 'expensive' petrol, or, more likely, a mixture of prices. No amount of expertise could determine this by a physical stock inspection, so *theoretical* pricing models have been created for this purpose (e.g. FIFO, AVCO, etc.) which are looked at later in the chapter.

The principle to be adopted is that the methods used in allocating costs to stock need to be selected with a view to providing the *fairest possible approximation to the expenditure actually incurred in bringing the product to its present location and condition.*

The explanatory note to the standard gives as an example, the case of retail stores holding a large number of rapidly changing individual items, where stocks on the shelves have often been stated at current selling prices less the normal gross profit margin. In *these particular circumstances* this may be acceptable as being the only practical method of arriving at a figure which approximates to cost.

In addition to the problem of determining the price paid for the stock, there is the added complication of determining any other relevant 'expenditure actually incurred in bringing the product to its present location and condition'. The standard recognises that the majority of problems arising in practice in determining both the cost and the net realisable value result from considerations which are relevant to *particular* businesses, and are 'not of such universal application that they can be the subject of a statement of standard accounting practice'. Because of this, Appendix 1 to the standard sets out general guidelines as to the particular areas of difficulty (*see* 'Practical difficulties' *below*).

To put these difficulties into context, the *full* definitions of key phrases used by the standard in connection with stocks are given below, while Figure 5.1 provides a summary of the components of cost.

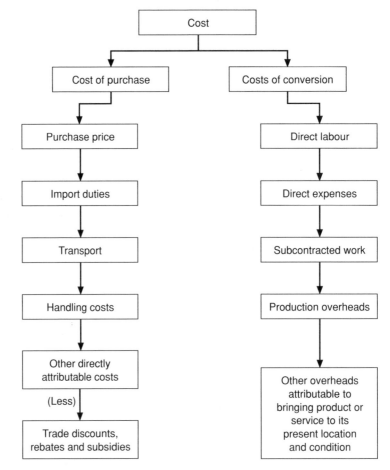

Fig. 5.1 Components of cost

Definitions

Cost is defined in relation to the different categories of stocks as being that expenditure which has been incurred in the normal course of business in bringing the product or service to its present location and condition. This expenditure should include, in addition to *cost of purchase*, such *costs of conversion* as are appropriate to that location or condition.

Cost of purchase comprises purchase price including import duties, transport and handling costs and any other directly attributable costs, less trade discounts, rebates and subsidies.

Cost of conversion comprises:

a) costs which are specifically attributable to units of production, e.g. direct labour, direct expenses and subcontracted work;

b) production overheads;

c) other overheads, if any, attributable in the particular circumstances of the business to bringing the product or service to its present location and condition.

Production overheads are those overheads incurred in respect of materials, labour or services for production, based on the normal level of activity, taking one year with another. For this purpose each overhead should be classified according to function (e.g. production, selling or administration) so as to ensure the inclusion, in cost of conversion, of those overheads (including depreciation) which relate to production, notwithstanding that these may accrue wholly or partly on a time basis.

Net realisable value is calculated as the actual or estimated selling price (net of trade but before settlement discounts) less:

a) all further costs to completion; and

b) all costs to be incurred in marketing, selling and distributing.

Practical difficulties

The allocation of overheads

The allocation of overheads included in the valuation of stocks needs to be based on the company's *normal* level of activity taking one year with another. *Normality* is determined by reference to such factors as:

a) the volume of production which the production facilities are intended by their designers and by management to produce under prevailing working conditions; and

b) the budgeted and actual levels of activity for the year under review and the ensuing year.

The definition of cost given earlier includes the words 'incurred in the normal course of business' when referring to the circumstances in which expenditure can be included in the valuation. The corollary of this is that all *abnormal* conversion costs need to be excluded.

The costing methods adopted by a business are usually designed to ensure that all *direct* costs (materials, labour and direct expenses) are identified and charged on a reasonable and consistent basis. Problems arise regarding certain overheads which require the exercise of subjective judgement as to their allocation.

Specific costs referred to in Appendix 1 of the standard are as follows:

Cost	Include in stock valuation?
Exceptional spoilage	No (abnormal)
Idle capacity	No (abnormal)
Design, marketing and selling costs incurred before manufacture	Yes (if firm sales contract)
Costs of general management (larger organisations)	No (not directly related to production)
Costs of general management (small organisation where management involved in daily admin. of the various functions)	Yes (if part of cost can be allocated to production function)
Central service departments (e.g. accounting)	Yes (but only those costs related to production function)
Marginal costs in management accounts	Yes (but add appropriate proportion of those production overheads not already included in the marginal cost)

Methods of costing

The difficulties of relating prices to stock items have been mentioned earlier, and Appendix 1 to the standard, whilst not explicitly favouring any one valuation method, does require management to:

'. . . exercise judgement to ensure that the methods chosen provide the fairest practicable approximation to cost'.

Appendix 2 to the standard contains a glossary of terms which includes seven stock valuation methods. The following is a summary of them, together with a comment regarding their 'acceptability' for the purposes of SSAP 9.

Method	Acceptable?
Unit Cost: The cost of purchasing or manufacturing identifiable units of stock.	Yes
Average Cost: Using an average price computed by dividing the total cost of units by the total number of such units.	Yes
FIFO (First In First Out): Using the assumption that the stock on hand represents the latest purchases or production.	Yes

LIFO (Last In First Out):
Using the assumption that the stock on hand represents the earliest purchases or production.

No, as costs are unlikely to bear a reasonable relationship to actual costs obtaining during the period.

Base Stock:
Ascribing a fixed unit value to a predetermined number of units in stock, any excess over this number being valued on the basis of some other method.

No, for the same reasons as given for LIFO.

Replacement Cost:
The cost at which an identical asset could be purchased or manufactured.

No, except in certain circumstances, e.g. materials, where the price has fluctuated considerably and which have not become subject to firm sales contracts by the time the financial statements are prepared.

Standard Cost:
Using predetermined costs calculated from management's estimates of expected levels of costs.

Yes, provided that the standard costs are reviewed frequently to ensure that they bear a reasonable relationship to actual costs.

In addition, two other methods are referred to in Appendix 1 of the Standard:

Selling price less estimated profit margin:
Sales prices of stock on hand, less the expected gross profit %.

No, unless it can be demonstrated that it gives a reasonable approximation of actual cost.

Latest purchase price:
Applying latest purchase price to the total units in stock.

No, as it is not necessarily the same as actual costs and, in times of rising prices, will result in the taking of a profit which has not been realised.

Long-term contracts

The definition of a long-term contract given in the standard is:

'A contract entered into for the design, manufacture or construction of a single substantial asset or the provision of a service (or of a combination of assets or services, which together constitute a single project), where the time taken substantially to complete the contract is such that the contract activity falls into different accounting periods. A contract that is required to be accounted for as long-term by this accounting standard will usually extend for a period exceeding one year. However, a duration exceeding one year is not an essential feature of a long-term contract. Some contracts with a shorter duration than one year should be accounted for as long-term contracts if they are sufficiently material to the activity of the period that not to record turnover and attributable profit would lead to a distortion of the period's turnover and results such that the financial statements would not give a true and fair view, provided that the policy is applied consistently within the reporting entity and from year to year.'

Where a company has contracts which come under the definition given above, and their outcome can be assessed with 'reasonable certainty before their conclusion', the standard allows it to record a proportion of turnover and profit arising while the contracts are in progress. Otherwise, the profit and loss account is likely to reflect the results of only those contracts *completed* in the year, rather than those on which the company has been actively working during the period.

The profit, to be calculated on a prudent basis, needs to reflect the proportion of the work carried out at the accounting date and to take into account any known inequalities of profitability in the various stages of the contract.

An appropriate proportion of total contract value is brought into the profit and loss account as *turnover* as the contract activity progresses, matched by the costs* incurred in reaching that stage of completion.

If the outcome of the contract is uncertain, then no profit should be taken to profit and loss account, though if no loss is expected it may be appropriate to show as turnover a proportion of the total contract value, using a zero estimate of profit.

If a *loss* is expected, then all the loss should be recognised *as soon as it is foreseen*. The standard gives worked examples of how this can be achieved, which are shown in Figure 5.2. Initially, the foreseeable loss will be deducted from the work-in-progress (WIP) figure of the particular contract, thereby reducing it to net realisable value. Any loss in excess of the WIP figure should be classified either as an accrual within *Creditors* or under *Provisions for liabilities and charges*, depending upon the circumstances. Where unprofitable contracts are of such magnitude that they can be expected to utilise a considerable part of the company's capacity for a substantial period, related administration overheads to be incurred to the completion of these contracts should also be included in the calculation of the provision for losses.

The accounting treatment of long-term contracts can be summarised therefore as follows:

> Long-term contracts should be assessed on a contract by contract basis and reflected in the profit and loss account by recording turnover and related costs as contract activity progresses. Turnover is ascertained in a manner appropriate to the stage of completion of the contract, the business and the industry in which it operates.

> Where it is considered that the outcome of a long-term contract can be assessed with reasonable certainty before its conclusion, the prudently calculated attributable profit should be recognised in the profit and loss account as the difference between the reported turnover and related costs for that contract.

---

* Interest on borrowed money is not normally included as a cost, except where sums borrowed can be identified as financing specific long-term contracts. In such cases a note should be given in the financial statements stating the fact of the inclusion of interest and the amount.

Fig. 5.2 Examples given in SSAP 9 of the treatment of various long-term contracts

	Project Number					Balance Sheet Total	Profit & Loss Account
	1	2	3	4	5		
Recorded as turnover – being value of work done	145	520	380	200	55		1,300
Cumulative payments on account	(100)	(600)	(400)	(150)	(80)		
Classified as amounts recoverable on contracts	45			50		95 DR	
Balance (excess) of payments on account		(80)	(20)		(25)		
Applied as an offset against long-term contract balances – see below.		60	20		15		
Residue classified as payments on account		(20)	–		(10)	(30) CR	
Total costs incurred	110	510	450	250	100		
Transferred to cost of sales	(110)	(450)	(350)	(250)	(55)		(1,215)
	–	60	100	–	45		
Provision/accrual for foreseeable losses charged to cost of sales				(40)	(30)		(70)
		60	100		15		
Classified as provision/accrual for losses				(40)		(40) CR	
Balance (excess) of payments on account applied as offset against long-term contract balances		(60)	(20)		(15)		
Classified as long-term contract balances		–	80		–	80 DR	
Gross profit (or loss) on long-term contracts	35	70	30	(90)	(30)		15

(Author's notes)
As can be seen from the last line of the example, Contracts 1, 2 and 3 are profitable, but Contracts 4 and 5 are showing a loss. The P & L account figures can be summarised as follows:

Contract	1	2	3	4	5
Sales	145	520	380	200	55
Cost of sales	(110)	(450)	(350)	(250)	(55)
Provision for foreseeable losses				(40)	(30)
Gross profit	35	70	30		
Gross loss				(90)	(30)

The balance sheet figures are more complex, but can also be summarised:

Contract	1	2	3	4	5
Cumulative turnover	145	520	380	200	55
Less Cumulative payments on account	(100)	(600)	(400)	(150)	(80)
Included in debtors	45			50	
Excess payments on account		(80)	(20)		(25)

▶

Fig. 5.2 continued

Notes:

Project 1   In this case, all the costs incurred to date relate to the activity recorded as turnover and are transferred to costs of sales, leaving a zero balance in stocks.

Project 2   The excess payments on account of 80 should firstly be offset against any debit balance on this contract included in stocks and then any residual amount (80 − 60 = 20) should be classified under creditors as a payment received on account.

The balance sheet note should disclose separately the net cost of 60 (510 − 450) and the applicable payments on account of 60 [(600 − 520) − 210].

Project 3   The excess payments on account of 20 should be offset against any debit balance on this contract included in stocks. Unlike Project 2, there is no residual amount.

The balance sheet note should disclose separately the net cost of 100 (450 − 350) and the applicable payments on account of 20 (400 − 380).

Project 4   The credit balance of 40 (the provision/accrual for losses) is not offset against the 50 which is included in debtors.

Project 5   The excess payment on account of 25 should firstly be offset against any debit balance on the contract (after deducting foreseeable losses) included in stocks and then a residual amount (25 − 15 = 10) should be classified under creditors as a payment received on account.

The balance sheet note should disclose separately the net cost of 15 [(100 − 55) − 30] and the applicable payments on account of 15 [(80 − 55) − 10].

The standard gives the following definitions of *attributable profit* and *foreseeable losses*:

Attributable profit: that part of the total profit currently estimated to arise over the duration of the contract, after allowing for likely estimated remedial and maintenance costs and increases in costs so far as not recoverable under the terms of the contract, that fairly reflects the profit attributable to that part of the work performed at the accounting date. (There can be no attributable profit until the profitable outcome of the contract can be assessed with reasonable certainty.)

Foreseeable losses: losses which are currently estimated to arise over the duration of the contract (after allowing for estimated remedial and maintenance costs, and increases in costs so far as not recoverable under the terms of the contract). This estimate is required irrespective of:

a) whether or not the work has yet commenced on such contracts;

b) the proportion of work carried out at the accounting date;

c) the amount of profits expected to arise on other contracts.

Summary

Figure 5.3 provides a summary of the accounting treatment of long-term contracts under SSAP 9.

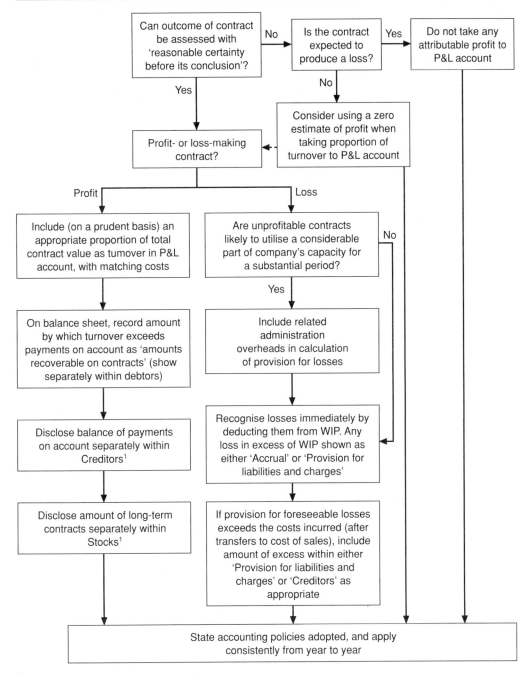

Fig. 5.3 SSAP 9 Long-term contracts

¹ See 'Disclosure' on p. 86 for full details

Worked example

A company has an uncompleted long-term contract at its financial year end. At that date the following figures are relevant.

Appropriate proportion of total contract value recognised in turnover	£3.0m
Total costs incurred on contract	£2.0m
Costs incurred on reaching stage of completion recognised in turnover	£1.8m
Progress payment invoiced to customer	£2.4m

Show the journal entries to record the above, and relevant extracts from the company's published accounts.

Journal

1. Dr Work in progress	£2.0m	
Cr Creditors		£2.0m

Costs incurred on long-term contract.

2. Dr Amounts recoverable on contracts	£3.0m	
Cr Profit and loss account		£3.0m

Appropriate proportion of total contract value reported as turnover for the year.

3. Dr Profit and loss account	£1.8m	
Cr Work-in-progress		£1.8m

Costs incurred in reaching stage of completion recognised in turnover.

4. Dr Debtors	£2.4m	
Cr Amounts recoverable on contracts		£2.4m

Progress payment invoiced to customer.

Extracts from financial statements

Profit and loss account

Turnover	£3.0m
Cost of sales	£1.8m
Gross profit	£1.2m

Balance sheet

Stocks	
Long-term contract balances (£2m − £1.8m)	£0.2m
Debtors	
Amounts recoverable under contracts (£3m − £2.4m)	£0.6m
Debtors	£2.4m
Creditors	£2.0m

DISCLOSURE IN FINANCIAL STATEMENTS

Relevant extracts from accounts of public companies are given below in *Application in practice*, p. 87. The standard requires:

Stocks

1. Accounting policies to be stated and applied consistently within the business and from year to year.

2. To be sub-classified in the balance sheet or in notes to the financial statements so as to indicate the amounts held in each of the main categories in the standard balance sheet formats.

Long-term contracts

1. Accounting policies, in particular the method of ascertaining turnover and attributable profit, to be stated and applied consistently within the business and from year to year.

2. Disclosed in the balance sheet as follows:

   a) the amount by which recorded turnover is in excess of payments on account should be classified as 'amounts recoverable on contracts' and separately disclosed within debtors;

   b) the balance of payments on account (in excess of amounts (i) matched with turnover; and (ii) offset against long-term contract balances) should be classified as payments on account and separately disclosed within creditors;

   c) the amounts of long-term contracts, at costs incurred, net of amounts transferred to cost of sales, after deducting foreseeable losses and payments on account not matched with turnover, should be classified as *long-term contract balances* and separately disclosed within the balance sheet heading *Stocks*; the balance sheet note should disclose separately the balances of:

      i)   net cost less foreseeable losses; and

      ii) applicable payments on account;

   d) the amount by which the provision or accrual for foreseeable losses exceeds the costs incurred (after transfers to cost of sales) should be included within either provisions for liabilities and charges or creditors as appropriate.

APPLICATION IN PRACTICE

Extracts from the accounts of Cammell Laird Holdings plc and Balfour Beatty plc are shown in Figure 5.4.

Fig. 5.4 Extracts from selected accounts showing treatment of stocks and long-term contracts

Cammell Laird Holdings plc

Accounting policies

Long-term contracts
The attributable profit on long-term contracts is recognised once the outcome can be assessed with reasonable certainty. The profit recognised reflects the proportion of work completed to date on the project.

Costs associated with long-term contracts are included in stock to the extent that they cannot be matched with contract work accounted for as turnover. Long-term contract balances included are stated at cost, after provision has been made for any foreseeable losses and the deduction of applicable payments on account.

Full provision is made for losses on all contracts in the year in which the loss is first foreseen.

Stocks
Stocks are stated at the lower of cost and net realisable value.

Balfour Beatty Group plc

Accounting policy

10. Stocks
Stocks and unbilled contract work in progress are valued at the lower of cost and net realisable value. Cost, where appropriate, includes a proportion of manufacturing overheads. Applications for progress payments are deducted from cost, with any excess included in other creditors as advance progress applications.

Note to the accounts

11. Stocks

	Group 2000 £m	Group 1999 £rn	Company 2000 £m	Company 1999 £m
Contract work in progress	89	66	–	–
Progress applications	(48)	(44)	–	–
Net contract balances	41	22	–	–
Development land and work in progress	2	5	2	5
Manufacturing work in progress	5	6	–	4
Raw materials and consumables	29	34	–	6
Finished goods and goods for resale	4	14	–	7
	81	81	2	22

CHAPTER SUMMARY

SSAP 9 Stocks and Long-term Contracts

- Stock stated at lower of cost and net realisable value.
- Cost is expenditure incurred in normal course of business in bringing the product or service to its present location and condition.
- LIFO, base stock and replacement stock (except in certain circumstances) are not acceptable valuation methods.
- Long-term contracts: attributable profit can be recognised in the profit and loss account by recording turnover and related costs as contract activity progresses. Foreseeable losses must be recognised immediately.

DISCUSSION QUESTIONS

1. 'SSAP 9 allows companies to bring in a profit before a long-term contract is completed. In most other circumstances, this would be unacceptable and imprudent.' Discuss.

2. 'Many non-UK companies use LIFO to value stocks. With the move to harmonisation of international accounting practices, it is only a matter of time before LIFO is acceptable in the UK.' Discuss.

(*See Appendix 3* for outline responses.)

EXAMINATION QUESTIONS

1. a) 'Both cost and net realisable value must be calculated for the stocks and work in progress at the balance sheet date and whichever of these gives the lower figure will appear in the accounts.'

   Critically evaluate this statement.

   (13 marks)

   b) Motac Enterprises commenced the manufacture of lockable petrol tank caps on 1 July X1. By 31 December X1 when the half yearly financial reports were prepared, 2000 complete petrol caps and 200 half-finished (as regards materials, labour and factory overheads) petrol caps were produced. No orders from customers had yet been taken. Costs in the six month period were as follows:

	£
Materials consumed	1,650
Labour	2,160
Production overheads	390
Administrative overheads	270
	4,470

   At 31 December X1 it was estimated that the net realisable value of each completed petrol cap was £2.75. At this date, the firm held stocks of raw materials as follows:

	Cost	Net realisable value
	£	£
Material X	1,200	1,370
Material Y	300	240
Material Z	530	680

Required:

Acceptable valuations for:

i)   raw materials;

ii) work in progress; and

iii) finished goods at 31 December X1.

(12 marks)
ICSA

2. Lytax Ltd is a company in the building construction industry. It has three regional offices, North Borders, Midlands and South Downs, which are constituted as separate units for accounting purposes.

On 25 May X3 Lytax Ltd acquired 90% of the ordinary share capital of Ceprem Ltd, a company which manufactures building materials.

Lytax Ltd has since X1 held 15% of the ordinary share capital of Bleco plc. This company carries out specialist research and development activities into building and construction materials, technology and techniques. It then sells the results of these activities to other companies.

Details of long-term contract work undertaken by Lytax Ltd.

At 31 October X3, Lytax Ltd was engaged in various contracts including five long-term contracts, details of which are given below:

	1	2	3	4	5
	£000	£000	£000	£000	£000
Contract price	1,100	950	1,400	1,300	1,200
At 31 October X3:					
Cumulative costs incurred	664	535	810	640	1,070
Estimated further costs to completion	106	75	680	800	165
Estimated cost of post-completion guarantee/rectification work	30	10	45	20	5
Cumulative costs incurred transferred to cost of sales	580	470	646	525	900
Progress payments:					
– cumulative receipts	615	680	615	385	722
– invoiced:					
– awaiting receipt	60	40	25	200	34
– retained by contractee	75	80	60	65	84

It is not expected that any contractees will default on their payments.

Up to 31 October X2, the following amounts had been included in the turnover and cost of sales figures.

	1	2	3	4	5
	£000	£000	£000	£000	£000
Cumulative turnover	560	340	517	400	610
Cumulative costs incurred transferred to cost of sales	460	245	517	400	610
Foreseeable loss transferred to cost of sales	–	–	–	70	–

It is the accounting policy of Lytax Ltd to arrive at contract turnover by adjusting contract cost of sales (including foreseeable losses) by the amount of contract profit or loss to be regarded as recognised, separately for each contract.

Required:

a) Calculate the amounts to be included within the turnover and cost of sales figures of the profit and loss account of Lytax Ltd for the year ended 31 October X3, in respect of the long-term contracts.

b) Prepare extracts from the balance sheet of Lytax Ltd at 31 October X3 incorporating the financial effects of the long-term contracts.

   Your answer should comply with the requirements of SSAP 9 (Revised) (Stocks and Long-Term Contracts) and should include any supporting notes required by that Standard.

   Workings for individual contracts which build up to the total for each item must be shown.

(33 marks)

ACCA

(*See Appendix 4* for suggested answers.)

Chapter 6

Capital instruments and derivatives: FRSs 4 & 13

Capital instruments; Derivatives and other financial instruments: disclosure

INTRODUCTION

These standards are highly specialised, and as such are unlikely to be examinable except at the final stages of the professional examinations. FRS 4 was issued to clamp down on hybrid financial instruments (also known as 'balance sheet gimmicks'!) such as convertible capital bonds which were popular in the 1980s. By various accounting magic tricks, short-term debts could appear to be long-term, or debt capital appear to be part of equity capital. In the words of the ASB's chairman 'The scene at the end of the 1980s was "anything goes".' A brief summary of the FRS 4 is as follows:

1. Capital instruments are to be classified as liabilities if they carry an obligation to transfer cash or other resources.

2. Shareholders' funds are to be analysed between equity and non-equity interests.

3. Convertible debt should be separately disclosed.

4. Minority interests in subsidiaries should be analysed between equity and non-equity interests.

5. Liabilities should be classified as current or non-current according to their contractual maturity dates except where the same lender is committed to refinance the debt on the same terms.

6. Liabilities should be recognised in the balance sheet at the amount received less any issue costs. The finance costs should be allocated to accounting periods so as to achieve a constant rate on the amount outstanding.

In practice, only those companies with complex capital structures will be greatly affected by FRS 4.

The ASB issued FRS 13 *Derivatives and other financial instruments: disclosure* in September 1998. This standard applies to all plcs (other than insurance companies) and banks. It came into effect for accounting periods ending on or after 23 March 1999. Again, this is a highly specialised standard requiring entities to provide a discussion of the major financial risks they face in their activities and how they manage their exposure to these risks. Numerical disclosures analysing borrowings, fair values of financial instruments, etc. must be made.

FRS 4 ACCOUNTING FOR CAPITAL INSTRUMENTS
(Issued December 1993)

Objective

The objective of FRS 4 is stated as

'. . . to ensure that financial statements provide a clear, coherent and consistent treatment of capital instruments, in particular as regards the classification of instruments as debt, non-equity shares or equity shares; that costs associated with capital instruments are dealt with in a manner consistent with their classification, and, for redeemable instruments, allocated to accounting periods on a fair basis over the period the instrument is in issue; and that financial statements provide relevant information concerning the nature and amount of the entity's sources of finance and the associated costs, commitments and potential commitments.'

Capital instruments are defined as:

'All instruments that are issued by reporting entities as a means of raising finance, including shares, debentures, loans and debt instruments, options and warrants that give the holder the right to subscribe for or obtain capital instruments. In the case of consolidated financial statements the term includes capital instruments issued by subsidiaries except those that are held by another member of the group included in the consolidation.'

Non-equity shares are defined as:

'Shares possessing any of the following characteristics:

a) any of the rights of the shares to receive payments . . . are for a limited amount that is not calculated by reference to the company's assets or profits or the dividends on any class of equity share;

b) any of the rights of the shares to participate in a surplus on a winding up are limited to a specific amount that is not calculated by reference to the company's assets or profits . . . ;

c) the shares are redeemable either according to their terms, or because their holder, or any party other than the issuer, can require their redemption.'

Equity shares are any shares other than non-equity shares.

Exceptions

The FRS does *not* apply to:

a) warrants issued to employees under employee share schemes;

b) leases (*see* SSAP 21, p. 58);

c) equity shares issued as part of a business combination that is accounted for as a merger.

Classification

All capital instruments should be accounted for in the balance sheet within *one* of the following three categories:

1. liabilities

2. shareholders' funds

3. minority interests.

Liabilities

Include:

1. **Capital instruments** (other than shares) if they contain an obligation to transfer economic benefits (including a contingent obligation to transfer economic benefits). This would include shares owned outside the group which have been issued by subsidiaries, where the group as a whole has an obligation to transfer economic benefits.

2. **Convertible debt** (note that the conversion should not be anticipated). This should be stated separately from other liabilities, and the finance cost (*see below*) should be calculated on the basis that the debt will never be converted.

   Details should be disclosed of:

   a) the dates of redemption;

   b) the amounts payable on redemption;

   c) number and class of shares into which the debt may be converted;

   d) dates at or periods within which the conversion may take place;

   e) whether conversion is at the option of the issuer or at that of the holder.

   Gains or losses arising on the repurchase or early settlement of debt should be disclosed in the profit and loss account as separate items within or adjacent to 'interest payable and similar charges'.

Shareholders' funds

Include:

1. shares and warrants;

2. capital instruments if they do not contain an obligation to transfer economic benefits;

3. shares issued on the conversion of debt. The amount recognised should be the same as the amount of the liability for the debt at the time of conversion. No gain or loss on conversion should be recognised.

The balance sheet should show the total amount of shareholders' funds. Where shareholders' funds are repurchased or redeemed, shareholders' funds should be reduced by the value of the consideration given.

Shareholders' funds should be analysed between equity interests and non-equity interests. A brief summary of the rights of each class of share should also be given, including:

1. the rights to dividends;

2. dates of redemption, and amounts payable on redemption;

3. their priority and amounts receivable on a winding up;

4. their voting rights.

This summary should be sufficient to explain why shares have been classified as equity or non-equity, but, if necessary, additional information should be given.

However, this summary need not be given where equity shares have:

1. no right to dividends except where recommended by directors;

2. no redemption rights;

3. an unlimited right to share in winding-up surpluses after all liabilities and participation rights of other classes of shares have been satisfied;

4. one vote per share.

Dividends should be analysed between those relating to:

1. equity shares;

2. participating dividends;

3. non-equity shares;

4. other appropriations of profit in respect of non-equity shares.

Minority interests (in the case of consolidated financial statements)

These include shares owned outside the group which have been issued by subsidiaries, where the group as a whole has no obligation to transfer economic benefits.

Minority interests should be analysed between equity interests and non-equity interests, both in the profit and loss account and the balance sheet. If any of the non-equity shares making up the minority interests are guaranteed by other group members, then they should be shown as liabilities.

Carrying amount and allocation of finance costs

Immediately after issue, debt should be stated at the amount of the net proceeds (i.e. after deduction of issue costs).

The finance costs associated with liabilities and non-equity shares are to be allocated to periods at a constant rate based on the carrying amount.

Finance costs are defined as:

> 'The difference between the net proceeds of an instrument and the total amount of the payments (or other transfer of economic benefits) that the issuer may be required to make in respect of the instrument.'

All finance costs should be charged in the profit and loss account, and the carrying amount of the debt should be increased by the finance cost in respect of the reporting period and reduced by payments made in respect of the debt in that period.

Gains or losses on the repurchase or early settlement of debt should be recognised in the profit and loss account in the period during which the repurchase or early settlement is made.

Example

Assume that convertible debt was issued on 1 January 1995 for £1,000 (net proceeds) and is redeemable at the same amount on 31 December 2009 (i.e. 15 years later). Interest at 5.9% is paid for the first five years, and 14.1% thereafter. The bond's internal rate of return is calculated at 10%. Calculate the annual finance cost and the carrying amount at each year-end.

Answer

The allocation is made on the basis that the greater the carrying amount, the greater the finance cost.

The finance cost is:

Total payments: $(1,000 + (5 \times 59) + (10 \times 141)) =$	2,705
Less net proceeds	1,000
Finance cost	1,705

The annual finance cost and year-end carrying amounts can be calculated as shown in Table 6.1.

Summary of disclosure

Table 6.2 summarises disclosure required under FRS 4.

Table 6.1 Calculation of annual finance cost and year-end carrying amounts

Year ending	Balance at beginning of year (£)	Finance cost for year (10%) (£)	Cash paid during year (£)	Balance at end of year (£)
31 Dec 1995	1,000	100	(59)	1,041
31 Dec 1996	1,041	104	(59)	1,086
31 Dec 1997	1,086	109	(59)	1,136
31 Dec 1998	1,136	114	(59)	1,190
31 Dec 1999	1,190	119	(59)	1,250
31 Dec 2000	1,250	125	(141)	1,234
31 Dec 2001	1,234	123	(141)	1,217
31 Dec 2002	1,217	122	(141)	1,198
31 Dec 2003	1,198	120	(141)	1,177
31 Dec 2004	1,177	118	(141)	1,154
31 Dec 2005	1,154	116	(141)	1,129
31 Dec 2006	1,129	113	(141)	1,101
31 Dec 2007	1,101	110	(141)	1,070
31 Dec 2008	1,070	107	(141)	1,036
31 Dec 2009	1,036	105*	(141)+(1,000)	0
		1,705		

* Adjusted for rounding differences

Table 6.2 Summary of disclosure under FRS 4

Item	Analysed between:	
Liabilities	Convertible liabilities	Non-convertible liabilities
Shareholders' funds	Equity interests	Non-equity interests
Minority interests in subsidiaries	Equity interests in subsidiaries	Non-equity interests in subsidiaries

Further required analysis

Debt maturity is to be analysed between amounts falling due:

a) in one year or less, or on demand;

b) between one and two years;

c) between two and five years;

d) in five years or more.

FRS 13 DERIVATIVES AND OTHER FINANCIAL INSTRUMENTS: DISCLOSURE
(Issued September 1998)

Introduction

As with FRS 4 *Accounting for capital instruments* (*see above*) this is a complex standard. It applies to all entities (other than insurance companies) that have one or more of their capital instruments listed or publicly traded on a stock exchange or market and to all banks and similar institutions. The standard is divided into three parts, each relevant to different types of reporting entities:

1. Part A: reporting entities other than financial institutions and financial institution groups;

2. Part B: banks and similar institutions and banking and similar groups;

3. Part C: other financial institutions and financial institution groups.

Due to the specialist nature of the standard, only the key elements of Part A are included in this text.

Objective

To ensure that disclosures are made within financial statements which enable users to assess the entity's objectives, policies and strategies for holding or issuing financial instruments. In particular, such information should enable users to assess:

a) the risk profile for each of the main financial risks that arise in connection with financial instruments and commodity contracts with similar characteristics; and

b) the significance of such instruments and contracts to the entity's reported financial position, performance and cash flows, regardless of whether the instruments and contracts are on the balance sheet (recognised) or off balance sheet (unrecognised).

Key definitions

Financial instrument: any contract that gives rise to both a financial asset of one entity and a financial liability or equity instrument of another entity.

Financial asset: any asset that is:

a) cash;

b) a contractual right to receive cash or another financial asset from another entity;

c) a contractual right to exchange financial instruments with another entity under conditions that are potentially favourable; or

d) an equity instrument of another entity.

Financial liability: any liability that is a contractual obligation to:

a) deliver cash or another financial asset to another entity; or

b) exchange financial instruments with another entity under conditions that are potentially unfavourable.

Equity instrument: an instrument that evidences an ownership interest in an entity, i.e. a residual interest in the assets of the entity after deducting all of its liabilities.

Commodity contract: a contract that provides for settlement by receipt or delivery of a commodity.

Disclosure

The standard requires disclosure of risks connected with financial instruments, including:

1. credit risk;
2. liquidity risk;
3. cash flow risk;
4. interest rate risk;
5. currency risk; and
6. other types of market price risk.

The information provided about these risks will usually be presented in the context of a discussion, in a statement such as the operating and financial review (*see* p. 228), of the entity's activities, structure and financing. For an example of such disclosures, *see Application in practice*, below.

APPLICATION IN PRACTICE

FRS 4 provides 'application notes' which show how to deal with a number of capital instruments, including convertible capital bonds, deep discount bonds and participating preference shares. A detailed consideration of these is outside the scope of this text, but it is helpful to see how FRS 4 has influenced the way in which companies are showing their borrowings. Figure 6.1 is an extract from the 2000 accounts of BAT Industries plc. The disclosure requirements of FRS 13 are reflected in Figure 6.2, showing an extract from the 2000 accounts of Kingfisher plc.

Fig. 6.1 BAT Industries plc: influence of FRS 4 on disclosure of borrowings

BAT Industries plc: Borrowings

	Currency	2000 £m	1999 £m
6⅞% Notes due 2003	US dollars	19	17
Medium term notes due 2001/2029	US dollars	88	408
5⅜% Eurobonds due 2006	Deutschmark	240	236
Eurobonds due 2002/2009	Euro	875	591
Eurobonds due 2002/2009	US dollars	1,542	1,671
Eurobonds due 2004/2009	Sterling	405	584
Euro medium term notes due 2001/2019	Various	119	115
Yen medium term notes due 2001	US dollars	247	
6½% and 6⅞% Notes due 2003/2008	US dollars	442	376
5½% Notes due 2005	Swiss francs	173	163
7¹⁄₁₀% and 7⁹⁄₁₀% Notes due 2004/2007	Malaysian ringgit	132	122
8⅜% to 10¼% Debentures due 2001/2003	Canadian dollars	201	
Medium term notes due 2001/2005	Canadian dollars	121	
Syndicated bank loan	US dollars	518	611
Other bank loans	Various	496	533
Commercial paper	Various	174	
Finance leases	Various	114	74
Miscellaneous	Various	103	65
Term borrowings (including finance leases)		6,009	5,566
Overdrafts	Various	142	110
Total		**6,151**	**5,676**
Amounts secured on Group assets including finance leases		143	120

Included in the finance leases above are obligations of **£31 million** 1999 £26 million payable within one year, **£26 million** 1999 £19 million payable between one and two years, **£39 million** 1999 £29 million payable between two and five years and **£18 million** 1999 £nil payable beyond five years.

Borrowings have been issued in a number of currencies and certain of these have been swapped into sterling, US dollars and Swiss francs and have been accounted for accordingly.

	2000 £m	1999 £m
The borrowings are repayable as follows:		
Due beyond 5 years (non-instalment)	1,821	1,931
Due between 2 and 5 years	2,133	2,506
Due between 1 and 2 years	1,112	206
Due beyond 1 year	5,066	4,643
Due within 1 year	1,085	1,033
	6,151	5,676

Fig. 6.1 continued

	2000 £m	1999 £m
Borrowings facilities		
Undrawn committed facilities expiring:		
within 1 year	**2,037**	385
beyond 1 year and within 2 years		1,879
beyond 2 years and within 5 years	**71**	1
beyond 5 years		50
	2,108	2,315

As explained on pages 23 and 24 of the Annual Review and Summary Financial Statement, the facilities include undrawn amounts in respect of the syndicated bank loan facility of US$1.5 billion (£1 billion), reduced from US$3 billion in the previous year. In addition 2000 includes Imperial Tobacco Canada's facilities of C$1.5 billion (£0.7 billion).

Fig. 6.2 Kingfisher plc: FRS 13 Disclosure requirements

Kingfisher plc

Accounting policies and standards (extract)
Derivative financial instruments
Financial assets are recognised on the balance sheet at the lower of cost and net realisable value. Discounts and premia are charged or credited to the profit and loss account over the life of the asset or liability to which they relate.

Derivative financial instruments are accounted for using hedge accounting to the extent that they are held to hedge a financial asset or liability. Where such instruments do not hedge an underlying asset or liability, they are accounted for using fair value accounting.

When a financial instrument ceases to be a hedge, either as a result of the underlying asset or liability being extinguished, or because a future event is no longer likely to occur, the instrument will thereafter be marked to its fair value in the financial statements.

Income and expenditure arising on financial instruments held for hedging purposes is recognised on an accruals basis, and credited or charged to the profit and loss account in the financial period in which it arises.

Gains or losses on financial instruments accounted for on a fair value basis are reflected in the profit and loss account as they arise.

For the purposes of notes 22, 23 and 25 to 28, short-term debtors and creditors have been excluded. The narrative disclosures required by FRS 13 are set out on pages 26 to 28 in the financial review.

▶

Fig. 6.2 continued

Notes to the accounts (extracts)
22 Interest rate and currency profile of gross financial liabilities

Currency	Gross liabilities £ millions	Floating liabilities £ millions	Fixed liabilities £ millions	Weighted average interest rate on fixed liabilities %	Weighted average time for which rate is fixed Years	Non-interest bearing liabilities £ millions	Weighted average time until maturity Years
At 29 January 2000							
Sterling	1,023.9	1,003.1	10.1	6.70	2.2	10.7	2.0
Euro	485.4	376.1	88.2	6.10	7.1	21.1	2.0
Other	45.3	42.5	2.8	8.90	10.4	–	–
Gross liabilities	1,554.6	1,421.7	101.1	6.20	6.7	31.8	2.0
At 30 January 1999							
Sterling	631.3	614.5	3.0	8.25	19.5	13.8	2.0
Euro	620.9	590.8	16.3	5.47	2.7	13.8	2.0
Other	21.7	18.2	3.5	6.06	1.9	–	–
Gross liabilities	1,273.9	1,223.5	22.8	5.93	4.8	27.6	2.0

The floating rate liabilities have interest rates based upon LIBOR and EURIBOR, fixed for periods of up to 12 months.

23 Interest rate and currency profile of gross financial assets

Currency	Gross assets £ millions	Floating rate assets £ millions	Fixed rate assets £ millions	Weighted average interest rate on fixed rate assets %	Weighted average time for which rate is fixed Years	Non-interest bearing assets £ millions
At 29 January 2000						
Sterling	597.5	411.1	2.7	5.00	3.0	183.7
Euro	108.5	36.5	1.8	4.01	4.8	70.2
Other	28.0	19.3	–	–	–	8.7
Gross financial assets	734.0	466.9	4.5	4.61	3.7	262.6

Of which	
Fixed asset investments (excluding ESOP shares)	9.0
Debtors due after more than one year	146.8
Consumer receivables (see note 18)	69.3
Current asset investments	352.3
Cash at bank and in hand	156.6
	734.0

Currency	Gross assets £ millions	Floating rate assets £ millions	Fixed rate assets £ millions	Weighted average interest rate on fixed rate assets %	Weighted average time for which rate is fixed Years	Non-interest bearing assets £ millions
At 30 January 1999						
Sterling	544.9	388.1	–	–	–	156.8
Euro	242.2	193.0	3.2	4.50	3.2	46.0
Other	2.2	2.1	–	–	–	0.1
Gross financial assets	789.3	583.2	3.2	4.50	3.2	202.9

Of which	
Fixed asset investments (excluding ESOP shares)	18.7
Debtors due after more than one year	144.1
Consumer receivables (see note 18)	73.6
Current asset investments	311.7
Cash at bank and in hand	241.2
	789.3

The floating rate financial assets have interest rates based upon LIBOR and EURIBOR, fixed for periods of up to 12 months.

Fig. 6.2 continued

24 Currency risk
The effect of currency exposures arising from the translation of overseas investments is mitigated by Group borrowings in the local currencies of its main operating subsidiaries. Gains and losses arising on net investments overseas and net foreign currency borrowings are recognised in the statement of recognised gains and losses.

After taking into account the effect of any hedging transactions entered into to manage currency exposures, there were no significant net foreign currency monetary assets or liabilities at the balance sheet date. Matched assets and liabilities are those that generate no gain or loss in the profit and loss account either because they are denominated in the same currency as the Group operations to which they belong or because they qualify under SSAP 20 as a foreign currency borrowing providing a hedge against a foreign equity investment.

25 Maturity of financial liabilities
The maturity of the Group's gross financial liabilities is as follows:

£ millions	2000	1999
Within one year	989.3	568.7
Between one and two years	110.0	35.4
Between two and five years	77.5	455.7
Over five years	377.8	214.1
	1,554.6	1,273.9

26 Borrowing facilities
At 29 January 2000 the Group had the following undrawn committed borrowing facilities available:

£ millions	2000	1999
Expiring within one year	236.9	470.0
Expiring in more than one year but no more than two years	4.6	–
Expiring beyond two years	400.7	182.5
	642.2	652.5

27 Fair values of financial assets and liabilites
Set out below is a year end comparison by category of the book, and fair values of the Group's financial assets and liabilities. Where available, market values have been used to determine fair values. Where market values are not available, fair values have been calculated by discounting cash flows at prevailing interest and exchange rates.

	2000		1999	
£ millions	Book Value	Fair Value	Book Value	Fair Value
Primary financial instruments held or issued to finance the Group's operations				
Fixed asset investments (excluding ESOP shares)	9.0	26.6	18.7	39.2
Long-term borrowings	(540.5)	(550.0)	(677.6)	(695.4)
	(531.5)	(523.4)	(658.9)	(656.2)
Derivative financial instruments held to manage the interest rate and currency profile				
Interest rate swaps and similar instruments	–	19.1	–	(0.7)
Cross currency interest rate swaps	–	1.0	–	–
Currency options	–	1.0	–	–
Forward foreign currency contracts	–	4.4	–	(0.1)
	–	25.5	–	(0.8)
	(531.5)	(497.9)	(658.9)	(657.0)

There are no material differences between the book and fair values of the Group's other financial assets and liabilities.

▶

Fig. 6.2 continued

28 Hedges

Derivative financial instruments are accounted for using hedge accounting to the extent that they are held to hedge a financial asset or liability. Where such instruments do not hedge an underlying asset or liability, they are accounted for using fair value accounting.

£ millions	Gains	Losses	Total net gains/ (losses)
Unrecognised gains and losses on hedges at 30 January 1999	0.3	(1.0)	**(0.7)**
Gains and losses arising in previous years or pre-acquisition periods that were recognised in the period to 29 January 2000	0.1	(0.1)	–
Gains and losses arising in the previous years or pre-acquisition periods that were not recognised in the period to 29 January 2000	0.2	(0.9)	**(0.7)**
Gains and losses arising in the period ending 29 January 2000 that were not recognised in that period	30.7	(4.5)	**26.2**
Unrecognised gains and losses on hedges at 29 January 2000	30.9	(5.4)	**25.5**
Of which			
Gains and losses expected to be recognised within one year	11.7	(2.8)	**8.9**
Gains and losses expected to be recognised after more than one year	19.2	(2.6)	**16.6**
	30.9	(5.4)	**25.5**

CHAPTER SUMMARY

FRS 4 Accounting for capital instruments

- Definition: all instruments that are issued by reporting entities as a means of raising finance, including shares, debentures, loans and debt instruments, options and warrants that give the holder the right to subscribe for or obtain capital instruments. In the case of consolidated financial statements the term includes capital instruments issued by subsidiaries except those that are held by another member of the group included in the consolidation.

- Capital instruments are to be classified as liabilities if they carry an obligation to transfer cash or other resources.

- Liabilities should be classified as current or non-current according to their contractual maturity dates unless where the same lender is committed to refinance the debt on the same terms.

- Liabilities should be recognised in the balance sheet at the amount received less any issue costs. The finance costs should be allocated to accounting periods so as to achieve a constant rate on the amount outstanding.

> **FRS 13 Derivatives and other Financial Instruments: Disclosure**
>
> - Requires entities to provide a discussion of the major financial risks they face in their activities and how they manage their exposure to these risks.
> - Numerical disclosures analysing borrowings, fair values of financial instruments etc. must be made.

DISCUSSION QUESTION

1. In introducing FRS 13, Sir David Tweedie (then chairman of the Accounting Standards Board) said: '. . . many companies now use types of financial instruments that can transform the business's risk profile overnight yet under previous practice would be hidden from view. This standard shines a torch into a darkened room, enabling users of accounts to understand the impact and significance of these instruments'. To what extent do you agree with these comments?

(*See Appendix 3* for outline responses.)

EXAMINATION QUESTION

On 1 January 2002, a company issued 100,000 £1 non-equity shares at a premium of 10p per share. It incurred issue costs of £2,000 related to the issue. The shares have a fixed cumulative dividend of 5% p.a. payable half-yearly and are redeemable on 31 December 2006 at a premium of 20%. Calculate the finance cost to be debited to profit and loss account in each of the five years to 31 December 2006, and the carrying value at the end of each of the five years. The internal rate of return has been calculated as 6.544%.

(20 marks)

(*See Appendix 4* for suggested answer.)

Chapter 7

Taxation: SSAP 5 and FRSs 16 & 19

Value added tax; Current tax; Deferred tax

INTRODUCTION

A major change in the corporation tax system took place in 1999, with the abolition of Advanced Corporation Tax (ACT) on dividends. This resulted in the need for a new taxation standard, FRS16, which replaced SSAP 8 in December of that year. There have been no major changes to the VAT system since it was introduced in the 1970s, so an old standard, SSAP 5, is still appropriate. Finally, the most recently issued standard at the time of writing, FRS 19 on Deferred Tax, was issued to bring UK practice in line with international accounting standards and US GAAP.

SSAP 5 ACCOUNTING FOR VALUE ADDED TAX
(Issued April 1974)

Value added tax (VAT) is a system of taxation whereby the tax is collected at each stage of the production and distribution chain (i.e. as value is added to the product) but is eventually borne by the final consumer. The trader acts, therefore, as a tax collector, accounting for VAT output tax (the VAT charged to customers on sales) and VAT input tax (the VAT charged by his or her suppliers on purchases, expenses, etc.), and either paying or receiving the balance at intervals to or from the taxation authorities (HM Customs and Excise in the UK), as follows:

If VAT output tax exceeds VAT input tax: difference paid to tax authority.

If VAT input tax exceeds VAT output tax: difference received from tax authority.

Note that only those traders who are *registered* for VAT purposes are allowed to charge VAT on their supplies and offset VAT suffered on their purchases and expenses. Registration is compulsory in the UK for traders who have an annual turnover which exceeds a prescribed amount (£54,000 at the time of writing). It is possible for certain businesses to opt for voluntary registration, even though their turnover is below that figure. This may prove beneficial to businesses with a small turnover whose customers are mainly registered traders.

Non-registered businesses, therefore, *suffer* the VAT input tax, i.e. the cost of goods and services will increase, as will the cost of fixed assets. No separate VAT accounting records need be kept, and the financial statements will include all relevant amounts at their *VAT-inclusive* prices.

Exempted activities

Whilst there are only two rates of VAT, standard rate ($17\frac{1}{2}\%$) and zero rate (0%), there are certain activities, such as insurance and banking services, which are treated as *exempt* from VAT. This means simply that whilst no VAT need be added to (e.g.) insurance premiums and bank charges, the insurance companies and banks cannot, in most circumstances, reclaim VAT on inputs relating to the provision of those exempted activities.

Non-deductible inputs

Not all VAT input tax can be offset against output tax. Examples include the VAT paid on motor cars and on most business entertaining. Such *irrecoverable* VAT must be included in the amounts to be disclosed in the published accounts where practicable and material.

Amounts due to or from the revenue authorities

At the end of the accounting period, the amount due to or from the revenue authorities should be included as part of debtors or creditors, and will not normally require separate disclosure.

Capital commitments

The estimated amount of capital commitments disclosed in a company's final accounts (in accordance with the Companies Act 1985) should include the amount, if any, of irrecoverable VAT.

Turnover

Turnover shown in the profit and loss account should exclude VAT on taxable outputs. If it is desired to show the *gross* turnover then the VAT relevant to that turnover should be shown as a deduction.

Summary of SSAP 5

Figure 7.1 provides a summary of SSAP 5 on value added tax.

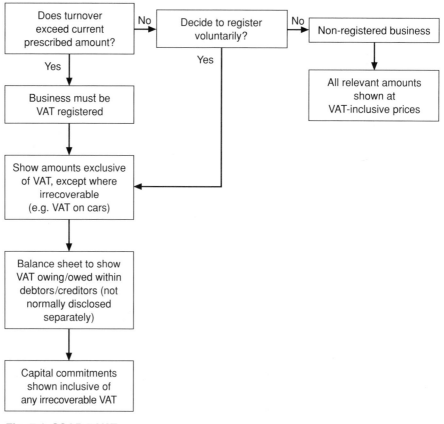

Fig. 7.1 SSAP 5 VAT

FRS 16 CURRENT TAX

(Issued December 1999)

Changes to the taxation system in 1999

A major change in the corporation tax system took place in 1999, with the abolition of Advanced Corporation Tax (ACT) on dividends from 6 April 1999. For corporation tax accounting periods (CTAPs) ending after 30 June 1999, companies with taxable profits of more than £1.5m pay their corporation tax in four quarterly instalments commencing six months and 14 days after the start of the CTAP. Small and medium-sized companies pay their full corporation tax liability nine months after the end of their CTAP. Despite the abolition of ACT, shareholders will still receive a tax credit on their dividend income.

Objective

The objective of the standard is to ensure that reporting entities recognise current taxes in a consistent and transparent manner.

Definitions

Current tax – the amount of tax estimated to be payable or recoverable in respect of the taxable profit or loss for the period, along with adjustments to estimates in respect of previous periods.

Tax credit – the tax credit given under UK tax legislation to the recipient of a dividend from a UK company.

Taxable profit or loss – the profit or loss for the period, determined in accordance with the rules established by the tax authorities, upon which taxes are assessed.

Withholding tax – Tax on dividends or income that is deducted by the payer of the income and paid to the tax authorities wholly on behalf of the recipient.

Recognition

Current tax – The way that current tax should be recognised in the financial statements is shown in Figure 7.2.

Dividends and interest – Whether paid, proposed, or receivable, they should be recognised at an amount that:

- includes any withholding taxes; but
- excludes any other taxes, such as attributable tax credits, not payable wholly on behalf of the recipient.

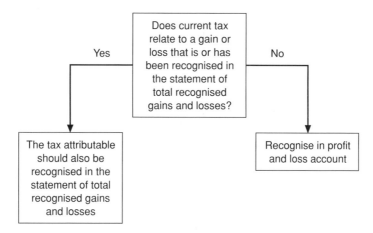

Fig. 7.2 Recognition of current tax

The effect of any withholding tax suffered should be taken into account as part of the tax charge.

Measurement of tax

Current tax should be measured at the amounts expected to be paid (or recovered) using the tax rates and laws that have been enacted or substantively enacted by the balance sheet date.

Disclosure

UK or Republic of Ireland tax should be disclosed separately from foreign tax, analysed between tax estimated for the current period and any prior period adjustments. The domestic tax should be disclosed before and after double taxation relief.

FRS 19 DEFERRED TAX

(Issued December 2000)

Introduction

Deferred tax arises because certain types of income and expenditure are not included in the measurement of *taxable* profits at the same time as they are included in the measurement of *accounting* profits. If no adjustment was made then the tax charge shown in the profit and loss account would be distorted and the 'true' overall liability not disclosed. Until FRS 19 was issued in late 2000, its predecessor standard SSAP 15 (see Appendix 2) had required a 'partial provision' method of deferred taxation, where only those potential liabilities which were expected to crystallise at some future date would be provided for.

Much of the deferred taxation provision relates to the way in which capital allowances on fixed assets tend to be more generous to companies when the assets are new. Companies that regularly replaced ageing assets argued that the generous tax allowances were continually being regenerated, thus putting off any potential tax liability. However, partial provisioning was criticised as being dependent on the management's own interpretation and expectation of future events. Also, International Accounting Standard 12 required deferred tax to be provided in full. With the strong move towards international harmonisation of accounting practices, the ASB recognised the need for a change of policy and accordingly issued FRS 19 which, whilst not completely mirroring IAS 12, has abandoned partial provisioning.

Objective

FRS 19's objective is to ensure that:

- future tax consequences of past transactions and events are recognised as liabilities or assets in the financial statements; and
- the financial statements disclose any other special circumstances that may have an effect on future tax charges.

Definitions

Current tax – the amount of tax estimated to be payable or recoverable in respect of the taxable profit or loss for a period, along with adjustments to estimates in respect of previous periods.

Deferred tax – estimated future tax consequences of transactions and events recognised in the financial statements of the current and previous periods.

Permanent differences – differences between an entity's taxable profits and its results as stated in the financial statements that arise because certain types of income and expenditure are non-taxable or disallowable, or because certain tax charges or allowances have no corresponding amount in the financial statements. Note that deferred tax is *not* recognised on permanent differences.

Timing differences – differences between an entity's taxable profits and its results as stated in the financial statements that arise from the inclusion of gains and losses in tax assessments in periods different from those in which they are recognised in financial statements. Timing differences originate in one period and are capable of reversal in one or more periods.

Summary of the standard

Deferred tax must be fully provided for on most types of timing differences as defined above. Examples of timing differences that require provision include:

- accelerated capital allowances, where tax deductions for the cost of an asset are received before the cost of the fixed asset is recognised in the profit and loss account;
- decelerated capital allowances, where tax deductions for the cost of an asset are received after the cost of the fixed asset is recognised in the profit and loss account;
- pension accruals which will only be tax-deductible when paid;
- interest charges or development costs, if capitalised on the balance sheet, are treated as revenue expenditure for tax purposes.

Examples of timing differences that are *not* to be recognised are those arising when:

- a fixed asset is revalued without there being any commitment to sell the asset (though if the asset is continuously revalued to fair value, with changes recognised in the profit and loss account, then deferred tax would be recognised);

- the gain on sale of an asset is rolled over into replacement assets;
- the remittance of a subsidiary, associate or joint venture's earnings would cause tax to be payable, but no commitment has been made to the remittance of the earnings.

If a deferred tax *asset* arises (e.g. where decelerated capital allowances result in tax deductions weighted towards the end of an assets life) it can only be recognised to the extent that it is regarded as more likely than not that they will be recovered.

The FRS permits but does not require entities to adopt a policy of discounting (allowing for the fall in value of money over time) deferred tax assets and liabilities. Under the previous standard, SSAP 15, the partial provisioning allowed in that standard had permitted many companies to provide for just a fraction of total potential deferred tax. For example, it was reported (*Accountancy Age, 26 August 1999*) that British Telecom had approximately £1,896m unprovided deferred tax whilst British Steel had provided only £16m of total deferred tax liabilities amounting to £386m. Forcing such companies to fully provide for deferred tax is likely to have a significant impact on levels of reserves and ability to pay dividends. Allowing deferred tax provisions to be discounted has 'sweetened the medicine' for such companies, but the effect is still likely to be dramatic.

Recognition

How deferred tax is recognised in the financial statements is shown in Figure 7.3.

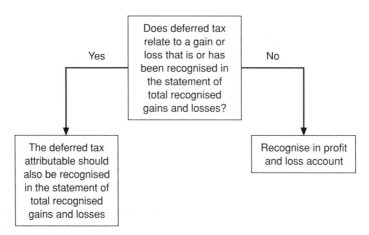

Fig. 7.3 Recognition of deferred tax

Discounting

The Standard allows companies to discount the deferred tax assets and liabilities to reflect the time value of money. The decision shall be based on such factors as:

- how material the impact of discounting would be to overall results and financial position;
- whether the benefits of discounting to users would outweigh the costs of collating the necessary information and performing discounting calculations; and
- whether there is an established industry practice, adherence to which would enhance comparability.

Presentation

Balance sheet: net deferred tax liabilities should be classified as provisions for liabilities and charges, whilst net deferred tax assets should be classified as debtors, with a separate subheading if material. If there are both debit and credit balances for deferred tax, they can only be offset if they relate to taxes levied by the same tax authorities, or arise within for example a group of companies where the tax losses of one group member can reduce the taxable profits of another.

Profit and loss account: deferred tax should be included within the heading 'tax on profit or loss on ordinary activities'.

Disclosures

Notes to the financial statements should disclose the amount of deferred tax charged or credited within:

1. The profit or loss account: tax on ordinary activities, separately disclosing material components, including those attributable to:
   - the origination and reversal of timing differences;
   - changes in tax rates and laws;
   - adjustments to the estimated recoverable amount of deferred tax assets arising in previous periods;
   - changes in the amounts of discount deducted in arriving at the deferred tax balance.
2. The statement of total recognised gains and losses: where tax has been recognised in this statement (*see* Figure 7.3), separately disclose within this statement the same information as listed above for the profit and loss account.

3. The balance sheet: the total deferred tax balance (before discounting where applicable) is stated, split between each significant type of timing difference. If the deferred tax has been discounted, the impact of discounting and the discounted amount is shown. An analysis reconciling the opening and closing net balance is given, showing separately:

- the amount charged or credited in the profit and loss account for the period;
- the amount charged or credited directly in the statement of total recognised gains and losses for the period; and
- movements arising from the acquisition or disposal of businesses.

In the case of a deferred tax *asset* being recognised, additional disclosures relating to its amount and evidence supporting its recognition must be made if:

- its recoverability is dependent on future taxable profits in excess of those arising from reversal of deferred tax liabilities; and
- a loss has been suffered in either the current or preceding period in the tax jurisdiction to which the deferred asset relates.

4. Notes to the financial statements should give a number of disclosures relating to deferred tax, including:

- a reconciliation of the tax charge or credit on ordinary activities for the period as reported in the profit and loss account, with the tax charge that would result from applying a relevant standard rate of tax to the profit on ordinary activities before tax. An example is given below.

	2002 £m	2001 £m
Profit on ordinary activities before tax	722	654
Profit on ordinary activities multiplied by standard rate of corporation tax in the UK of 31% (2001: 30%)	224	196
Effects of:		
Expenses not deductible for tax purposes (primarily goodwill amortisation)	44	20
Capital allowances for period in excess of depreciation	(116)	(108)
Utilisation of tax losses	(34)	(36)
Rollover relief on profit on disposal of property	(20)	–
Higher tax on overseas earnings	6	12
Adjustment to tax charge in respect of previous periods	8	(12)
Current tax charge for period	112	72

- If assets have been revalued (or market values of unrevalued assets shown in a note) and no deferred tax recognised, an estimate must be given of the tax that could be payable or recoverable if the assets were sold at the values shown.

Differences between the UK standard and the International standard

Although FRS 19 was issued to bring UK accounting practice into harmony with international standards, a number of key differences remain between it and IAS 12. Significantly, the UK standard:

- does not in general require deferred tax to be provided for when assets are revalued or adjusted to their fair values on the acquisition of a business;
- allows (but does not require) deferred tax liabilities that will not be settled for some time to be discounted to reflect the time value of money. IAS 12 prohibits this.

When FRS 19 was issued, Sir David Tweedie, the then chairman of the ASB, said 'It was inevitable that UK companies would have to move to a full provision method of accounting for deferred tax. But we don't think that they should be expected to accept the present international approach, which we believe requires companies to make provisions for tax that they may never have to pay. By developing FRS 19 based on a different approach, we hope to show the rest of the world that there is a better way of implementing full provision for deferred tax.'

APPLICATION IN PRACTICE

Figure 7.4 provides extracts from the published annual report of Kingfisher plc showing how that company treats the various taxation items appearing in its financial statements. Note that this annual report was published before the implementation of FRS 19.

Fig. 7.4 Kingfisher plc: treatment of taxation

Consolidated profit and loss account (extract)

Kingfisher plc and subsidiary companies for the financial year ended 29 January 2000

£ millions	Notes	2000	1999
Profit on ordinary activities before taxation		**726.2**	629.3
Tax on profit on ordinary activities	10	**(204.4)**	(183.5)
Profit on ordinary activities after taxation		**521.8**	445.8

Balance sheets (extract)

Kingfisher plc and subsidiary companies as at 29 January 2000

		Group	
£ millions	Notes	2000	1999
Creditors			
Provisions for liabilities and charges	29	**(18.6)**	(21.8)

▶

Fig. 7.4 continued

Accounting policies (extract)

Deferred taxation

Provision is made for deferred taxation, using the liability method, on all material timing differences to the extent that it is probable that the liability or asset will crystallise.

Notes to the accounts (extract)

10 Taxation

£ millions	2000	1999
Tax charge on profit for the year:		
United Kingdom corporation tax at 30.16% (1999: 31.00%)	**123.9**	148.6
Relief for double taxation	**(3.2)**	(1.2)
Overseas taxation	**93.6**	40.2
Deferred tax	**(0.3)**	(0.2)
Joint ventures	**0.7**	–
Associated undertakings	**0.8**	1.5
	215.5	188.9
Prior year adjustments	(11.1)	(5.4)
	204.4	183.5

The 1999 comparative UK tax charge includes tax on the exceptional VAT accrual release.

29 Provisions for liabilities and charges

£ millions	Pensions	Deferred tax	Onerous property contracts	Total
Balance at 30 January 1999	11.0	0.9	9.9	21.8
Transfer to/(from) profit and loss account	1.0	(0.3)	0.9	1.6
Utilised in the year	(0.3)	–	(3.8)	(4.1)
Effect of foreign exchange rate changes	(0.6)	–	(0.1)	(0.7)
Balance at 29 January 2000	11.1	0.6	6.9	18.6

£ millions	2000	1999
Deferred taxation not provided		
Accelerated capital allowances	**50.4**	42.8
Potential chargeable gains on properties	**223.2**	144.2
Losses	**(39.0)**	(41.3)
Other	**(2.9)**	(6.1)
	231.7	139.6

Within the pensions provision, the final salary pension fund provision for the UK pension scheme has remained unchanged at £6.7m. This provision arises through accounting for the UK pension costs under SSAP 24 (see note 34). The remaining pension provision of £4.4m relates to overseas pension schemes.

The deferred tax provision represents £0.6m (1999: £0.9m) in respect of taxation on future remittances of the accumulated reserves of overseas subsidiary undertakings. Except for the above, deferred tax has not been provided on earnings retained overseas where it is not currently intended to remit these earnings to the UK.

Within deferred taxation not provided, the prior year amounts have been restated to reflect the final closing position of Castorama at the date of acquisition.

CHAPTER SUMMARY

SSAP 5 Accounting for Value Added Tax

- Registered traders show amounts exclusive of VAT, except where irrecoverable.
- Non-registered traders show amounts at VAT-inclusive prices.
- VAT owed/owing included within debtors/creditors.

FRS 16 Current Tax

- Current tax relating to a gain or loss that is or has been recognised in the statement of total recognised gains and losses should also be recognised in that statement.
- Other current tax should be recognised in the profit and loss account.
- Dividends and interest received is shown gross (before any withholding tax), with the related tax suffered being shown as part of the total tax charge for the period.

FRS 19 Deferred Tax

- Deferred tax must be fully provided for on most types of timing differences.
- Timing differences *not* to be recognised include a fixed asset revalued without there being any commitment to sell the asset, and when the gain on the sale of an asset is rolled over into replacement assets.
- Deferred tax relating to a gain or loss that is or has been recognised in the statement of total recognised gains and losses should also be recognised in that statement.
- Other deferred tax should be recognised in the profit and loss account.

DISCUSSION QUESTION

1. 'Although FRS 19 brings the UK closer to international practice, differences of treatment over deferred taxation still exist. The goal of international harmony on this topic is as far away as ever.' Discuss.

(*See Appendix 3* for outline responses.)

EXAMINATION QUESTIONS

1. A company buys and sells goods some of which are:

a) subject to VAT at a standard rate of 17.5%;

b) zero rated (those where no VAT is chargeable on sales but any VAT charged on purchases is recoverable);

c) exempt (those where no VAT is chargeable on sales and where any VAT charged is not recoverable).

You are given the following information:

1. The balance on the VAT account at the end of July was £4,700. This amount was paid on 30 August.

2. Purchases, including VAT at 17.5%, during the quarter were:

   £80,000 for standard-rated goods;

   £12,000 for zero-rated goods;

   £2,300 for exempt goods.

3. Sales, not including VAT, during the quarter were:

   £100,000 for standard-rated goods;

   £10,000 for zero-rated goods;

   £5,000 for exempt goods.

4. All items purchased are for resale.

Required:

Write up the company's Value Added Tax account, sales account and purchases account in its ledger for the months of August, September and October, and show the balance outstanding on the VAT account at the end of the quarter.

(10 marks)

CIMA

2. In connection with FRS 19, deferred taxation must be fully provided for on most types of timing differences.

   a) Explain what is meant by 'timing differences'.

   b) Give two examples of timing differences that do *not* require a provision for deferred taxation.

(20 marks)

(*See Appendix 4* for suggested answers.)

Chapter 8

Reporting financial performance, earnings per share: FRSs 3 & 14

INTRODUCTION

FRS 3 was issued on 29 October 1992, replacing the much derided SSAP 6 *Extraordinary items and prior year adjustments*. SSAP 6 had been described as a 'useless standard' (*Accountancy Age*, April 1992), due to the scope it gave to companies to distort profits by a liberal use of 'extraordinary' items (often relating to closure and redundancy costs), which appeared 'below the line' in the profit and loss account. As the key *earnings per share* (eps) figure was then calculated without regard to extraordinary items, company results appeared far better than they should have done. Extraordinary items have been almost eliminated by FRS 3.

On its introduction, Sir David Tweedie, chairman of the ASB, described it as:

'. . . a landmark standard . . . the Board has virtually abolished the extraordinary item which has been the source of so much confusion and manipulation. Ensuring that almost all transactions will be recorded 'above the line' will relieve preparers of accounts from having to meet competitive pressures by stretching to breaking point the definitions of exceptional (above the line) and extraordinary (below the line) items. We believe that the proposals of FRS 3 will dispose of most of the arguments over the definition of extraordinary and exceptional items and will remove one of the major abuses of UK accounting.'

One of the main reasons for developing the standard was to destroy the reliance on a single figure (eps) to measure and predict a company's earnings. However, investment analysts were unhappy about what they perceived as too much volatility in the earnings figures as reported under the new standard. One firm of stockbrokers accused the ASB of 'throwing the baby out with the bath water' in its reform of the profit and loss account, and creating a recipe for chaos. However, this criticism can be ascribed to the 'shock of the new', and it should be borne in mind that not one analyst took the opportunity to comment on the proposals contained in FRED 1 (the precursor of FRS 3) when they had the opportunity to do so.

In October 1998, the ASB published FRS 14 *Earnings per share* which superseded SSAP 3 which had the same title.

The new standard was introduced to bring UK practice in line with the International Accounting Standard 33 issued in February 1997.

FRS 3 REPORTING FINANCIAL PERFORMANCE

(Issued October 1992, amended June 1993)

Overview

FRS 3 introduced:

1. changes to the format of the profit and loss account;
2. changes to the calculation of earnings per share (*see* FRS 14, p. 129);
3. a requirement for companies to provide:

    a) a statement of total recognised gains and losses (a primary statement);

    b) a note of historical cost profits and losses;

    c) a reconciliation of movements in shareholders' funds;

4. the virtual abolition of extraordinary items.

A minor amendment to the standard in June 1993 gave insurance companies limited relief from particular requirements relating to the recognition of gains and losses on investments.

Objective of the standard

The standard states its objective as being to 'aid users in understanding the performance achieved by a reporting entity in a period and to assist them in forming a basis for their assessment of future results and cash flows'.

Definitions

The key definitions contained within FRS 3 are as follows.

Ordinary activities

These are any activities which are undertaken by a reporting entity as part of its business and such related activities in which the reporting entity engages in furtherance of, incidental to or arising from these activities. Ordinary activities include the effects on the reporting entity of any event in the various environments in which it operates. This includes the political, regulatory, economic and geographical environments, irrespective of the frequency or unusual nature of the events.

Extraordinary items

These are material items possessing a high degree of abnormality which arise from events or transactions that fall outside the ordinary activities of the reporting entity and which are not expected to recur. They do not include exceptional items nor do they include prior period items merely because they relate to a prior period.

However, note that the FRS states in an explanatory paragraph that (author's italics):

'. . . extraordinary items are *extremely rare* as they relate to highly abnormal events or transactions that fall outside the ordinary activities of the reporting entity and which are not expected to recur. *In view of the extreme rarity of such items no examples are provided.*'

Exceptional items

These are material items which derive from events or transactions that fall within the ordinary activities of the reporting entity and which individually or, if of a similar type, in aggregate need to be disclosed by virtue of their size or incidence if the financial statements are to give a true and fair view.

Prior period adjustments

These are material adjustments applicable to prior periods arising from changes in accounting policies or from the correction of fundamental errors. They do not include exceptional items nor do they include prior period items merely because they relate to a prior period (*see* Figure 8.7 on p. 128).

Acquisitions

These are operations of the reporting entity that are acquired in the period.

Discontinued operations

These are operations of the reporting entity that are sold or terminated and that satisfy all of the following conditions.

a) The sale or termination is completed either in the period or before the earlier of three months after the commencement of the subsequent period and the date on which the financial statements are approved.

b) If a termination, the former activities have ceased permanently.

c) The sale or termination has a material effect on the nature and focus of the reporting entity's operations and represents a material reduction in its operating facilities resulting either from its withdrawal from a particular market (whether class of business or geographical) or from a material reduction in turnover in the reporting entity's continuing markets.

d) The assets, liabilities, results of operations and activities are clearly distinguishable, physically, operationally and for financial reporting purposes.

Operations not satisfying all these conditions are classified as continuing.

Total recognised gains and losses

This is the total of all gains and losses of the reporting entity that are recognised in a period and are attributable to shareholders.

How FRS 3 has changed company reporting

1. The profit and loss account

A layered format is to be used for the profit and loss account to highlight:

a) results of continuing operations (including the results of acquisitions);

b) results of discontinued operations;

Fig. 8.1 Profit and loss account

	2002 £m	2002 £m	2001 £m
Turnover			
Continuing operations	550		500
Acquisitions	50		
	600		
Discontinued operations	175		190
		775	690
Cost of sales		(620)	(555)
Gross profit		155	135
Net operating profit		(104)	(83)
Operating profit			
Continuing operations	50		40
Acquisitions	6		
	56		
Discontinued operations	(15)		12
Less 2001 provision	10		
		51	52
Profit on sale of properties in continuing operations		9	6
Provision for loss on operations to be discontinued			(30)
Loss on disposal of discontinued operations	(17)		
Less 2001 provision	20		
		3	
Profit on ordinary activities before interest		63	28
Interest payable		(18)	(15)
Profit on ordinary activities before taxation		45	13
Tax on profit on ordinary activities		(14)	(4)
Profit on ordinary activities after taxation		31	9
Minority interests		(2)	(2)
[Profit before extraordinary items]		29	7
[Extraordinary items] (included only to show positioning)		–	–
Profit for the financial year		29	7
Dividends		(8)	1
Retained profit for the financial year		21	6
Earnings per share		**39p**	**10p**
Adjustments			
[to be itemised and an adequate description given]		*xp*	*xp*
		yp	*yp*

Fig. 8.1 continued

Note	2002 Continuing £m	2002 Discontinued £m	2002 Total £m	2001 Continuing £m	2001 Discontinued £m	2001 Total £m
Cost of sales	455	165	620	385	170	555
Net operating expenses						
Distribution costs	56	13	69	46	5	51
Administrative costs	41	12	53	34	3	37
Other operating income	(8)	0	(8)	(5)	0	(5)
	89	25	114	75	8	83
Less 2001 provision	0	(10)	(10)			
	89	15	104			

The total figures for continuing operations in 2002 include the following amounts relating to acquisitions: cost of sales £40m and net operating expenses £4m (namely distribution costs £3m, administrative expenses £3m and other operating income £2m).

c) profits or losses on the sale or termination of an operation, costs of a fundamental reorganisation or restructuring and profits or losses on the disposal of fixed assets;

d) extraordinary items (extremely rare).

Figure 8.1 shows an example of the profit and loss account which, though not part of the standard, is given by way of illustration to it. Figure 8.2 shows an alternative presentation.

Continuing and discontinued operations

The minimum disclosure requirements are explained in Figure 8.3.

Exceptional items

Exceptional items (*see definition above*) should be disclosed separately by way of note, or on the face of the profit and loss account if such prominence is necessary to give a true and fair view. An adequate description should be given. They should be credited or charged in arriving at the profit or loss on ordinary activities by inclusion under the statutory Companies Act headings to which they relate.

The following items should be shown separately on the face of the profit and loss account, after operating profit and before interest, and included under the appropriate heading of continuing or discontinued operations:

a) profits or losses on the sale or termination of an operation;

b) costs of a fundamental reorganisation or restructuring having a material effect on the nature and focus of the reporting entity's operations; and

c) profits or losses on the disposal of fixed assets.

Relevant information regarding the effect of these items on the taxation charge and (where applicable) any minority interest should be given as a note to the profit and loss account.

Extraordinary items

Any extraordinary items (*see definition above*) should be shown separately on the face of the profit and loss account, after the profit or loss on ordinary

Fig. 8.2 Profit and loss account (alternative format)

	Continuing operations 2002 £m	Acquisitions 2002 £m	Discontinued operations 2002 £m	Total 2002 £m	Total 2001 £m
Turnover	550	50	175	775	690
Cost of sales	(415)	(40)	(165)	(620)	(555)
Gross profit	135	10	10	155	135
Net operating expenses	(85)	(4)	(25)	(114)	(83)
Less 2001 provision			10	10	
Operating profit	50	6	(5)	51	52
Profit on sale of properties	9			9	6
Provision for loss on operations to be discontinued					(30)
Loss on disposal of discontinued operations			(17)	(17)	
Less 2001 provision			20	20	
Profit on ordinary activities before interest	59	6	(2)	63	28
Interest payable				(18)	(15)
Profit on ordinary activities before taxation				45	13
Tax on profit on ordinary activities				(14)	(4)
Profit on ordinary activities after taxation				31	9
Minority interests				(2)	(2)
[Profit before extraordinary items]				29	7
[Extraordinary items] (included only to show positioning)				–	–
Profit for the financial year				29	7
Dividends				(8)	(1)
Retained profit for the financial year				21	6
Earnings per share				39p	10p
Adjustments [to be itemised and an adequate description given]				*xp*	*xp*
				yp	*yp*

Fig. 8.2 continued

Note	2002			2001		
	Continuing £m	Discontinued £m	Total £m	Continuing £m	Discontinued £m	Total £m
Turnover				500	190	690
Cost of sales				385	170	555
Net operating expenses						
Distribution costs	56	13	69	46	5	51
Administrative costs	41	12	53	34	3	37
Other operating income	(8)	0	(8)	(5)	0	(5)
	89	25	114	75	8	83
Operating profit				40	12	52

The total figure of net operating expenses for continuing operations in 2002 includes £4m in respect of acquisitions (namely distribution costs £3m, administrative expenses £3m and other operating income £2m).

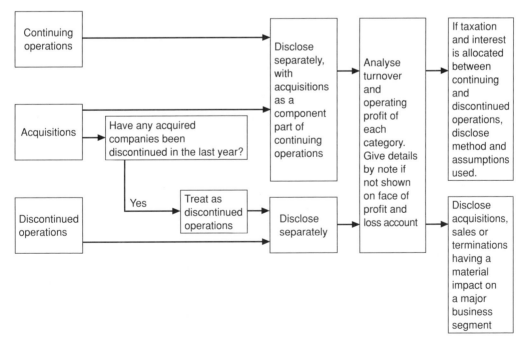

Fig. 8.3 Continuing and discontinued operations

activities after taxation, but before appropriations such as dividends paid or payable, or minority interests where applicable. Taxation and any minority interests relating to the extraordinary item should be shown separately, either on the face of the profit and loss account or as a note to it. The explanatory note published with the standard states that 'extraordinary items are extremely rare as they relate to highly abnormal events or transactions that fall outside the ordinary activities of a reporting entity and which are not expected to recur. In view of the extreme rarity of such items no examples are provided.'

Taxation

Any special circumstances (including those relating to exceptional or extraordinary items) should be disclosed by way of note to the profit and loss account, and their individual effects quantified.

2. Statement of total recognised gains and losses

This is a primary financial statement (i.e. of equal standing to the profit and loss account, balance sheet and cash flow statement). It enables users to consider all recognised gains and losses of a reporting entity in assessing its overall performance. It includes the profit or loss for the period together with all other movements on reserves reflecting recognised gains and losses attributable to shareholders. Transfers between reserves are not shown, but should be shown in notes to the financial statements. Figure 8.4 shows an example of the statement.

If the reporting entity has no recognised gains or losses other than the profit or loss for the period, a statement to this effect should be made immediately

Fig. 8.4 Statement of total recognised gains and losses

	2002	2001 as restated
	£m	£m
Profit for the financial year	29	7
Unrealised surplus on revaluation of properties	4	6
Unrealised (loss)/gain on trade investment	(3)	7
	30	20
Currency translation differences on foreign currency net investments	(2)	5
Total recognised gains and losses relating to the year	28	25
Prior year adjustment	(10)	
Total gains and losses recognised since last annual report	18	

Fig. 8.5 Note of historical cost profits and losses

	2002	2001 as restated
	£m	£m
Reported profit on ordinary activities before taxation	45	13
Realisation of property revaluation gains over previous years	9	10
Difference between a historical cost depreciation charge and the actual depreciation charge of the year calculated on the revalued amount	5	4
Historical cost profit on ordinary activities before taxation	59	27
Historical cost profit for the year retained after taxation, minority interests, extraordinary items and dividends	35	20

below the profit and loss account, and no statement of total recognised gains and losses need be given.

3. Note of historical cost profits and losses

This is a memorandum statement, designed to present the profits or losses of companies which have revalued their assets on a more comparable basis with those that have not. Figure 8.5 shows an example of the statement. It is a summary of the profit and loss account, adjusting the reported profit or loss, if necessary, so as to show it as if no asset revaluations had been made.

Adjustments are made for such items as:

a) the difference between the profit on the disposal of an asset calculated on depreciated historical cost and that calculated on a revalued amount, and

b) the difference between a historical cost depreciation charge and the depreciation charge calculated on the revalued amount included in the profit and loss account for the period.

Unless the historical cost information is unavailable, the note is required whenever there is a material difference between the result as disclosed in the profit and loss account and the result on an unmodified historical cost basis. It should be presented immediately after either the profit and loss account or the statement of total recognised gains and losses (*see above*).

4. Reconciliation of movements in shareholders' funds

This statement reconciles the opening and closing totals of shareholders' funds of the period. Figure 8.6 shows an example of the statement, while Figure 8.7 shows an example of the note to the financial statements which explains the overall movements on reserves. Note how the prior year adjustment has been shown.

Fig. 8.6 Reconciliation of movements in shareholders' funds

	2002	2001 as restated
	£m	£m
Profit for the financial year	29	7
Dividends	(8)	(1)
	21	6
Other recognised gains and losses relating to the year (net)	(1)	18
New share capital subscribed	20	1
Goodwill written-off	(25)	
Net addition to shareholders' funds	15	25
Opening shareholders' funds (originally £375m before deducting prior year adjustment of £10m)	365	340
Closing shareholders' funds	380	365

Fig. 8.7 Reserves (note to financial statements)

	Share premium account	Revaluation reserve	Profit and loss account	Total
	£m	£m	£m	£m
At beginning of year as previously stated	44	200	120	364
Prior year adjustment			(10)	(10)
At beginning of year as restated	44	200	110	354
Premium on issue of shares (nominal value £7m)	13			13
Goodwill written-off			(25)	(25)
Transfer from profit and loss account of the year			21	21
Transfer of realised profits		(14)	14	0
Decrease in value of trade investment		(3)		(3)
Currency translation differences on foreign currency net investments			(2)	(2)
Surplus on property valuations		4		4
At end of year	57	187	118	362

Note: Nominal share capital at end of year £18m (2001 £11m)

Comparative figures

Comparative figures should be given for all items in the primary statements and notes required by the standard. Comparative figures for the 'continuing operations' in the profit and loss account should relate only to those operations which were classified as continuing in the current year.

Prior year adjustments

These arise due to changes in accounting policies or the correction of fundamental errors. Figure 8.8 shows a summary of their treatment.

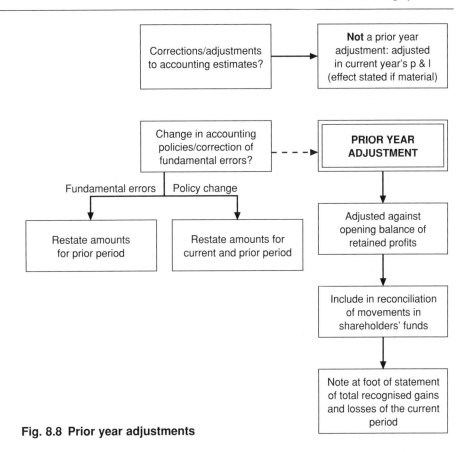

Fig. 8.8 Prior year adjustments

Current position of FRS 3

The ASB issued an Exposure Draft in December 2000 (FRED 22) proposing a new standard to replace FRS 3. The major change would be to combine the existing profit and loss account and statement of total recognised gains and losses into one statement divided into three sections:

- operating;
- financing and treasury; and
- other gains and losses.

FRS 14 EARNINGS PER SHARE
(Issued October 1998)

This standard applies only to *publicly traded* companies, i.e. those whose shares are, or are about to be, quoted on a recognised stock exchange. Other companies which choose to disclose their eps must also follow FRS 14. The earnings per share (eps) is widely used by investors and analysts as an indicator of a company's performance, and the *price–earnings (p/e) ratio*, shown in the *Financial Times* and the financial pages of certain other newspapers is perhaps the clearest indication of the stock market's rating of any particular company. The p/e ratio is simply the market price divided by the eps.

While 'market price' is derived from the forces of supply and demand which exist in the stock markets, eps is, as the name implies, the proportion of a company's earnings which is attributable to each equity share, as based on the company's most recently reported profits. For the p/e ratio to have meaning, the eps must be reliable, and consistently calculated both between one company and another and between one financial period and another. The eps calculation is based on the following formula, as stated in the definition of basic eps contained within the standard:

'Basic earnings per share should be calculated by dividing the net profit or loss for the period attributable to ordinary shareholders by the weighted average number of ordinary shares outstanding during the period.'

The formula can be expressed as follows:

$$\frac{\text{Net profit (or loss) after tax, extraordinary and exceptional items, minority interests and preference dividends}}{\text{Weighted average* number of ordinary shares outstanding during the period}}$$

* The weighted average uses the number of days that the specific shares are outstanding as a proportion of the total number of days in the period. A reasonable approximation of the weighted average is reasonable in many circumstances.

Until FRS 3 was issued, the eps calculation had *excluded* extraordinary items from the calculation of profit, with consequent major distortions occurring for many companies who were able to publish eps figures which were unaffected by such material losses as redundancy or closure costs. This has now changed, as FRS 3 has almost eliminated extraordinary items, and any which a company does decide to disclose are to be adjusted when calculating eps.

It is still possible for companies to calculate additional 'alternative' eps figures based on other levels of profit, but they should be calculated on a consistent basis and reconciled to the 'official' eps based on the stated formula by itemising and quantifying the adjustments made. In terms of presentation, the additional version must not be more prominent than the FRS 14 version, and the reason for presenting an additional eps figure must be stated.

Although the p/e ratio continues to be a key statistic in the evaluation of company shares, it is worth noting the ASB's view that:

'It is not possible to distil the performance of a complex organisation into a single measure. Undue significance, therefore, should not be placed on any one such measure which may purport to achieve this aim. To assess the performance of a reporting entity during a period all components of its activities must be considered.'

Complications

In practice, the calculation of eps is more complicated than simply applying the given FRS 14 formula, due to two factors:

1. changes in share capital;

2. future dilution of earnings.

1. Changes in share capital

The formula contained within the definition of eps uses as divisor the weighted average number of ordinary shares outstanding during the period. Problems arise due to the following events which may take place between the start and end of the accounting period:

1. a bonus issue;

2. a bonus element in any other issue or buyback, e.g. a bonus element in a rights issue to existing shareholders;

3. a share split;

4. a share consolidation.

In each of the above cases, the formula used for determining eps must be amended, as follows:

1. **Bonus issue and share splits,** i.e. where reserves have been converted into equity capital by means of a bonus issue, or where equity shares are split into shares of a smaller nominal value. The eps formula is:

$$\frac{\text{Net profit (or loss) after tax, extraordinary and exceptional items, minority interests and preference dividends}}{\text{Weighted average number of ordinary shares, including those issued by way of bonus or share split, outstanding during the period}}$$

(The corresponding eps figure for the previous period should be adjusted by using the divisor in the above formula.)

An example is as follows:

Net profit Year 1	£300
Net profit Year 2	£500
Ordinary shares outstanding through to 31 October Year 1	400
Bonus issue 1 November Year 1	Two ordinary shares for each ordinary share outstanding at 31 October Year 1 $(400 \times 2 = 800)$

Eps Year 2 $\qquad \dfrac{£500}{(400 + 800)} = 41.7p$

Adjusted Eps Year 1 $\qquad \dfrac{£300}{(400 + 800)} = 25p$

2. **Rights issue at less than fair value,** i.e. where existing shareholders have been invited to buy shares at a discount to 'the pre-rights' market price. Because of this bonus element, the eps for previous years must be adjusted for the purpose of comparisons, and the following factor is applied:

$$\frac{\text{Fair value per share immediately before the exercise of rights}}{\text{Theoretical ex-rights fair value per share}^*}$$

* calculated as follows:

$$\frac{\text{Pre-rights fair value of shares + Proceeds from rights issue}}{\text{Shares outstanding after rights issue}}$$

An example is as follows:

Net profit Year 1	£12,000
Net profit Year 2	£18,000
Net profit Year 3	£24,000
Ordinary shares outstanding before rights issue	600,000
Rights issue	One new ordinary share for each three ordinary shares outstanding (200,000 in total) at an exercise price of £4. Last date to exercise rights 1 April Year 2
Fair value at 31 March Year 2	£7

Calculation of theoretical ex-rights value per share:

$$\frac{\text{Pre-rights fair value of shares + Proceeds from rights issue}}{\text{Shares outstanding after rights issue}}$$

$$\frac{(£7 \times 600,000) + (£4 \times 200,000)}{(600,000 + 200,000)} = \frac{£5m}{0.8m} = £6.25$$

Computation of adjustment factor:

$$\frac{\text{Fair value per share immediately before exercise of rights}}{\text{Theoretical ex-rights fair value per share}} = \frac{£7}{£6.25} = 1.12$$

Computation of earnings per share – shown in Table 8.1.

3. **Share consolidations.** A share consolidation occurs where two or more shares are amalgamated into another share with a higher nominal value. This usually takes place as a confidence-boosting move following a major drop in the market value of a company's shares. For example, a loss-making company with shares of 25p nominal value may have seen its share price fall to 15p. By increasing nominal values to £1 (i.e. 4 × 25p shares being exchanged for one share of £1 nominal value), this should have the effect of quadrupling the share price to 60p.

In calculating the eps following a straightforward consolidation, the number of ordinary shares outstanding before the event is adjusted for

Table 8.1 Computation of earnings per share

	Year 1	Year 2	Year 3
Year 1 (original eps) £12,000/600,000 shares	2p		
Year 1 eps restated for rights issue £12,000/(600,000 × 1.12)	1.8p		
Year 2 eps including effects of rights issue: $$\frac{£18,000}{(600,000 \times 1.12 \times 3/12) + (800,000 \times 9/12)}$$		2.3p	
Year 3 eps £24,000/800,000 shares			3p

the proportionate change in the number of ordinary shares outstanding as if the event had occurred at the beginning of the earliest period reported.

2. Future dilution of earnings

If a company has certain types of convertible loan stocks, options or warrants which carry the right for holders to convert into equity shares at some future date, the effect of these may be to *dilute* the eps in future.

In each of these cases, in addition to the basic eps, the *fully diluted* eps figure should be shown on the face of the profit and loss account. Full information as to the rights of holders of the stock, warrants, etc. and the basis of the calculation of the diluted eps figure should be given.

The calculation of diluted earnings per share is based on the following formula:

Net profit (or loss) after tax, extraordinary and exceptional items, minority interests and preference dividends, plus post-tax effect of dividends, interest or other income or expense relating to the dilutive potential ordinary shares[1]

Weighted average number of ordinary shares outstanding during the period plus the weighted average number of all potential ordinary shares, deemed to have been converted at the beginning of the period[2]

Notes:
1. e.g. interest on convertible loan stock which would be saved if the conversion rights are exercised by the stockholders.
2. Or date of issue if not in existence at the beginning of the period.

APPLICATION IN PRACTICE

Figures 8.9 to 8.13 show relevant extracts from the accounts of Wembley plc and Kingfisher plc.

Fig. 8.9 Wembley plc: consolidated profit and loss account

	Note	£'000	2000 £'000	£'000	1999 £'000
Turnover					
Continuing operations			115,044		106,146
Discontinued operations			–		3,550
Turnover	1		115,044		109,696
Operating costs			(71,613)		(69,562)
Gross profit	2		43,431		40,134
Administrative expenses			(15,652)		(15,085)
Operating profit					
Continuing operations		27,779		24,349	
Discontinued operations	2	–		700	
Operating profit	1		27,779		25,049
Profit on sale of tangible fixed assets	3		1,643		–
Sale or termination of businesses	4		2,058		–
Share of operating loss in associate	5		(1,029)		–
Interest receivable and similar income			3,365		4,299
Interest payable and similar charges	6		(1,770)		(2,702)
Profit on ordinary activities before taxation			32,046		26,646
Tax on profit on ordinary activities	10		(5,328)		(10,232)
Profit for the financial year			26,718		16,414
Ordinary dividend	11		(4,369)		(3,844)
Retained profit for the year			22,349		12,570
Earnings per share	12		61.7p		31.3p
Diluted earnings per share	12		61.1p		31.2p
Adjusted earnings per share	12		40.2p		31.3p
Dividend per share	11		11.0p		8.0p

Fig. 8.10 Wembley plc: extract from notes to the accounts

Notes on the Accounts (extract)

12 Earnings per share	2000	1999
The earnings per share figures have been calculated as follows:		
Profit for the financial year (£'000)	26,718	16,414
Weighted average number of shares in issue ('000)	43,321	52,447
Earnings per share	61.7p	31.3p

Fig. 8.10 continued

	2000	1999
	No. '000	No. '000
The diluted earnings per share of 61.1p [1999: 31.2p] is based on the profit for the financial year of £26,718,000 (1999: £16,414,000) and on 43,746,000 (1999: 52,563,000) ordinary shares, the latter calculated as follows:		
Basic weighted average number of shares	43,321	52,447
Dilutive potential ordinary shares:		
Executive Share Option Schemes	258	–
Employee Sharesave Schemes	112	60
Warrants (note 22 – Share capital)	55	56
	43,746	52,563

The fair value (average price for the year) of Wembley plc shares during 2000 was £5.22 (1999: £3.61).

	2000	1999
	pence per share	pence per share
The adjusted earnings per share figures have been calculated as follows:		
Basic earnings per share	61.7	31.3
Adjustment in respect of profit on sale of tangible fixed assets (note 3)	(3.8)	–
Adjustment in respect of sale or termination of businesses (note 4)	(4.8)	–
Adjustment in respect of tax on sale or termination of businesses (note 4)	(12.9)	–
Adjusted earnings per share	40.2	31.3

An adjusted earnings per share figure is included as, in the opinion of the Directors, this gives a more useful indication of underlying performance.

Fig. 8.11 Wembley plc: statement of total recognised gains and losses

	2000	1999
STATEMENT OF TOTAL RECOGNISED GAINS AND LOSSES	£'000	£'000
Profit for the financial year	26,718	16,414
Exchange differences	8,456	2,930
Total recognised gains relating to the year	**35,174**	**19,344**

A note of historical cost profits and losses has not been provided on the basis that the difference, when compared to the reported result in the profit and loss account, is not material.

Fig. 8.12 Wembley plc: movement in shareholders' funds

	2000	1999
RECONCILIATION OF MOVEMENTS IN SHAREHOLDERS' FUNDS	£'000	£'000
Profit for the financial year	26,718	16,414
Ordinary dividend	(4,369)	(3,844)
Retained profit for the year	22,349	12,570
Issue of shares (share capital plus share premium)	1,745	314
Expenditure in relation to the purchase and cancellation of shares	(43,248)	(27,539)
Exchange adjustments	8,456	2,930
Net movement in shareholders' funds	**(10,698)**	(11,725)
Shareholders' funds at 1 January	**227,867**	239, 592
Shareholders' funds at 31 December	**217,169**	227,867

Fig. 8.13 Kingfisher plc: earnings per share

Earnings per share (pence)

	Note	2000	1999
Basic	12	**30.9**	32.3
Basic before exceptional items	12	**30.1**	31.7
Fully diluted	12	**32.8**	30.3
Fully diluted before exceptional items	12	**31.9**	29.7

Note 12 Earnings per share

12 Earnings per share

Basic earnings per share is calculated by dividing the earnings attributable to ordinary shareholders by the weighted average number of ordinary shares in issue during the year, excluding those held in the ESOP (see note 36) which are treated as cancelled.

For diluted earnings per share, the weighted average number of ordinary shares in issue is adjusted to assume conversion of all dilutive potential ordinary shares. These represent share options granted to employees where the exercise price is less than the average market price of the Company's shares during the year.

Supplementary earnings per share figures are presented. These exclude the effects of exceptional items, acquisition goodwill amortisation and e-commerce and other new channel losses in the year and are presented to allow comparison to prior year on a like for like basis.

Fig. 8.13 continued

	2000			1999		
	Earnings	Weighted average number of shares	Per share amount	Earnings	Weighted average number of shares	Per share amount
	£ millions	millions	pence	£ millions	millions	pence
Basic earnings per share Earnings attributable to ordinary shareholders	**419.4**	**1,357.1**	**30.9**	436.9	1,351.2	32.3
Effect of dilutive securities Options		**33.3**	**(0.7)**		25.5	(0.6)
Convertible loan stock in subsidiary undertakings	**(1.5)**		**(0.1)**	(0.5)		–
Diluted earnings per share	**417.9**	**1,390.4**	**30.1**	436.4	1,376.7	31.7
Supplementary earnings per share **Basic earnings per share**	**419.4**	**1,357.1**	**30.9**	436.9	1,351.2	32.3
Effect of exceptionals Aborted merger costs	**3.5**		**0.2**	–		–
VAT release (post tax)	**–**		**–**	(30.9)		(2.3)
Profit on disposal of properties	**(6.2)**		**(0.4)**	(2.1)		(0.1)
Basic earnings per share before exceptional items	**416.7**	**1,357.1**	**30.7**	403.9	1,351.2	29.9
Acquisition goodwill amortisation	**10.5**		**0.8**	2.2		0.2
E-commerce and other new channels (post tax)	**18.5**		**1.3**	2.7		0.2
Basic – adjusted earnings per share	**445.7**	**1,357.1**	**32.8**	408.8	1,351.2	30.3
Diluted earnings per share	**417.9**	**1,390.4**	**30.1**	436.4	1,376.7	31.7
Effect of exceptionals Aborted merger costs	**3.5**		**0.2**	–		–
VAT release (post tax)	**–**		**–**	(30.9)		(2.3)
Profit on disposal of properties	**(6.2)**		**(0.4)**	(2.1)		(0.1)
Diluted earnings per share before exceptional items	**415.2**	**1,390.4**	**29.9**	403.4	1,376.7	29.3
Acquisition goodwill amortisation	**10.5**		**0.7**	2.2		0.2
E-commerce and other new channels (post tax)	**18.5**		**1.3**	2.7		0.2
Diluted – adjusted earnings per share	**444.2**	**1,390.4**	**31.9**	408.3	1,376.7	29.7

CHAPTER SUMMARY

FRS 3 Reporting Financial Performance

- Introduced changes to the profit and loss format (continuing/discontinued activities, acquisitions).
- Introduced a statement of total recognised gains and losses, a note of historical cost profits and losses and a reconciliation of movements in shareholders' funds.
- Abolished extraordinary items.

FRS 14 Earnings Per Share

- Basic formula:

$$\frac{\text{Net profit (or loss) after tax, extraordinary and exceptional items, minority interests, and preference dividends}}{\text{Weighted average number of ordinary shares outstanding during the period}}$$

- Formula if there has been a bonus issue or share split: as basic eps, but divisor includes ordinary shares issued by way of bonus or share split during the year.
- If there has been a rights issue at less than fair value, previous year's eps must be adjusted by the factor:

$$\frac{\text{Fair value per share immediately before the exercise of rights}}{\text{Theoretical ex-rights fair value per share*}}$$

*calculated as follows:

$$\frac{\text{Pre-rights fair values of shares + Proceeds from rights issue}}{\text{Shares outstanding after rights issue}}$$

- *Diluted earnings* refers to the effect of potential conversion rights of loan stocks, warrants etc. into ordinary shares at future dates. Formula is:

$$\frac{\text{(numerator as in basic eps) plus post-tax effect of dividends, interest or other income or expense relating to the dilutive potential ordinary shares}}{\text{(divisor as in basic eps) plus the weighted average number of all potential ordinary shares, deemed to have been converted at the beginning of the period}}$$

DISCUSSION QUESTIONS

1. 'Extraordinary items were a useful way of showing unusual occurrences in a business's finances, but FRS 3 abolished them.' Discuss.

2. If the ASB's view is that it is not possible to distil the performance of a complex organisation into a single measure, why does it give 'Earnings per share' the accolade of having a complete accounting standard dedicated to it?

(*See Appendix 3* for outline responses.)

EXAMINATION QUESTIONS

1. Answer the following questions in accordance with FRS 14 *Earnings per share* (eps).

a) Why is it considered important to measure eps and what figure for earnings should you use when calculating eps for a group of companies with ordinary and preference shares?

(8 marks)

b) How should you deal with the following situations when calculating eps?

i) The issue of a separate class of equity shares which do not rank for any dividend in the period under review, but will do so in the future.

(2 marks)

ii) A scrip (or bonus) issue of shares during the year.

(2 marks)

iii) Shares issued during the period as consideration for shares in a new subsidiary.

(2 marks)

c) On 1 January 2001 a company had 3 million ordinary shares of £1 each in issue. On 1 July 2001 the company made a rights issue of 1 for 2 at a price of £1.50. The market price of the existing shares immediately before the rights issue was £2.00.
The earnings of the company for the year ended 31 December 2001 were £750,000.
Calculate the eps for the year ended 31 December 2001.

(4 marks)

ACCA (amended)

2. You are given the following information relating to S plc:

	£000	£000
Profit on ordinary activities before taxation		4,131
UK. tax on profit on ordinary activities		1,629
Profit on ordinary activities after taxation		2,502
Minority interest		90
		2,412
Retained profits at 1 January 2001		5,268
		7,680
Dividends:		
Preference	45	
Ordinary	669	
		714
Retained profits at 31 December 2001		6,966

i) From 1 January 2000 until 31 March 2001 the share capital of S plc consisted of 12 million ordinary shares of 25 pence each (authorised, issued and fully paid) and 900,000 preference shares of £1 each (authorised, issued and fully paid).

ii) On 1 April 2001 S plc made a 1 for 4 rights issue of ordinary shares at £1. The market price of an ordinary share of S plc on the last day of quotation cum rights was £1.50.

iii) The earnings per share for the year ended 31 December 2000 had been calculated at 15.0 pence.

In accordance with the requirements of FRS 14 *Earnings per share*, you are required to:

a) calculate the earnings per share of S plc for the year ended 31 December 2001;

b) calculate the adjusted earnings per share of S plc for the year ended 31 December 2000;

c) show how the results of your calculations, together with any necessary notes, would be disclosed in the financial statements of S plc.

(15 marks)

CIMA (amended)

(*See Appendix 4* for suggested answers.)

Chapter 9

The substance of transactions, related parties: FRSs 5 & 8

Reporting the substance of transactions; Related party disclosures

INTRODUCTION

FRS 5 is the ASB's attempt to crack down on 'off balance sheet financing', whereby companies have taken advantage of loopholes in company law and existing standards to misrepresent and distort the values of assets and liabilities shown on their balance sheets.

Described as 'conceptual and judgmental' by a partner in a major accounting firm, FRS 5 requires auditors to be more vigilant than ever before when their clients come up with schemes which are aimed at moving debts off their balance sheets.

In Chapter 4, it was seen how the standard on leasing (SSAP 21) was based on the principle of substance over form, so that assets which were not legally owned by a business were to be included on the lessee's balance sheet under certain circumstances. This plugged one of the 'off balance sheet' loopholes as, before SSAP 21 was issued, leased assets were never shown on the lessee's balance sheet. This led to unreal situations where, for example, manufacturing companies with millions of pounds of leased assets showed neither the value of the assets nor the liability to the finance companies on their balance sheets.

FRS 5 continues this theme of 'substance over form', and tackles a number of schemes which creative accountants have used, such as the 'quasi subsidiary' deals which kept £148m off Burton Group plc's 1990 balance sheet; the sale and leaseback deals which kept £41m debt out of Queens Moat Houses plc's 1991 accounts while adding £18m to the company's profits; and the securitisation deals which kept £1.7bn of mortgages off National Home Loans plc's 1991 balance sheet. It is alleged that merchant banks in the 1980s were actively touting schemes to companies which allowed funds to be raised without being reflected in the balance sheet.

The FRS addresses general principles, but 'application notes' (not part of the standard) are also given, showing how it is to be applied to five specific transaction types. The ASB is aware that if it is too specific loopholes will again be found. The four main areas covered by FRS 5 are:

1. how to determine the substance of a transaction;
2. whether any resulting assets and liabilities should be included in the balance sheet;
3. what disclosures are necessary;
4. whether any special-purpose vehicle companies (quasi-subsidiaries) involved in a transaction should be included in the consolidation.

FRS 5 does not change the accounting treatment and disclosure of the vast majority of transactions, but the substance of more complex transactions may mean that the commercial effect may not be readily apparent. Such transactions include:

1. those where the party that gains the principal benefits generated by an asset is not its legal owner;
2. where a transaction is linked by others in such a way that the commercial effect can be understood only by considering the series as a whole;
3. where an option is included on terms that make its exercise highly likely.

Regarding FRS 8 *Related party disclosures*, this standard marked the last instalment of the ASB's drive to stamp out accounting abuses such as so-called 'back-door' directors' deals, and brought UK practice into line with international standards (IAS 24). Put simply, the standard requires companies to disclose all material transactions and balances with related parties and also to disclose the controlling party or ultimate controlling party.

In a typically memorable phrase, Sir David Tweedie, Chairman of the ASB, said: 'In financial matters it is not enough to look at the puppets; users need to see the strings and know who is pulling them.' However, a somewhat cynical note was struck by Gerry Acher, head of accounting and auditing at KPMG, who said 'A fraudster who is beyond the law is unlikely to be deterred by a new accounting standard.'

FRS 5 REPORTING THE SUBSTANCE OF TRANSACTIONS
(Issued April 1994, amended December 1994 and September 1998)

Objective

The objective of FRS 5 is stated as '. . . to ensure that the substance of an entity's transactions is reported in its financial statements. The commercial effect of the entity's transactions, and any resulting assets, liabilities, gains or losses, should be faithfully represented in its financial statements.'

Assets are defined as 'rights or other access to future economic benefits controlled by an entity as a result of past transactions or events'.

Liabilities are defined as 'an entity's obligations to transfer economic benefits as a result of past transactions or events'.

A key step in determining the substance of a transaction is to identify whether it has given rise to new assets or liabilities for the entity and whether it has increased or decreased the entity's existing assets or liabilities.

Exclusions

The FRS does *not* apply to:

1. forward contracts and futures (e.g. for foreign currencies or commodities)

2. foreign exchange and interest rate swaps

3. contracts where a net amount will be paid or received based on the movement in a price index

4. expenditure commitments and orders placed

5. employment contracts

unless they are part of a transaction that falls within the scope of FRS 5.

Relationship with other standards

Where there is an overlap between FRS 5 and another SSAP (e.g. SSAP 21 *Accounting for hire purchase and leases*), FRS or statutory provision, the standard or statute that contains the more specific provisions should be applied.

The four key areas

As stated in the introduction, the FRS is based on general principles divided into four key areas, followed by 'application notes' on several specific types of off balance sheet transactions. The four key areas are:

1. the substance of transactions;

2. recognition of assets and liabilities;

3. disclosures;

4. quasi-subsidiaries.

1. The substance of transactions

This is the core of the standard: that an entity should report the substance of the transactions into which it has entered. In determining the substance of a transaction (or group or series of transactions where appropriate), all its aspects and implications should be identified and greater weight given to those more likely to have a commercial effect in practice.

In determining the substance of a transaction it is necessary to identify:

1. whether the transaction has given rise to *new* assets or liabilities for the reporting entity;

2. whether it has *changed* the entity's existing assets and liabilities.

According to the definition of an asset (*see above*), the entity must enjoy rights or other access to benefits arising from the transaction. Evidence of this is given if the entity is exposed to the risks inherent in the benefits, taking into account the likelihood of those risks having a commercial effect in practice. A liability is defined as an obligation to *transfer* economic benefits, so evidence of this is given where an entity is unable to avoid, legally or commercially, an outflow of benefits.

2. Recognition of assets and liabilities

Recognition is defined as 'the process of incorporating an item into the primary financial statements under the appropriate heading. It involves depiction of the item in words and by a monetary amount and inclusion of that amount in the statement totals.'

The standard requires recognition in the balance sheet of assets and liabilities if:

1. there is sufficient evidence of the existence of the item (including the inflow/outflow of benefit referred to above); and

2. the item can be measured at a monetary amount with sufficient reliability.

Transactions in previously recognised assets

Where an asset which has been previously recognised in the financial statements is involved in a transaction, it should continue to be recognised if the asset definition (*see above*) still applies. However, if the transaction transfers all rights to benefits or exposure to the risks inherent in those benefits, then the asset should no longer be recognised. An example given is where debts are 'sold', but with recourse to the seller in the event of bad debts, and where the finance charge is linked to the speed with which debtors pay. In such cases, the seller would continue to recognise an asset equal to the amount of the debts, even though the legal title has passed to the buyer of the debts.

Linked presentation

In certain defined cases, the standard allows a 'linked presentation' to be used on the balance sheet, whereby finance associated with a particular asset is deducted from the asset it finances. For example, the finance received from the sale of debts (see previous paragraph) could be deducted (i.e. 'linked') from the debts themselves. The key requirement for the 'linked presentation' is that the finance is repaid from the asset it finances and that there is no provision for the asset to be kept on repayment of the finance.

Assets and liabilities should not be offset.

3. Disclosure of the substance of transactions

Although the vast majority of transactions will not require any more disclosure than that currently required, in the case of more complex transactions further information will be needed. For example, certain assets may not be available for use as security for liabilities of the entity, in which case full details should be given.

Even where neither an asset nor a liability is recognised as a result of a transaction, further details may be needed where the transaction gives rise to guarantees, commitments or other rights and obligations.

4. Quasi-subsidiaries

A **quasi-subsidiary** is defined as 'a company, trust, partnership or other vehicle that, though not fulfilling the definition of a subsidiary, is directly or indirectly controlled by the reporting entity and gives rise to benefits for that entity that are in substance no different from those that would arise were the vehicle a subsidiary.'

In determining control, regard should be given as to who, in practice, directs its financial and operating policies.

Where the entity has a quasi-subsidiary, the assets, liabilities, profits, losses and cash flows should be reported in the consolidated financial statements as if they were those of a subsidiary. The only exception is where the interest in the quasi-subsidiary is held with a view to subsequent resale, and it has not previously been included in the consolidated financial statements. Disclosure is also required, in summary form, of the financial statements of quasi-subsidiaries.

Application notes

An appendix to FRS 5 includes five 'application notes' which give detailed information concerning the treatment of specific transactions. The notes are not part of the standard, being seen as an 'aid to understanding'. The five areas are:

1. consignment stock;
2. sale and repurchase agreements;
3. factoring of debts;
4. securitised assets (i.e. where specific groups of assets are financed, rather than the whole business);
5. loan transfers.

These application notes are outside the scope of this text.

Private Finance Initiatives and similar contracts

In September 1998, the ASB issued an amendment which explains how the standard should apply to transactions conducted under the government's Private Finance Initiative (PFI), whereby private operators construct capital assets such as roads, schools and hospitals and use the assets to provide services to a public sector 'purchaser', e.g. the Department of the Environment, Transport and the Regions. The amendment addresses the key question of which party to the contract (purchaser or operator) should record the asset.

Some PFI contracts contain a 'service' element such as laundry, cleaning, etc. These should be excluded from the consideration of who has an asset of the property. The remaining elements of the property are classed into:

1. those where the remaining elements are payments for the property, in which case SSAP 21 *Accounting for leases and hire purchase contracts* should apply;

2. other contracts, which would come under the scope of FRS 5. The key question of the extent to which each party to the contract ('purchaser' or 'operator') records an asset of the property depends on the extent to which each party bears the potential variations in property profits or losses. The criteria for determining this are set out in considerable detail in the amendment to the standard and are outside the scope of this text.

FRS 8 RELATED PARTY DISCLOSURES
(Issued October 1995)

Objective

The standard's objective is to ensure that financial statements contain the disclosures necessary to draw attention to the possibility that the reported financial position and results may have been affected by the existence of related parties and by material transactions with them. The standard is applicable to all companies, regardless of size.

Definitions

A **related party transaction** is defined as the transfer of assets or liabilities or the performance of services by, to or for a related party irrespective of whether a price is charged.

A **related party relationship** is defined as existing where at any time during the financial period,

a) one party has direct or indirect control of the other party; or

b) the parties are subject to common control from the same source; or

c) one party has influence over the financial and operating policies of the other party to an extent that that other party might be inhibited from pursuing at all times its own separate interests; or

d) the parties, in entering a transaction, are subject to influence from the same source to such an extent that one of the parties to the transaction has sub-ordinated its own separate interests.

Control is defined as 'the ability to direct the financial and operating policies of an entity with a view to gaining economic benefits from its activities'.

Close family is defined as '. . . those family members, or members of the same household, who may be expected to influence, or be influenced by, that person in their dealings with the reporting entity'.

Key management are 'those persons in senior positions having authority or responsibility for directing or controlling the major activities and resources of the reporting entity'.

Who are related parties?

In brief, the definition includes companies in the same group as the reporting entity, associated companies, directors and their close families, and pension funds for the benefit of employees of the reporting entity.

Furthermore, key management and those controlling 20% or more of the voting rights are presumed to be related parties unless it can be demonstrated that neither party has influenced the financial and operating policies of the other in such a way as to inhibit the pursuit of separate interests.

Disclosure of control

When the reporting entity is controlled by another party, there should be disclosure of:

a) the related party relationship; and

b) the name of the related party (and, if different, the ultimate controlling party), or, if the controlling party or ultimate controlling party is not known, a disclosure of that fact.

These disclosures should be made irrespective of whether any transactions have taken place between the controlling parties and the reporting entities.

Disclosure of transactions and balances

Material transactions (irrespective of whether a price is charged for them) should be disclosed within the financial statements as follows:

a) names of the transacting related parties;

b) description of the relationship between the parties;

c) description of the transactions;

d) amounts involved;

e) any other elements of the transactions necessary for an understanding of the financial statements;

f) the amounts due to or from related parties at the balance sheet date and provisions for doubtful debts due from such parties at that date; and

g) amounts written off in the period in respect of debts due to or from related parties.

Exemptions from disclosure

No disclosure is required:

a) in consolidated financial statements of intra-group transactions and balances eliminated on consolidation;

b) by parent undertakings where its own group provides the necessary disclosures;

c) in subsidiary undertakings, 90% or more of whose voting rights are controlled within the group, of transactions with other group entities, provided that consolidated financial statements which include that subsidiary are readily available.

APPLICATION IN PRACTICE

The related party transactions of Flying Brands plc are shown in Figure 9.1.

Fig. 9.1 Flying Brands plc: related party transactions

32 – Related party transactions

Freehold land and building additions of £112,000 were supplied by a company in which Mr T Dunningham has a 50% beneficial interest. The additions relate to building works carried out at Retreat Farm, Jersey which were provided at cost. Staff accommodation was provided at a cost of £49,000 by a company in which Mr T Dunningham has a 50% beneficial interest.

Company secretarial services were provided by Communitie.com Limited at a cost of £5,000. Information technology services were provided by the Company to Communitie.com for a total consideration of less than £5,000.

CHAPTER SUMMARY

FRS 5 Reporting the Substance of Transactions

- Four main areas:
  - the substance of transactions – has the transaction given rise to new assets or liabilities and has it changed the entity's existing assets and liabilities;
  - recognition of assets and liabilities in the balance sheet – if sufficient evidence of the existence of the item and the item can be measured at a monetary amount with sufficient reliability;

▶

- disclosures, e.g. where assets are not available for use as security against liabilities;
- quasi-subsidiaries – definition: 'a company, trust, partnership or other vehicle that, though not fulfilling the definition of a subsidiary, is directly or indirectly controlled by the reporting entity and gives rise to benefits for that entity that are in substance no different from those that would arise were the vehicle a subsidiary.'

FRS 8 Related Party Disclosures

- Definition of related party transaction: the transfer of assets or liabilities or the performance of services by, to or for a related party irrespective of whether a price is charged.
- Disclosure of transactions to be made include the names of related parties, their relationship and description of the transactions and amounts involved.

DISCUSSION QUESTIONS

1. 'No matter how many standards are issued, there will always be dishonest directors who find loopholes in them.' Discuss.

2. 'The excessive detail required to be disclosed by FRSs 5 and 8 will act as a restraint on entrepreneurial initiatives taken by directors for the company's good.' Discuss.

(*See Appendix 3* for outline responses.)

EXAMINATION QUESTION

The board of D plc has been offered the opportunity to make use of a slightly unusual financing package and are worried about its effect on the company's balance sheet.

Explain what is meant by off balance sheet financing (OBF) and briefly explain how FRS 5 – Reporting the Substance of Transactions – distinguishes between matters which must be included in the balance sheet and those which do not.

(20 marks)
CIMA

(*See Appendix 4* for suggested answer.)

Chapter 10

Segmental reporting: SSAP 25

INTRODUCTION

This is a straightforward statement, requiring companies to disclose information relating to performance in their main classes of business and the geographical areas in which they trade. Although both Stock Exchange listing requirements and the 1985 Companies Act state that certain information must be disclosed, the standard goes further, for example by requiring that the net assets are shown, broken down by both business and geographical segments.

SSAP 25 SEGMENTAL REPORTING
(Issued June 1990)

The explanatory note to the standard states that the purpose of segmental information is to provide information to assist the users of financial statements:

a) to appreciate more thoroughly the results and financial position of the entity by permitting a better understanding of the entity's past performance and thus a better assessment of its future prospects; and

b) to be aware of the impact that changes in significant components of a business may have on the business as a whole.

The standard applies to the following classes of company:

a) a plc, or a company with a plc as a subsidiary;

b) a banking or insurance company or group;

c) a company which exceeds the criteria, multiplied by 10, for definition as a middle-sized company as per CA 1985.

However, a subsidiary that is not a plc or a banking or insurance company need not comply with the standard if its parent provides segmental information in compliance with the standard.

As with the relevant provisions of the CA 1985, the standard gives exemption from disclosure where such disclosure would be 'seriously prejudicial to the interests of the reporting entity'. The fact that information has been withheld must be stated.

How many segments?

It is up to the directors to decide how many different classes of business the company has and how many markets it has traded with. However, they should have regard to the purpose of segmental reporting as set out above, and also the need of the user of the financial statements to be informed where different classes of business or geographical areas:

a) earn a return on investment that is out of line with the rest of the business; or

b) are subject to different degrees of risk; or

c) have experienced different rates of growth; or

d) have different potentials for future development.

If a class of business or geographical segment is *significant* to an entity as a whole, it should be identified as a reportable segment. A segment is significant if:

a) its third-party turnover is 10 per cent or more of the total third-party turnover of the entity; or

b) its segment result, whether profit or loss, is 10 per cent or more of the combined result of all segments in profit or of all segments in loss, whichever combined result is the greater; or

c) its net assets are 10 per cent or more of the total net assets of the entity.

Business segments

The decision as to whether or not a company operates in different classes of business depends upon the following factors:

a) the nature of the products, services or production processes;

b) the markets in which the products or services are sold;

c) the distribution channels for the products;

d) the manner in which the entity's activities are organised;

e) any separate legislative framework relating to part of the business (e.g. a bank or insurance company).

Geographical segments

A geographical segment is defined as a geographical area comprising an individual country or group of countries in which an entity operates, or to which it supplies products or services.

By giving an analysis of results by geographical segment, the user of the financial statements is able to assess factors such as:

a) expansionist or restrictive economic climates;

b) stable or unstable political regimes;

c) exchange control regulations;

d) exchange rate fluctuations.

Disclosure

Where an entity has two or more classes of business, or operates in two or more geographical segments which differ substantially from each other, it should define each segment in its financial statements, and report with respect to each class the following financial information:

a) turnover, split between that derived from external customers and that derived from other segments;

b) profit or loss (before tax, minority interests and extraordinary items);

c) net assets.

The geographical segmentation of turnover by origin* should be disclosed, as well as the turnover to third parties by destination† (unless this is not materially different from turnover by origin).

The segment result will normally be disclosed before taking account of interest. However, where all or part of the entity's business is to earn and/or incur interest, or where interest income or expense is central to the business, interest should normally be included in arriving at the segment profit or loss. To the extent that the segment result is disclosed after accounting for interest, the corresponding interest-bearing assets or liabilities should be included.

If the amounts disclosed in the segmental report differ from the related total in the financial accounts, a reconciliation should be given.

Comparative figures for the previous accounting period should be given. Directors should redefine segments when appropriate, and disclose the nature of, and reasons for, any such changes made. Comparative figures will need restating in this event.

Consolidated accounts

Segmental information should be based on consolidated financial statements where both parent and consolidated results are given.

---

* *Origin* of turnover is defined as the geographical segment from which products services are supplied to a third party or to another segment.

† *Destination* of turnover is defined as the geographical segment to which products or services are supplied.

Associated companies

If associated companies account for at least 20% of the total result or total net assets, then the following information will be disclosed:

a) the group's share of the associate's results (before tax, minorities and extra-ordinary items);

b) the group's share of the associate's net assets (including goodwill not written off) stated, where possible, at fair values at the date of acquisition.

If the information is unobtainable or considered prejudicial to the business of the associate, then it need not be disclosed. A note stating reasons for the non-disclosure, together with a brief description of the omitted business or businesses should be given.

Common costs

In reporting the results of segments, there is a problem of how to allocate costs which are common to several different segments. Many companies have their own methods of apportionment which they use for internal management purposes, and these can be similarly apportioned for external reporting.

If, however, apportionment would be misleading, then it is acceptable to deduct common costs from the combined total of the segment results.

APPLICATION IN PRACTICE

Figure 10.1 shows the segmental analysis provided by Wembley plc in its 2000 accounts.

CHAPTER SUMMARY

SSAP 25 Segmental Reporting

- If an entity has two or more classes of business or operates in two or more geographical segments, it should define them and report for each class:
  - turnover, split between that arising from external customers and that arising from other segments;
  - profit or loss;
  - net assets.

Fig. 10.1 Wembley plc: segmental analysis

1 Segmental analysis	2000 Turnover £'000	2000 Profit £'000	2000 Net assets £'000	1999 Turnover £'000	1999 Profit £'000	1999 Net assets £'000
Class of business						
Continuing operations:						
Entertainment						
US venues	63,161	27,876	129,560	52,559	22,021	118,613
UK greyhounds	20,850	3,648	37,404	19,455	3,802	35,953
24dogs/New Media Services	43	(1,993)	119	–	–	–
Events services						
Keith Prowse	16,245	902	615	19,752	1,076	1,882
Wembley Complex	14,570	505	36,965	14,380	(341)	27,112
Event Management Services	175	(995)	4,143	–	–	–
Central management	–	(2,164)	(2,489)	–	(2,209)	(3,175)
	115,044	27,779	206,317	106,146	24,349	180,385
Discontinued operations:						
Sports stadium management	–	–	(140)	3,550	700	(695)
Leisure services	–	–	(1,206)	–	–	(18,108)
Total turnover	115,044			109,696		
Operating profit		27,779			25,049	
Profit on sale of tangible fixed assets		1,643			–	
Sale or termination of businesses		2,058			–	
Share of operating loss in associate		(1,029)			–	
Net interest		1,595			1,597	
Profit before tax		32,046			26,646	
Capital employed			204,971			161,582
Net cash			12,198			66,285
Net assets			217,169			227,867
Geographical area						
Continuing operations:						
United Kingdom and Ireland	51,883	(97)	76,757	53,587	2,328	61,772
North America (USA)	63,161	27,876	129,560	52,559	22,021	118,613
	115,044	27,779	206,317	106,146	24,349	180,385
Discontinued operations:						
United Kingdom	–	–	(1,206)	3,550	700	(1,355)
North America (USA)	–	–	–	–	–	(16,753)
Far East	–	–	(140)	–	–	(695)
	–	–	(1,346)	3,550	700	(18,803)

Turnover represents sales (excluding VAT) to external customers. Turnover between business segments is not material. The analysis of turnover by geographical area is based on the origin of the supply. The analysis by destination is not materially different and so is not shown.

The analyses of capital employed by activity and geographical area are calculated on net assets excluding inter company balances and investments and all cash and borrowings. The Group's financing is centrally arranged and accordingly the cash and borrowings and net interest are not attributed to individual activities or geographical areas.

The results for US venues include income from gaming, greyhound and horse racing venues.

DISCUSSION QUESTION

1. 'As SSAP 25 (and the 1985 Companies Act) gives exemption from disclosure where such disclosure would be seriously prejudicial to the interests of the reporting entity, this effectively negates the usefulness of the standard.' Discuss.

(*See Appendix 3* for outline responses.)

EXAMINATION QUESTION

You are required to discuss

a) the benefits, to readers of financial statements, of including detailed segmental financial information in a group's financial report;

b) the reasons why a group may resist disclosing such detailed segmental financial information in its annual report.

(15 marks)
CIMA

(*See Appendix 4* for suggested answer.)

Chapter 11

Post balance sheet events, provisions and contingencies: SSAP 17 and FRS 12

Post balance sheet events; Provisions, contingent liabilities and contingent assets

INTRODUCTION

According to the 'official terminology' published by the Chartered Institute of Management Accountants, a balance sheet is:

> 'A statement of the financial position of an entity at a given date disclosing the value of the assets, liabilities and accumulated funds such as shareholders' contributions and reserves, prepared to give a true and fair view of the state of the entity at that date.'

The 'true and fair view' cannot be given solely by listing the relevant balances as appear in the ledger at the 'given date'. Comprehensive notes are appended which not only explain the accounting policies adopted but also give detailed information to ensure compliance with company law, accounting standards and possibly Stock Exchange requirements. This chapter concerns two standards which may be referred to in notes, relating firstly to certain events which occur *after* the balance sheet date and secondly to conditions which, though *in existence at the balance sheet date*, will be confirmed only on the occurrence (or non-occurrence) of one or more uncertain future events.

SSAP 17 ACCOUNTING FOR POST BALANCE SHEET EVENTS
(Issued August 1980)

It may come as a surprise to students that events occurring after the date of the balance sheet need be considered when drawing up the financial statements. In practice, they need to be reflected in the statements only if they are material and provide additional evidence of conditions that existed at the balance sheet date.

The 'post balance sheet period' during which such events might arise starts at the date of the balance sheet and ends with the date on which the financial statements are approved by the board of directors. This is usually the date of the company's (or holding company's, in the case of group accounts) board meeting at which the approval is given. The date is always shown in the statements, usually at the foot of the 'Directors' Report'.

The standard excludes any *preliminary consideration* given by directors within the post balance sheet period to matters which may lead to decisions being taken at some future date. However, relevant information concerning any material events occurring after the end of the post balance sheet period *should* be published to avoid misleading the users of the financial statements. An example is given in *Application in practice*, p. 163.

Classification

The definition of a post balance sheet event is given in the standard as follows:

'. . . those events, both favourable and unfavourable, which occur between the balance sheet date and the date on which the financial statements are approved by the board of directors.'

They are divided between *adjusting* events (i.e. those which require figures to be adjusted within the financial statements) and *non-adjusting* events which, as their name implies, do not require any changes to amounts, but need only be 'noted'.

The distinction between the two depends upon whether they relate to conditions existing at the balance sheet date as the following example illustrates.

Example

A company has a financial year which ends on 31 March 2002. Before the accounts are approved by the directors, consideration is given to the following matters.

1. A plot of land was sold on 10 March 2002, at a price which was determined by an independent valuation in April 2002.
2. A factory building was acquired in April 2002.

Both are regarded as material events.

The first item is an *adjusting* event, as the valuation provides additional evidence of conditions existing at the balance sheet date. As such, the determined price will be incorporated within the financial statements for the year ended 31 March 2002.

The second item is *non-adjusting*, as it concerns conditions which did not exist at the date of the balance sheet. The accounts will include a note giving details of the acquisition, for the purpose of providing users with additional and relevant information on which to judge the company's performance and prospects.

Adjusting events

In addition to the subsequent determination of the purchase price of assets as illustrated in the previous section, an appendix to the standard gives the following examples of 'adjusting events'.

a) Fixed assets:

The subsequent determination of the proceeds of sale of assets purchased or sold before the year end.

b) Property:

A valuation which provides evidence of a permanent diminution in value.

c) Investments:

The receipt of a copy of the financial statements or other information in respect of an unlisted company which provides evidence of a permanent diminution in the value of a long-term investment.

d) Stocks and work in progress:

i) The receipt of proceeds of sales after the balance sheet date or other evidence concerning the net realisable value of stocks.

ii) The receipt of evidence that the previous estimate of accrued profit on a long-term contract was materially inaccurate.

e) Debtors:

The renegotiation of amounts owing by debtors, or the insolvency of a debtor.

f) Dividends receivable:

The declaration of dividends by subsidiaries and associated companies relating to periods prior to the balance sheet date of the holding company.

g) Taxation:

The receipt of information regarding rates of taxation.

h) Claims:

Amounts received or receivable in respect of insurance claims which were in the course of negotiation at the balance sheet date.

i) Discoveries:

The discovery of errors or frauds which show that the financial statements were incorrect.

Note that there is usually no necessity to disclose adjusting events as separate items in the financial statements.

Adjusting events and the 'going concern' concept

As stated in FRS 18 *Accounting policies* (*see* p. 25), the going concern concept assumes that the enterprise will continue in operational existence for the foreseeable future. It sometimes happens that events occur during the post balance sheet period which give cause for doubt as to the appropriateness of applying the concept when preparing the financial statements. Examples might include the liquidation of a major debtor or the existence of worsening cash flow problems. The standard requires such matters to be treated as adjusting events where they indicate that the application of the going concern concept to the whole or a material part of the company is not appropriate.

Non-adjusting events

In addition to a list of suggested adjusting events, the appendix to the standard provides examples of non-adjusting events, as follows.

a) Mergers and acquisitions.

b) Reconstructions and proposed reconstructions.

c) Issues of shares and debentures.

d) Purchases and sales of fixed assets and investments.

e) Losses of fixed assets or stocks as a result of a catastrophe such as a fire or flood.

f) Opening new trading activities or extending existing trading activities.

g) Closing a significant part of the trading activities if this was not anticipated at the year end.

h) Decline in the value of property and investments held as fixed assets, if it can be demonstrated that the decline occurred after the year end.

i) Changes in rates of foreign exchange.

j) Government action, such as nationalisation.

k) Strikes and other labour disputes.

l) Augmentation of pension benefits.

In exceptional circumstances, the need for prudence may require non-adjusting events to be reclassified as adjusting, with full details being given in the financial statements.

Post balance sheet events and 'window dressing'

Window dressing has been defined* as:

'Transactions, the purpose of which is to arrange affairs so that the financial statements of the concern give a misleading or unrepresentative impression of its financial position.'

Examples of window dressing include circular transactions, where two or more companies enter into transactions with each other of equivalent values, the purpose being to inflate amounts stated in the financial statements of one or more of the companies, with the transactions being reversed after the year end.

SSAP 17 requires that such alterations be disclosed where they are material, to avoid misleading the users of the financial statements.

---

* Technical Release 603, ICAEW, issued December 1985.

Information to be given on disclosure

As stated previously, those post balance sheet events which are non-adjusting or represent the reversal of 'window dressing' transactions require disclosure in the financial statements. In such cases, the following information should be given:

a) the nature of the event;

b) an estimate of the financial effect, or a statement that it is not practicable to make such an estimate.

Relevant extracts from published company accounts are given in *Application in practice* p. 163.

Summary of SSAP 17

Figure 11.1 provides a flowchart summarising the accounting treatment of post balance sheet events laid down in SSAP 17.

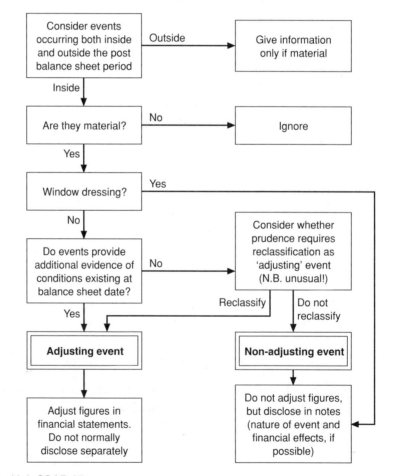

Fig. 11.1 SSAP 17

FRS 12 PROVISIONS, CONTINGENT LIABILITIES AND CONTINGENT ASSETS
(Issued September 1998)

Provisions are liabilities of uncertain timing or amount. However, there are some liabilities (and assets) which are 'contingent' in the sense that their existence will be confirmed only by the occurrence of an *uncertain* future event or events not wholly within an entity's control. An example could be a legal case for damages against a company – if the court's decision has not been made at the date of preparation of the financial statements, but there are *potential* damages, what if anything should be stated in the accounts?

Although the term 'provisions' is also used in the context of depreciation, doubtful debts, etc., these are regarded as adjustments to *the carrying amounts of assets* (*see* FRS 15, p. 40) and are not covered by FRS 12. Other liabilities such as trade creditors and accruals are not provisions as they are either certain in amount or can be estimated with far less uncertainty than in the case of a provision.

Objectives

The FRS has been issued to ensure that provisions, contingent liabilities and contingent assets have appropriate recognition criteria and measurement bases, and that sufficient information is to be disclosed regarding their nature, timing and amount.

Key definitions

Provision – a liability of uncertain timing or amount.

Contingent liability – a possible obligation that arises from past events and whose existence will be confirmed only by the occurrence of one or more uncertain future events not wholly within the entity's control; *or* a present obligation that arises from past events but is not recognised because:

a) it is not probable that a transfer of economic benefits will be required to settle the obligation; or

b) the amount of the obligation cannot be measured with sufficient reliability.

Contingent asset – a possible asset that arises from past events and whose existence will be confirmed only by the occurrence of one or more uncertain future events not wholly within the entity's control.

Recognition

Provisions

Provisions should be recognised (i.e. created by transfer from profit and loss account) when an entity has:

1. a present obligation (legal or constructive) as a result of a past event; and

2. a transfer of economic benefits will probably be required to settle the obligation; and

3. the amount of the obligation can be reliably estimated.

Some of these terms are explained as follows:

A **constructive obligation** exists where an entity has established a pattern of past practice that it will accept certain responsibilities and has created a valid expectation that it will discharge those responsibilities.

Past events in this context refers to obligations existing independently of an entity's future actions (i.e. the future conduct of its business). Examples include clean-up costs for past environmental damage.

However, potential costs for adapting plant to meet strict pollution control limits at some future date would *not* be regarded as a provision to be recognised as it has no present obligation for the future expenditure.

A past event which leads to a present obligation is known as an **obligating event**.

A **reliable estimate** is the best estimate of the expenditure required to settle the present obligation at the balance sheet date. Where the time value of money is material, the provision will be calculated on the basis of the present value of the expenditures expected to be required to settle the obligation.

Reviewing provisions

Provisions should be reviewed at each balance sheet date and adjusted to reflect the best estimate. The provision should be reversed if a transfer of economic benefits to settle the obligation is no longer probable. Note that provisions should not be created for potential future operating losses.

Onerous contracts

An **onerous contract** is one in which the unavoidable costs of meeting the contract's obligations exceed the economic benefits expected to be received. In such circumstances, the present obligation under the contract should be recognised and provided for.

Reimbursements

If some or all of the expenditure required to settle a provision is expected to be **reimbursed** by another party, the reimbursement should be recognised as a separate asset only when it is virtually certain that it will be received. In the profit and loss account, the expense relating to the provision may be shown net of the amount recognised for the reimbursement.

Contingent liabilities and contingent assets

Neither contingent liabilities nor contingent assets should be recognised by an entity.

A contingent liability is disclosed (i.e. as a note to the accounts) unless a transfer of economic benefits is remote.

A contingent asset is disclosed where an inflow of economic benefits is probable, but is not recognised within the profit and loss account due to the possibility of overstatement of profit by an amount which may never be realised.

If the realisation of profit is virtually certain then it is not regarded as a contingent asset and therefore can be recognised.

Summary of FRS 12

Figure 11.2 provides a flowchart summarising the treatment of provisions, contingent liabilities and contingent assets as laid down in FRS 12.

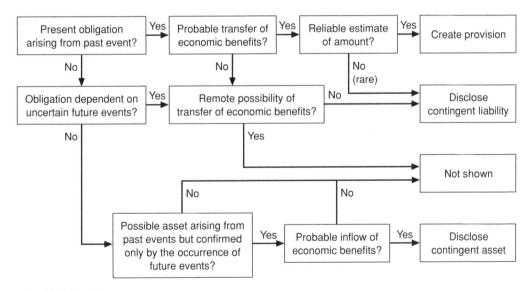

Fig. 11.2 FRS 12

APPLICATION IN PRACTICE

Figures 11.3 to 11.5 show relevant extracts from the published accounts of several UK public limited companies.

Fig. 11.3 Manchester United plc: contingent liabilities

Transfer fees payable
Under the terms of certain contracts with other football clubs in respect of player transfers, certain additional amounts would be payable by the Group if conditions as to future team selection are met. The maximum that could be payable is £3,158,500 (1999 – £2,607,500) of which £178,500 could arise within one year.

Fig. 11.4 Cammell Laird Holdings plc: post balance sheet events

32. Post balance sheet events
On 7 July 2000 the Group entered into a 20 year lease arrangement with the Port of Marseilles for the three large dry docks, one of which is the largest repair dock in Europe. Co-terminus with this agreement, the Group acquired one of the ship repair companies, Compagnie Marseillaise de Reparation (CMR), that operates within the port for a consideration of $1.2m.

Fig. 11.5 BAT Industries plc: contingent liabilities and financial commitments

Contingent liabilities and financial commitments

23 Contingent liabilities and financial commitments
There are contingent liabilities in respect of litigation, overseas taxes and guarantees in various countries.

Group companies, notably Brown & Williamson Tobacco Corporation ('B&W'), as well as other leading cigarette manufacturers, are defendants, principally in the United States, in a number of product liability cases, including a substantial number of new cases filed in 2000, although a number of cases were discontinued by claimants (without payment by any defendants) in the year. In a number of these cases, the amounts of compensatory and punitive damages sought are significant.

US litigation
The total number of US product liability cases pending at year end involving Group companies was approximately 4,740 (31 December 1999 537 cases). UK based group companies were named as co-defendants in some 1,345 of those cases (1999 161 cases). Only perhaps a couple of dozen cases or fewer are likely to come to trial in 2001. Since many of these pending cases seek unspecified damages, it is not possible to determine the total amount of claims pending, but the aggregate amounts involved in such litigation are significant. The cases fall into four broad categories:

(1) Medical reimbursement cases. These civil actions seek to recover amounts spent by government entities and other third party providers on health care and welfare costs claimed to result from illnesses associated with smoking.

Despite the almost uniform success of the industry's defence to these actions, to date, the United States Department of Justice has filed suit against the leading US cigarette manufacturers, certain affiliated companies (including parent companies), and others seeking reimbursement for Medicare and other health expenses incurred by the US federal government as well as various equitable remedies, including paying over of

▶

Fig. 11.5 continued

proceeds from alleged unlawful acts. The court has dismissed the reimbursement claims but is allowing the government to proceed with its claims for equitable relief. The court has tentatively scheduled trial for July 2003. At 31 December 2000, similar reimbursement suits were pending against B&W amongst others by seven Indian tribes and by five county or other political subdivisions of certain states. The settlement of the states' suits includes a credit for any amounts paid in suits brought by the states' political subdivisions; nevertheless, B&W intends to defend these cases vigorously.

Based on somewhat different theories of claim are some 34 non-governmental medical reimbursement cases and health insurers claims, the majority of which were filed by labour union health and welfare funds on behalf of their members. To date, seven federal appellate courts have issued decisions dismissing this type of case entirely and some but not all state courts have issued similar decisions. Only one union health fund case (Ohio Iron Workers) has been tried, resulting in a verdict for defendants, including B&W, in March 1999. Four third party reimbursement cases are currently scheduled for trial in 2001.

(2) Class actions. As at 31 December 2000, B&W was named as a defendant in some 35 (31 December 1999 38) separate actions attempting to assert claims on behalf of classes of persons allegedly injured by smoking. While most courts refused to do so, ten courts have certified classes of tobacco claimants in cases involving B&W but five of these classes have subsequently been decertified. Even if the classes remain certified and the possibility of class-based liability is eventually established, it is likely that individual trials will still be necessary to resolve any actual claims. If this happens, it is possible that many of the defences that have contributed to more than 600 individual cases being successfully disposed of over the years by B&W will be available.

In the first phase of the trifurcated trial in Engle (Florida), the jury returned a verdict that included general findings that smoking causes several specified diseases and other findings including that the defendants' conduct rose to a level that would permit a potential award of punitive damages. The second phase of the trial included two parts. The first portion of phase two was a trial of the three named class representatives' compensatory damages claims. In that portion, the jury awarded a total of $12.7 million to the three class representatives but found that one of the representatives' claims ($5.8 million of that total) was time-barred. In the second portion of phase two, the jury assessed $17.6 billion in punitive damages against B&W and $127 billion in total punitive damages against the other major companies in the US tobacco industry. Although the trial court has entered a final judgement on those verdicts, B&W contends that that judgement was improperly entered. In any event, B&W continues to believe confidently that the pending Engle decisions will eventually be reversed on appeal given the inappropriateness of class certification, the numerous errors committed during trial, and the significant constitutional issues involved in the case. Immediate payment of punitive damages pursuant to the verdict is unlikely for numerous reasons that will be presented to the trial and appellate courts, including, among others, that the punitive damages cannot be final until completion of a series of further individual trials for every member of the class (the so-called phase three of the Engle trial plan, which will take many years); that the jury's determination of punitive damages violates several provisions of Florida law; and that, pursuant to recently adopted legislation, in Florida any enforcement of punitive damages must be stayed upon the posting of a bond in an amount equal to the lower of 10 per cent of the defendant's net worth or $100 million. Although the Florida legislation is intended to apply to the Engle case, the outcome of any challenge to its application cannot be predicted. B&W has delivered a surety bond that meets the requirements of Florida's legislation to stay enforcement of punitive damages in class actions.

Fig. 11.5 continued

Trial of a class action in West Virginia (Blankenship), in which a class of smokers sought funding for medical monitoring of their health, ended in a mistrial. Another medical monitoring class action in Louisiana (Scott) is currently scheduled for trial in June 2001.

(3) Individual cases. Approximately 4,637 cases were pending against B&W at 31 December 2000 (31 December 1999 421) filed by or on behalf of individuals in which it is contended that diseases or deaths have been caused by cigarette smoking or by exposure to environmental tobacco smoke (ETS). Of these cases: (a) approximately two thirds are ETS cases brought by flight attendants who were members of a class action (Broin) that was settled on terms that allow compensatory but not punitive damage claims by class members; (b) approximately one quarter of the individual cases against B&W are cases brought in consolidated proceedings in West Virginia; and (c) less than eight per cent are cases filed by other individuals.

A jury verdict against B&W for $750,000 (Carter) was recently reinstated by the Florida Supreme Court. B&W is currently seeking review of that decision by the US Supreme Court.

(4) Other claims. At 31 December 2000, eight cases were pending on behalf of asbestos companies. Those companies seek reimbursement for costs and judgements paid in litigation brought by third parties against them. These companies claim that but for the smoking of the claimants against them, their damages would have been less.

A reimbursement case brought by a trust established to pay asbestos litigation claims (Falise) ended in mistrial in January 2001 because the jury was unable to reach a unanimous decision. According to press reports, 10 jurors favoured the tobacco company defendants while two would have found for plaintiffs.

At 31 December 2000, B&W was named as defendant in 18 US cases brought by foreign government entities seeking reimbursement of medical costs which they incurred for treatment for persons in their own countries who are alleged to have smoked imported cigarettes including those manufactured by B&W. Four foreign government cases had been dismissed at 31 December 2000. One foreign government case (Marshall Islands) is set for trial in 2001.

In addition, conduct-based claims, including antitrust and RICO claims, have been filed in the US. Among these are some 37 class action antitrust cases brought by wholesalers or retailers alleging that B&W and other major US cigarette manufacturers conspired to fix prices for cigarettes. Although plaintiffs in these class actions have not specified the damages they claim, the amounts could be significant. None of these conduct-based claims is considered to be meritorious.

B.A.T Industries has been named as a co-defendant in the US in most of the medical reimbursement cases, in a quarter or fewer of the class actions and even fewer of the individual cases. It is contesting the jurisdiction of the US courts since it is a 'holding' company not transacting business in the United States. In the 53 cases that have decided this issue to date, 30 courts have dismissed them prior to trial. In the balance of 23 cases, there has been no adverse ruling on the issue of jurisdiction affirmed on the merits through appeal. Some 135 plaintiffs have voluntarily agreed to drop the Company (or B.A.T Industries) or substitute the Company's indirectly held subsidiary British American Tobacco (Investments) Limited (formerly called British-American Tobacco Company Ltd.), as a co-defendant.

Legal matters outside the United States
At year end, there were no active claims against Group companies in respect of health-related claims outside Argentina, Australia, Brazil, Canada, Chile, Finland, France, Germany, Israel, the Netherlands, Pakistan, the Philippines, Republic of Ireland, Sri Lanka and Uganda.

Fig. 11.5 continued

Conclusion

While it is impossible to be certain of the outcome of any particular case or of the amount of any possible adverse verdict, the Company believes that the defences of the Group companies to all these various claims are meritorious both on the law and the facts, and a vigorous defence is being made everywhere. If an adverse judgement were entered against any of the Group companies in any case, an appeal would be made. Such appeals could require the posting of appeal bonds or substitute security by the appellants in amounts which could in some cases equal or exceed the amount of the judgement. At least in the aggregate and despite the quality of defences available to the Group, it is not impossible that the results of operations or cash flows of the Group in particular quarterly or annual periods could be materially affected by this and by the final outcome of any particular litigation.

Having regard to all these matters, the Directors (i) do not consider it appropriate to make any provision in respect of any pending litigation and (ii) do not believe that the ultimate outcome of all this litigation will significantly impair the financial condition of the Group.

Guarantees

Performance guarantees given to third parties in respect of Group companies were **£123 million** 1999 £76 million.

	2000 £m	1999 £m
Operating leases		
Annual commitments under operating leases comprise leases which expire:		
Land and buildings		
Within 1 year	17	10
Between 2 and 5 years	23	20
Beyond 5 years	18	12
	58	42
Others		
Within 1 year	8	11
Between 2 and 5 years	19	24
Beyond 5 years	3	12
	30	47

CHAPTER SUMMARY

SSAP 17 Post Balance Sheet Events

- A post balance sheet period is between the balance sheet date and the date on which the board of directors approve the financial statements.

- Adjusting post balance sheet events provide additional evidence of conditions existing on the balance sheet date and require figures to be adjusted accordingly.

- Non-adjusting post balance sheet events are material events that occur in the post balance sheet period and are sufficiently important to be brought to the attention of users by way of note.

▶

FRS 12 Provisions, Contingent Liabilities and Contingent Assets

- Provisions (liability of uncertain timing or amount) are recognised if there is a present obligation arising from a past event, a probable transfer of economic benefits and a reliable estimate can be made.
- Neither contingent liabilities nor contingent assets can be recognised, but can be disclosed by note if there is the likelihood of a transfer of economic benefits.

DISCUSSION QUESTIONS

1. An adjusting post balance sheet event might concern stock that reduces in value in the post balance sheet period due to factors such as cheap imports or increased competition. How can we be sure that this fall occurs as a result of factors that related to conditions existing at the balance sheet date?

2. FRS 12 clamped down on provisions for future operating losses. Why was this?

(*See Appendix 3* for outline responses.)

EXAMINATION QUESTIONS

1. With reference to SSAP 17 *Accounting for post balance sheet events* and FRS 12 *Provisions, contingent liabilities and contingent assets*:

a) define the following terms:
   i)   post balance sheet events;
   ii) adjusting events;
   iii) non-adjusting events;
   iv) contingent asset;
   v)   contingent liability.

(10 marks)

b) give FOUR examples of adjusting events and FOUR examples of non-adjusting events; and

(8 marks)

c) state how

   i) a material contingent liability, and
   ii) material contingent assets should be accounted for in financial statements.

(7 marks)
AAT (amended)

2. State, with reasons, how you would account for the following items:

i) The directors of a company have discovered a painting in a cupboard and have sent it to an auction house, who have confirmed that it should sell for £1 million in the following month's auction.

(3 marks)

ii) A claim has been made against a company for injury suffered by a pedestrian in connection with building work by the company. Legal advisers have confirmed that the company will probably have to pay damages of £200,000 but that a claim can be made against the building sub-contractors for £100,000.

(3 marks)

iii) A company uses 'recourse factoring' whereby the company agrees with the factor to repurchase any debts not paid to the factor within 90 days of the sales invoice date. In the year ended 30 June 1999 the factored credit sales of the company were £2 million, of which £1.8 million had been paid to the factor, £150,000 was unpaid but due within 90 days and £50,000 was unpaid for more than 90 days.

(3 marks)

iv) The manufacturer of a snooker table has received a letter from a professional snooker player who was defeated in the final of a major snooker competition, threatening to sue the manufacturer for £1 million, being his estimate of his loss of earnings through failing to win the competition, on the grounds that the table was not level.

(3 marks)
ACCA (amended)

(*See Appendix 4* for suggested answers.)

Chapter 12

Cash flow statements: FRS 1

INTRODUCTION

FRS 1 superseded SSAP 10 *Source and application of funds statements*, which placed emphasis on how the components of working capital (stock, debtors, creditors, bank) changed in the year. On the introduction of FRS 1 in 1991, the Chairman of the ASB, Professor David Tweedie said:

> 'It is right that cash flow should be the subject of the board's first standard. Recent experience has demonstrated all too clearly that adequate information on cash is an essential element of a company's financial statements. Cash is the lifeblood of a business. If it dwindles the business will die. But it is also a very difficult figure to fiddle.'

The 'recent experience' referred to much publicised cases where apparently solvent companies had collapsed due to lack of liquidity. In particular, the demise of the Polly Peck group (an international group trading in various goods and commodities ranging from fruit to electronics) was highlighted. In its Source and Application of Funds Statement, the group recorded a healthy 'funds' inflow of £172m in 1989. Had the figures been restated as a *cash flow statement*, an outflow of £129m would have been shown.

Although an extreme case, it does serve to illustrate that a *funds* flow statement could be misinterpreted, as its emphasis was on working capital rather than cash. Consequently, a significant decrease in cash could be obscured by an increase in stock or debtors. FRS 1 lists other advantages of using a cash flow statement rather than a working capital based funds flow statement:

1. cash flow is a concept more widely understood than working capital changes;

2. cash flows can be a direct input into a business valuation model, unlike working capital changes;

3. funds flow statements are based mainly on the difference between two balance sheets without introducing new data, whereas cash flow statements (and associated notes) may introduce additional information to that disclosed in a funds flow statement.

FRS 1 includes a standard layout for the cash flow statement, which is an innovation when compared with SSAP 10 which it replaced. SSAP 10 allowed individual companies certain discretion over presentation of funds flow statements which did little to promote comparability between companies or limit the scope for creative presentation.

Cash flow statements can be complex to prepare, particularly for international groups, though FRS 1 has introduced wide exemptions for smaller companies. Although acknowledged as a significant improvement on SSAP 10, cash flow statements are still based on historical data and should not be seen as an infallible guide to a company's future financial performance.

FRS 1 CASH FLOW STATEMENTS
(Issued September 1991, revised October 1996 and November 1997)

Objective

The first objective of the FRS is for those companies covered by the standard (*see below*) to report the cash generation and cash absorption for a period by highlighting the significant components of cash flow in a way that facilitates comparison with the cash flow performance of different businesses.

The second objective is to provide information that assists in the assessment of the company's:

a) liquidity;

b) solvency;

c) financial adaptability.

Comparative figures are required for all items in the cash flow statement and notes.

The standard requires the following standard headings, which are considered in detail below.

1. Operating activities (using the direct or indirect method)

2. Dividends from joint ventures and associates

3. Returns on investments and servicing of finance

4. Taxation

5. Capital expenditure and financial investment*

6. Acquisitions and disposals

7. Equity dividends paid

8. Management of liquid resources

9. Financing

---

* Shown as 'Capital expenditure' if there is no financial investment.

The first seven headings must be in the stated sequence, but the last two headings can be shown in a single section provided a sub-total is given for each heading.

Scope

The standard exempts small companies (as defined in the 1985 Companies Act) from the requirement to prepare a cash flow statement, and also:

1. subsidiary undertakings where 90% or more of the voting rights are controlled within the group, provided that consolidated financial statements including the subsidiary are publicly available;
2. mutual life assurance funds;
3. pension funds;
4. open-ended investment funds (subject to certain stated conditions);
5. building societies (subject to certain stated conditions);
6. non-corporate entities which would have been exempt under Companies Act legislation as a 'small company'.

The exemption for small companies was reviewed as part of the discussion concerning the Financial Reporting Standard for Smaller Entities (*see* p. 7). The rationale for the exemption stated in the original standard was that 'the costs . . . for small entities, which are often owner managed, of producing historical cash flow information in a highly standardised form are likely to be disproportionate to the benefits'. The revised FRSSE issued in December 1998 states that smaller entities are '. . . encouraged, but not required, to provide a cash flow statement . . .'.

The exemption for '90%+' groups was based on the likelihood that the liquidity, solvency and financial adaptability of the subsidiary essentially depends on the group rather than its own cash flows.

Format

The standard gives four illustrative examples of cash flow statements in an appendix, for the following types of business entity:

a) single company
b) group
c) bank
d) insurance company.

The example for a single company is reproduced opposite (Figure 12.1), while Figure 12.2 on pp. 175–8 shows the example for a group of companies. The other examples are outside the scope of this text.

Fig. 12.1 Illustrative example of a cash flow statement for a single company

XYZ Limited
Cash flow statement for the year ended 31 December 2001

Reconciliation of operating profit to net cash inflow from operating activities	£000	£000
Operating profit		6,022
Depreciation charges		899
Increase in stocks		(194)
Increase in debtors		(72)
Increase in creditors		234
Net cash inflow from operating activities		6,889

Cash flow statement		
Net cash inflow from operating activities		6,889
Returns on investments and servicing of finance (note 1)		2,999
Taxation		(2,922)
Capital expenditure		(1,525)
		5,441
Equity dividends paid		(2,417)
		3,024
Management of liquid resources (note 1)		(450)
Financing (note 1)		57
Increase in cash		**2,631**

Reconciliation of net cash flow to movement in net debt (note 2)		
Increase in cash in the period	2,631	
Cash repurchase of debenture	149	
Cash used to increase liquid resources	450	
Change in net debt*		3,230
Net debt at 1.1.01		(2,903)
Net funds at 31.12.01		327

* In this example all changes in net debt are cash flows.

▶

Fig. 12.1 continued

Notes to the cash flow statement

Note 1 – Gross cash flows	£000	£000
Returns on investments and servicing of finance		
Interest received	3,011	
Interest paid	(12)	
		2,999
Capital expenditure		
Payments to acquire intangible fixed assets	(71)	
Payments to acquire tangible fixed assets	(1,496)	
Receipts from sales of tangible fixed assets	42	
		(1,525)
Management of liquid resources		
Purchase of treasury bills	(650)	
Sale of treasury bills	200	
		(450)
Financing		
Issue of ordinary share capital	211	
Repurchase of debenture loan	(149)	
Expenses paid in connection with share issues	(5)	
		57

Note 2 – Analysis of changes in net debt

	At 1 Jan 2001 £000	Cash flows £000	Other changes £000	At 31 Dec 2001 £000
Cash in hand, at bank	42	847		889
Overdrafts	(1,784)	1,784		
		2,631		
Debt due within 1 year	(149)	149	(230)	(230)
Debt due after 1 year	(1,262)		230	(1,032)
Current asset investments	250	450		700
Total	(2,903)	3,230	–	327

Fig. 12.2 Illustrative example of a cash flow statement for a group

XYZ Group plc
Cash flow statement for the year ended 31 December 2001

	£000	£000
Cash flow from operating activities (note 1)		15,772
Dividends received from associates		250
Returns on investments and servicing of finance (note 2)		(2,239)
Taxation		(2,887)
Capital expenditure and financial investment (note 2)		(865)
Acquisitions and disposals (note 2)		(17,824)
Equity dividends paid		(2,606)
Cash outflow before use of liquid resources and financing		**(10,399)**
Management of liquid resources (note 2)		700
Financing (note 2) – Issue of shares	600	
Increase in debt	2,347	
		2,947
Decrease in cash in the period		**(6,752)**

Reconciliation of net cash flow to movement in net debt (note 3)

	£000	£000
Decrease in cash in the period	**(6,752)**	
Cash inflow from increase in debt and lease financing	(2,347)	
Cash inflow from decrease in liquid resources	(700)	
Change in net debt resulting from cash flows		(9,799)
Loans and finance leases acquired with subsidiary		(3,817)
New finance leases		(2,845)
Translation difference		643
Movement in net debt in the period		**(15,818)**
Net debt at 1.1.01		**(15,215)**
Net debt at 31.12.01		**(31,033)**

Notes to the cash flow statement

Note 1 – Reconciliation of operating profit to operating cash flows

	Continuing £000	Discontinued £000	Total £000
Operating profit	18,929	(1,616)	17,313
Depreciation charges	3,108	380	3,488
Cash flow relating to previous year restructuring provision (note 4)		(560)	(560)
Increase in stocks	(11,193)	(87)	(11,280)
Increase in debtors	(3,754)	(20)	(3,774)
Increase in creditors	9,672	913	10,585
Net cash inflow from continuing operating activities	16,762		
Net cash outflow in respect of discontinued activities		(990)	
Net cash inflow from operating activities			15,772

▶

Fig. 12.2 continued

Note 2 – Analysis of cash flows for headings netted in the cash flow statement

	£000	£000
Returns on investments and servicing of finance		
Interest received	508	
Interest paid	(1,939)	
Preference dividend paid	(450)	
Interest element of finance lease rentals payments	(358)	
Net cash outflow for returns on investments and servicing of finance		(2,239)
Capital expenditure and financial investment		
Purchase of tangible fixed assets	(3,512)	
Sale of trade investment	1,595	
Sale of plant and machinery	1,052	
Net cash outflow for capital expenditure and financial investment		(865)
Acquisitions and disposals		
Purchase of subsidiary undertaking	(12,705)	
Net overdrafts acquired with subsidiary	(5,516)	
Sale of business	4,208	
Purchase of interest in a joint venture	(3,811)	
Net cash outflow for acquisitions and disposals		(17,824)
Management of liquid resources*		
Cash withdrawn from 7 day deposit	200	
Purchase of government securities	(5,000)	
Sale of government securities	4,300	
Sale of corporate bonds	1,200	
Net cash inflow from management of liquid resources		700
Financing		
Issue of ordinary share capital		600
Debt due within a year: *increase in short-term borrowings*	2,006	
repayment of secured loan	(850)	
Debt due beyond a year: *new secured loan repayable in 2005*	1,091	
new unsecured loan repayable in 2004	1,442	
Capital element of finance lease rental payments	(1,342)	
		2,347
Net cash inflow from financing		2,947

*XYZ Group plc includes as liquid resources term deposits of less than a year, government securities and AA rated corporate bonds.

▶

Fig. 12.2 continued

Note 3 – Analysis of net debt

	At 1 Jan 2001	Cash flow	Acquisition* (excl. cash and overdrafts)	Other non-cash changes	Exchange movement	At 31 Dec 2001
	£000	£000	£000	£000	£000	£000
Cash in hand, at bank	235	(1,250)			1,392	377
Overdrafts	(2,528)	(5,502)			(1,422)	(9,452)
		(6,752)				
Debt due after 1 year	(9,640)	(2,533)	(1,749)	2,560	(792)	(12,154)
within 1 year	(352)	(1,156)	(837)	(2,560)	1,465	(3,440)
Finance leases	(4,170)	1,342	(1,231)	(2,845)		(6,904)
		(2,347)				
Current asset investments	1,240	(700)				540
Total	(15,215)	(9,799)	(3,817)	(2,845)	643	(31,033)

* This column would include any net debt (excluding cash and overdrafts) disposed of with a subsidiary undertaking.

Note 4 – Cash flow relating to exceptional items
The operating cash outflows include under discontinued activities an outflow of £560,000, which relates to the £1,600,000 exceptional provision for a fundamental restructuring made in the 2000 accounts.

Note 5 – Major non-cash transactions
a. During the year the group entered into finance lease arrangements in respect of assets with a total capital value at the inception of the leases of £2,845,000.
b. Part of the consideration for the purchases of subsidiary undertakings and the sale of a business that occurred during the year comprised shares and loan notes respectively. Further details of the acquisitions and the disposal are set out below.

Note 6 – Purchase of subsidiary undertakings

	£000
Net assets acquired	
Tangible fixed assets	12,194
Investments	1
Stocks	9,384
Debtors	13,856
Taxation recoverable	1,309
Cash at bank and in hand	1,439
Creditors	(21,715)
Bank overdrafts	(6,955)
Loans and finance leases	(3,817)
Deferred taxation	(165)
Minority shareholders' interests	(9)
	5,522
Goodwill	16,702
	22,224

Fig. 12.2 continued

Satisfied by	
Shares allotted	9,519
Cash	12,705
	22,224

The subsidiary undertakings acquired during the year contributed £1,502,000 to the group's net operating cash flows, paid £1,308,000 in respect of net returns on investments and servicing of finance, paid £522,000 in respect of taxation and utilised £2,208,000 for capital expenditure.

Note 7 – Sale of business

	£000
Net assets disposed of	
Fixed assets	775
Stocks	5,386
Debtors	474
	6,635
Loss on disposal	(1,227)
	5,408
Satisfied by	
Loan notes	1,200
Cash	4,208
	5,408

The business sold during the year contributed £200,000 to the group's net operating cash flows, paid £252,000 in respect of net returns on investments and servicing finance, paid £145,000 in respect of taxation and utilised £209,000 for capital expenditure.

Definitions

The key definitions contained in the FRS are as follows:

Cash: cash in hand and deposits repayable on demand with any qualifying financial institution, less overdrafts from any qualifying financial institution repayable on demand. Deposits are repayable on demand if they can be withdrawn at any time without notice and without penalty or if a maturity or period of notice of not more than 24 hours or one working day has been agreed. Cash includes cash in hand and deposits denominated in foreign currencies.

Cash flow: an increase or decrease in an amount of cash.

Qualifying financial institution: an entity that as part of its business receives deposits or other repayable funds and grants credits for its own account.

Groups

A group cash flow statement should exclude internal flows of cash within the group. The cash flows of any entity which is equity accounted (*see* FRS 9,

p. 199) should only be included in the group cash flow statement to the extent of the actual cash flows between the group and entity concerned, for example dividends received in cash and loans made or repaid.

Companies with foreign operations

The cash flow statement should be translated using the same rate as the profit and loss account (*see* SSAP 20, p. 211), unless the actual rate at the date of transaction is used.

The nine standard headings

The standard gives detailed guidance on each of the standard headings.

1. Operating activities

Cash flows from operating activities are in general the cash effects of transactions and other events relating to operating or trading activities normally shown in the profit and loss account in arriving at operating profit.

There are two methods, 'indirect' and 'direct', which can be used for reporting net cash flows generated from operating activities.

The *indirect method* (as shown in note 1 in Figure 12.2) starts with operating profit (as stated in the profit and loss account) and adjusts for non-cash charges and credits to arrive at the net cash flow from operating activities.

The principal advantage claimed for this method is that it highlights the differences between operating profit and net cash flow from operating activities. As some investors and creditors assess future cash flows by estimating future income and then allowing for accruals adjustments, knowledge of past accruals adjustments may be useful for this purpose.

The *direct method* shows operating cash receipts and payments, aggregating to the net cash flow from operating activities. For example, if Figure 12.2 had been presented using the direct method, the amounts in the first part of the statement may have appeared as follows (using assumed figures):

Operating activities	£000	£000
Cash received from customers	132,876	
Cash payments to suppliers	(56,299)	
Cash paid to and on behalf of employees	(47,709)	
Other cash payments	(12,846)	
Net cash inflow from operating activities		16,022

This information is optional, and would be in addition to the reconciliation provided in note 1 in Figure 12.2. The reconciliation must show separately:

179

a) movements in stocks;

b) movements in debtors;

c) movements in creditors;

d) other differences between cash flows and profits (e.g. depreciation, profits/losses on sales of assets).

The principal advantage of the direct method is that it shows the specific sources of operating cash receipts and payments which may be useful in assessing future cash flows.

Summary

Companies *must* give the information required by the **indirect method**, but *may* also give the additional information required by the **direct method** (*see* Figure 12.3).

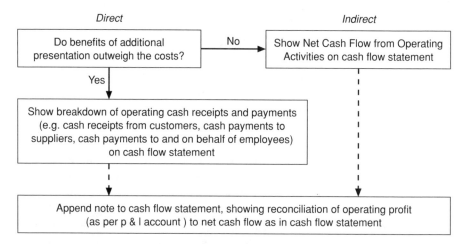

Fig. 12.3 Determining direct or indirect method of reporting net cash flow from operating activities

2. Dividends from joint ventures and associates

This heading was introduced by an amendment contained within FRS 9 *Associates and joint ventures* published in November 1997 (*see* p. 199), and, as its title suggests, shows dividends received in the period from joint ventures and associates.

3. Returns on investments and servicing of finance

In general terms, these are receipts resulting from the ownership of an investment (e.g. dividends and interest received), and payments to providers of finance (e.g. interest paid). Equity dividends *paid* are shown in a separate heading (*see below*).

Cash inflows and taxation

Taxation implications relating to cash inflows are that interest received is shown 'gross'.

Note that dividends from 'equity accounted entities' (associated undertakings – *see* FRS 9, p. 199) must be shown separately.

Cash outflows and taxation

Interest paid is shown at the gross amount.

Note that the interest element of finance lease rental payments is shown separately (*see* SSAP 21, p. 58)

4. Taxation

This heading represents cash flows to or from taxation authorities relating to both revenue and capital profits. In practice, this means:

Outflows:

a) corporation tax paid;

b) purchase of certificates of tax deposit;

c) tax paid on overseas income.

Inflows:

a) tax rebates;

b) claims;

c) returns of overpayments.

Value added tax is excluded from cash flows reported in the statement, unless it is irrecoverable, in which case the cash flows from operating activities would be shown gross. The net movement on the amount payable to or receivable from the taxing authority (HM Customs and Excise in the UK) should be allocated to cash flows from operating activities, unless the particular circumstances warrant a different treatment. The standard gives no guidance as to what the 'particular circumstances' might be.

Any taxation cash flows other than those listed above should be included in the cash flow statement under the same standard heading as the cash flow that gave rise to the taxation cash flow. Again, a different treatment for particular circumstances is allowed.

5. Capital expenditure and financial investment

This shows cash flows related to acquisitions and disposals of any fixed assets other than those relating to the purchase or sale of a trade or business, which are shown separately in the heading 'Acquisitions and disposals' (*see below*). 'Financial investment' includes cash inflows arising from the repayment of loans made to other entities or sales of debt instruments of other entities, and cash outflows due to loans made by the reporting entity and payments to acquire debt instruments of other entities.

6. Acquisitions and disposals

Cash inflows under this heading include:

a) receipts from sales of investments in subsidiary undertakings, showing separately any balances of cash and overdrafts transferred as part of the sale;

b) receipts from the sales of investments in associates or joint ventures;

c) receipts from the sales of trades or businesses.

Cash outflows under this heading include:

a) payments to acquire investments in subsidiary undertakings, showing separately any balances of cash and overdrafts acquired;

b) payments to acquire investments in associates or joint ventures;

c) payments to acquire trades or businesses.

7. Equity dividends paid

These are cash outflows relating to the company's equity dividends.

8. Management of liquid resources

This shows the cash flows relating to items such as withdrawals from, and payments into, short-term deposits. Liquid resources are defined in the standard as 'current asset investments held as readily disposable stores of value'. A 'readily disposable investment' is one that is disposable by the reporting entity without curtailing or disrupting its business and is either readily convertible into known amounts of cash at or close to its carrying amount, or traded in an active market.

9. Financing

Financing cash flows are receipts or repayments of principal from or to external providers of finance.

Financing cash inflows include receipts from issuing:

a) shares;

b) other equity instruments;

c) debentures;

d) loans;

e) notes;

f) bonds;

g) other long and short-term borrowings (other than overdrafts).

Financing cash outflows include:

a) repayments of amounts borrowed (other than overdrafts);

b) the capital element of finance lease rental payments (*see* SSAP 21, p. 58);

c) payments to re-acquire or redeem the entity's shares;

d) payments of expenses or commissions on any issue of equity shares.

The amounts of any financing cash flows received from or paid to equity accounted entities (*see* FRS 9, p. 199) should be disclosed separately.

Exceptional and extraordinary items

If the company's cash flows are affected by exceptional and/or extraordinary items (*see* FRS 3, p. 120), these items should be shown under the appropriate standard headings according to the nature of each item. A note to the cash flow statement should disclose the details of the transactions. (*See* Note 4 in Figure 12.2 as an example.)

Further required analysis

In addition to the reconciliation between operating profit and the net cash flow from operating activities, the standard requires a number of analyses and notes, as follows.

Reconciliation to net debt

Another requirement is for a note to be given which reconciles the movement in cash in the period with the movement in net debt. Note 2 in Figure 12.1 and Note 3 in Figure 12.2 show alternative acceptable presentations.

Additional disclosure for groups of companies: acquisition or disposal of subsidiary undertakings

Where a group buys or sells a subsidiary a note to the cash flow statement should show a summary of the effects of acquisitions and disposals indicating how much of the consideration comprised cash.

In the case of a subsidiary joining or leaving a group during a year, the cash flows of the subsidiary will be included in the group cash flow statement for the same period as the group's profit and loss account includes the subsidiary's results.

Where the sale or purchase of a subsidiary has a material effect on the amounts reported under the standard headings in the cash flow statement, a note should be appended showing these effects as far as practicable.

(*See* Notes 6 and 7 in Figure 12.2 as an example of how this information is to be shown.)

APPLICATION IN PRACTICE

The 2000 annual report of Manchester United plc contains a cash flow statement as shown in Figure 12.4.

Fig. 12.4 Manchester United plc: cash flow statement

Consolidated Cash Flow Statement

For the year ended 31 July 2000

	Note	2000 £'000	2000 £'000	1999 £'000	1999 £'000
Net cash inflow from operating activities			35,761		32,514
Returns on investments and servicing of finance					
Interest received		828		1,987	
Interest paid		(327)		(422)	
Net cash inflow from returns on investments and servicing of finance			501		1,565
Taxation paid			(7,328)		(4,962)
Capital expenditure and financial investment					
Proceeds from disposal of players		2,698		4,793	
Purchase of intangible fixed assets		(20,547)		(11,423)	
Sale of tangible fixed assets		761		1,089	
Purchase of tangible fixed assets		(33,685)		(17,164)	
Net cash outflow from capital expenditure and financial investment			(50,773)		(22,705)
Acquisitions and disposals					
Investment in associated company		(126)		–	
Investment in joint venture		(275)		(700)	
Net cash outflow from acquisitions and disposals			(401)		(700)
Equity dividends paid			(4,754)		(4,494)
Cash (outflow)/inflow before management of liquid resources and financing			(26,994)		1,218
Management of liquid resources					
Sale of marketable securities		52,686		113,976	
Purchase of marketable securities		(17,071)		(132,031)	
Net cash inflow/(outflow) from management of liquid resources			35,615		(18,055)
Financing					
Repayment of borrowings	19	(1,722)		(1,598)	
Net cash outflow from financing			(1,722)		(1,598)
Increase/(decrease) in cash in the year	27		6,899		(18,435)

	2000 £'000	1999 £'000
Net cash generated from operating activities		
Operating profit	15,681	20,311
Depreciation charges	5,052	4,565
Amortisation of cost of players' registrations	13,092	10,192
Loss on disposal of tangible fixed assets	392	453
Grants released	(219)	(259)
Increase in stocks	(702)	(1,401)
Increase in debtors	(2,443)	(2,228)
Increase in creditors	4,908	881
Net cash inflow from operating activities	35,761	32,514

▶

Fig. 12.4 continued

Notes to the accounts (extract)

27 Reconciliation of net cash flow to movement in net funds

	Group	
	2000 £'000	1999 £'000
Increase/(decrease) in cash in the year	6,899	(18,435)
Cash outflow from decrease in debt	1,722	1,598
Cash (inflow)/outflow from management of liquid resources	(35,615)	18,055
Movement in net funds	(26,994)	1,218
Opening net funds	37,557	36,339
Closing net funds	10,563	37,557

The Group includes as liquid resources its holding of marketable securities.

28 Analysis of changes in net funds

Group	At 1 August 1999 £'000	Cash flows £'000	Non-cash movements £'000	At 31 July 2000 £'000
Cash at bank and in hand	5,520	6,899	–	12,419
Debt due within one year	(1,722)	1,722	(1,856)	(1,856)
Debt due after more than one year	(1,856)	–	1,856	–
Marketable securities	35,615	(35,615)	–	–
Total	37,557	(26,994)	–	10,563

CHAPTER SUMMARY

FRS 1 Cash Flow Statements

- Standard layout with the following headings:
  - Operating activities;
  - Dividends from joint ventures and associates;
  - Returns on investments and servicing of finance;
  - Taxation;
  - Capital expenditure and financial investment;
  - Acquisitions and disposals;
  - Equity dividends paid;
  - Management of liquid resources;
  - Financing.

DISCUSSION QUESTION

1. 'If cash is the lifeblood of a business, does that make it more important than profit?' Discuss.

(*See Appendix 3* for outline responses.)

EXAMINATION QUESTION

1. Y Ltd's profit and loss account for the year ended 31 December 2001 and balance sheets at 31 December 2001 and 31 December 2000 were as follows:

Y Ltd
Profit and Loss Account for the year ended 31 December 2001

	£000	£000
Sales		360
Raw materials consumed	35	
Staff costs	47	
Depreciation	59	
Loss on disposal	9	
		150
Operating profit		210
Interest payable		14
Profit before tax		196
Taxation		62
		134
Dividend		36
Profit retained for year		98
Balance brought forward		245
		343

Y Ltd
Balance sheets

	31 December 2001		31 December 2000	
	£000	£000	£000	£000
Fixed assets				
Cost		798		780
Depreciation		159		112
		639		668
Current assets				
Stock	12		10	
Trade debtors	33		25	
Bank	24		28	
	69		63	
Current liabilities				
Trade creditors	6		3	
Taxation	51		43	
Proposed dividend	10		8	
	67		54	
Working capital		2		9
		641		677
Long-term liabilities				
Long-term loans		100		250
		541		427
Share capital		180		170
Share premium		18		12
Profit and loss		343		245
		541		427

During the year the company paid £45,000 for a new piece of machinery.
  You are required

a) to prepare a cash flow statement for Y Ltd for the year ended 31 December 2001
    in accordance with the requirements of Financial Reporting Standard 1 (FRS 1)
                                                                  (19 marks)

b) to explain what is meant by the term 'cash' in the context of statements prepared
    under the requirements of FRS 1 (revised)

                                                                  (3 marks)
                                                          (Total: 22 marks)
                                                          CIMA (amended)

(*See Appendix 4* for suggested answers.)

Chapter 13

Consolidated financial statements: FRSs 2, 6, 7 & 9

Subsidiary undertakings; Acquisitions and mergers; Fair values in acquisition accounting; Associates and joint ventures

INTRODUCTION

The whole area of accounting for groups of companies is one which has seen radical changes in the past few years. In introducing FRS 2, the ASB stated:

'The Board's aim is to see consolidated financial statements that give a full picture of the economic activities and financial position of the groups concerned. The legislation on the subject is very detailed. We have therefore taken some care to dovetail the FRS's requirements and commentary with the provisions of the (Companies) Act, and we believe that the FRS will be of real service to preparers of accounts in this complex area.'

More recently, on the introduction of FRSs 6 and 7, Sir David Tweedie, chairman of the ASB said 'Accounting for acquisitions has long been seen as fertile ground for manipulating figures. This is in no one's interests as it creates an atmosphere of suspicion and it puts unfair pressure on the many companies that try to present their results honestly.' Pressure to tighten up the regulations in these areas has been building up for several years. For example, Coloroll plc paid £213m in shares and cash in 1988 for John Crowther plc and then made so many fair value adjustments and provisions that by the time it had finished it had written off £11m more than the total cost of the company!

FRS 2 ACCOUNTING FOR SUBSIDIARY UNDERTAKINGS
(Issued July 1992)

Consolidated financial statements are defined as 'the financial statements of a group prepared by consolidation'. *Consolidation* is defined as 'the process of adjusting or combining financial information from the individual financial statements of a parent undertaking and its subsidiary undertakings to prepare consolidated financial statements that present financial information for the group as a single economic entity'.

The decision as to whether companies have a parent/subsidiary relationship depends upon either the proportion of voting rights owned or the degree of influence which exists as shown in Figure 13.1.

Requirements of the standard

The standard does not concern itself with the technicalities of how consolidated accounts are produced, but instead concentrates on the circumstances under which they should be prepared.

The requirements of the standard are dealt with under the following major headings:

1. Scope
2. Consolidated financial statements
3. Consolidation adjustments
4. Changes in composition of a group
5. Changes in stake
6. Distributions.

Scope

Parent undertakings that prepare consolidated financial statements intended to give a true and fair view of the financial position and profit or loss of their group should prepare such statements in accordance with the FRS's requirements. If a parent undertaking uses an exemption from the requirements to prepare consolidated accounts (*see below*) it must provide a statement to the effect that its financial statements present information about it as an individual undertaking and not about its group.

Consolidated financial statements

Preparation

A parent undertaking should prepare consolidated financial statements for its group unless it uses one of the exemptions set out below. (*See* 'Application in practice', p. 205, for the relevant extract from the annual report of Tate and Lyle plc.)

Exempt parent undertakings

Consolidated financial statements do not have to be prepared by a parent undertaking if:

1. its group is small or medium sized (unless any of its members is a plc, a bank, an insurance company or an 'authorised person' under the Financial Services Act);

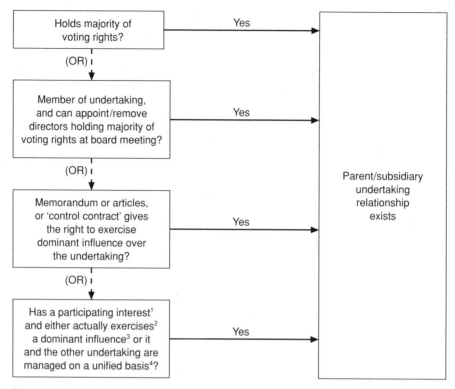

Notes:

1. Participating interest is defined as 'an interest held by an undertaking which it holds on a long-term basis for the purpose of securing a contribution to its activities by the exercise of control or influence arising from or related to that interest'. An interest of 20% or more in the shares (or conversion rights or options to acquire 20% or more) is presumed to be a participating interest, unless the contrary is shown.

2. Actual exercise of dominant influence is the situation whereby major decisions are taken in accordance with the wishes of the holder of the influence, for the holder's benefit whether or not those wishes are explicit.

3. Dominant influence is influence that can be exercised to achieve the operating and financial policies desired by the holder of the influence, notwithstanding the rights or influence of any other party.

4. Management on a unified basis exists if the whole of the operations of two or more undertakings are integrated and are managed as a single unit. Unified management does not arise solely because one undertaking manages another.

Fig. 13.1 Parent/subsidiary relationship

2. it is a wholly-owned subsidiary undertaking and its immediate parent undertaking is established under the law of an EU country (unless its own securities are listed on a stock exchange within the EU);

3. all of its subsidiary undertakings are permitted or required to be excluded from consolidation by section 229 of the Companies Act (*see* 'Exclusions from consolidation' below).

Undertakings to be included in the consolidation

The consolidated financial statements should include the parent undertaking and all its subsidiary undertakings, other than those required to be excluded (*see* 'Exclusions from consolidation' below).

Disproportionate expense and undue delay

If subsidiaries are individually or collectively material in the group context, they cannot be excluded from consolidation by virtue of disproportionate expense or undue delay in obtaining information.

Exclusions from consolidation

The circumstances whereby subsidiaries can be excluded from consolidation are as follows:

1. severe long-term restrictions substantially hinder the exercise of the parent's rights over the subsidiary's assets or management; or

2. the group's interest in the subsidiary is held exclusively with a view to subsequent resale and the subsidiary has not previously been consolidated; or

3. the subsidiary's activities are so different from those of other undertakings to be included in the consolidation that its inclusion would be incompatible with the obligation to give a true and fair view. Note that this would be exceptional, and the FRS gives no examples of dissimilar activities. It points out that the Act does not permit exclusion 'merely because some of the undertakings are industrial, some commercial and some provide services, or because they carry on industrial or commercial activities involving different products or provide different services'.

The names of any subsidiaries excluded from the consolidation and the reasons why they have been excluded should be given. Further information, including particulars of balances between the excluded subsidiary undertakings and the rest of the group, must be disclosed.

Accounting for excluded subsidiaries

The three types of excluded subsidiary should be accounted for as follows.

1. **Severe long-term restrictions.** Subsidiaries excluded on these grounds are to be treated as fixed asset investments. They are to be treated at their

carrying amount when the restrictions came into force, subject to any write down for permanent diminution of value. No further accruals are to be made for profits or losses of such subsidiaries, unless the parent still exercises significant influence (in which case they are to be treated as associated undertakings – *see* FRS 9, p. 199).

2. *Held exclusively with a view to subsequent resale.* These are to be included as current assets at the lower of cost and net realisable value.

3. *Different activities.* These are to be accounted for under the equity method (*see* p. 204).

Disclosures

In addition to disclosures required by the Companies Act, principal subsidiaries (i.e. those whose results or financial position principally affect the figures in the consolidated financial statements) must disclose:

1. the proportion of voting rights held by the parent and its subsidiary undertakings; and

2. an indication of the nature of its business.

Additionally, where a subsidiary has been consolidated because of the parent actually exercising dominant influence, the basis of the dominant influence should be stated.

Minority interests

If a subsidiary is not wholly owned by its parent, then it has a minority amongst its members whose interest needs to be calculated and disclosed as a liability within the consolidated financial statements. This interest is effectively the value of the minority's proportion of the subsidiaries' net assets or liabilities as disclosed in their own balance sheets.

The standard requires that minority interests in total should be reported separately in the consolidated balance sheet and profit and loss account. Whether the assets and liabilities of the subsidiary are included at fair values or adjusted carrying amounts, those attributable to the minority interest should, for consistency, be included on the same basis as those attributable to the interests held by the parent and its other subsidiaries.

The FRS requires that any goodwill arising on the acquisition of a subsidiary that is not wholly owned should be recognised only in relation to the group's interest and that none should be attributed to the minority interest.

Consolidation adjustments

Intra-group transactions

Profits or losses included in the book value of assets at consolidation must be eliminated, as are loans or other debts to and from group companies. The adjustment for intra-group profits or losses is set against the respective interests held by the group and the minority interest in the company whose financial statements recorded the eliminated profit or losses.

Accounting policies

Uniform group accounting policies should generally be used in preparing the consolidated financial statements, if necessary by adjusting amounts reported by individual subsidiaries in their own financial statements. In exceptional cases, different accounting policies may be used, but the particulars must be disclosed.

Accounting periods and dates

In preparing the consolidation, all the subsidiaries should have the same financial year end and be for the same accounting period. Where dates differ, then interim accounts for a subsidiary should be prepared, covering the same accounting period as the parent undertaking. If this is impracticable, then earlier (no more than three months prior to the parent's year-end) financial statements of the subsidiary can be used. Any changes in the intervening period which materially affect the view given in the group's financial statements should be adjusted for when preparing the consolidation. In such cases, the following information should be given:

a) the name of the subsidiary undertaking;

b) the accounting date or period of the subsidiary undertaking; and

c) the reason for using a different accounting date or period for the subsidiary undertaking.

Changes in composition of a group

Date of changes in group membership

An undertaking becomes a subsidiary on the date when control passes to the parent. It ceases to be a subsidiary when the parent relinquishes control over the subsidiary. Control is defined as 'the ability of an undertaking to direct the financial and operating policies of another undertaking with a view to gaining economic benefits from its activities'.

Subsidiaries ceasing to be group members

Where a subsidiary ceases to be part of the group during a period, the consolidated financial statement should include the results of that subsidiary up to the date of cessation and any gain or loss arising on that cessation (other than where already provided for). The gain or loss is calculated by comparing the carrying amount of the group's interest in the subsidiary's net assets (including any goodwill not previously written off through profit and loss) before and after the cessation, together with any proceeds received.

Changes in the membership of the group should be disclosed. Where an undertaking has become or ceased to be a subsidiary other than as a result of a purchase or exchange of shares, the circumstances should be explained by way of a note in the consolidated financial statements.

Changes in stake

Acquiring a subsidiary in stages

Assets and liabilities of a subsidiary are to be included at fair value at the date of its acquisition (the date it becomes a subsidiary). This also applies where the parent's interest is acquired in stages.

Increasing an interest

Where a group increases its interest in an existing subsidiary, the assets and liabilities of that subsidiary should be revalued to fair value (unless the difference between net fair values and carrying amounts of the net assets relating to the increased stake is immaterial).Goodwill arising on the increase should be calculated by reference to those fair values.

Reducing an interest

Where a group reduces its interest in a subsidiary it should record any profit or loss arising, calculated by comparing the carrying amount of the group's interest in the subsidiary's net assets (including any goodwill not previously written off through profit and loss) before and after the reduction, together with any proceeds received. An adjustment must be made to the minority interest in the subsidiary, which will increase by their proportion of the carrying amount of the net assets.

Distributions

Restrictions

Where there are material limitations to the parent's access to distributable profits due to significant statutory, contractual or exchange control restrictions, the nature and extent of the restrictions should be disclosed.

Tax on accumulated reserves of overseas subsidiaries

Disclosure should be made of the extent to which deferred tax has (or has not) been provided in respect of future remittances of accumulated reserves of overseas subsidiaries.

Quasi-subsidiaries

FRS 5 (*see* p. 142) has introduced new rules regarding quasi-subsidiaries.

A *quasi-subsidiary* is defined as 'a company, trust, partnership or other vehicle that, though not fulfilling the definition of a subsidiary, is directly or indirectly controlled by the reporting entity and gives rise to benefits for that entity that are in substance no different from those that would arise were the vehicle a subsidiary'.

In determining control, regard should be had to who, in practice, directs its financial and operating policies.

Where the entity has a quasi-subsidiary, the assets, liabilities, profits, losses and cash flows should be reported in the consolidated financial statements *as if they were those of a subsidiary*. The only exception is where the interest in the quasi-subsidiary is held with a view to subsequent resale, and it has not previously been included in the consolidated financial statements. Disclosure is also required, in summary form, of the financial statements of quasi-subsidiaries.

FRS 6 ACQUISITIONS AND MERGERS
(Issued September 1994)

In the previous part of the chapter on FRS 2 *Accounting for subsidiary undertakings*, the section headed 'Changes in composition of a group' referred to certain requirements in the event of subsidiaries being acquired or disposed of. FRS 6 gives details of the two alternative accounting methods available for accounting for business combinations, those of acquisition accounting and merger accounting.

Acquisition accounting

This is the traditional method of consolidation accounting, where the business combination results from the acquisition of one company by another; the identifiable net assets acquired are included in the consolidated balance sheet at their fair value from the date of acquisition, and its results included in the profit and loss account from the date of acquisition. Goodwill arises on the difference between the consideration given and the fair value of the net assets of the business acquired.

Merger accounting

This treats two or more parties as combining on an equal footing, usually without any restatement of net assets to a fair value. However, appropriate adjustments should be made to achieve uniformity of accounting policies between the combining companies. It includes the results for each party for the whole of the accounting period. Any shares issued on the merger are not regarded as an application of resources at fair value. Merger accounting is only permissible if specific conditions are met.

Goodwill does not arise as in acquisition accounting, but when consolidating under the merger method, differences may arise if the carrying value of the investment in the subsidiary (i.e. the nominal value of shares issued plus the fair value of any additional consideration given) is greater or less than the nominal value of the shares being acquired. The difference is accounted for as follows.

a) Where the carrying value of the investment is less than the nominal value of the shares acquired, the difference (credit balance) is treated as a non-distributable reserve arising on consolidation.

b) Where the carrying value of the investment is greater than the nominal value of the shares acquired, the difference (debit balance) is treated as a capitalisation of reserves, which are reduced by an equivalent amount.

Conditions whereby merger accounting is permissible

FRS 6 requires acquisition accounting to be used for any business combination where one party is being acquired by the other. Merger accounting is restricted to, and required for, those business combinations where the use of acquisition accounting would not properly reflect the true nature of the combination. Note that in its predecessor standard, SSAP 23, companies could choose whether or not to use merger accounting. With FRS 6, the restrictions are such that the use of merger accounting in future will be 'very rare'. Indeed, the US Financial Accounting Standards Board announced in April 1999 an end to merger accounting in that country.

FRS 6 defines a merger as:

'. . . a business combination in which, rather than one party acquiring control of another, the parties come together to share in the future risks and benefits of the combined entity. It is not the augmentation of one entity by the addition of another, but the creation of what is effectively a new reporting entity from the parties to the combination'

The five criteria for merger accounting

Merger accounting can only be used if the combination meets the following five criteria:

1. neither party is portrayed as acquirer or acquired by their boards or management or by any other party to the combination;

2. all parties participate in the formation of the management structure and the selection of personnel. Decisions are made by consensus rather than by the exercise of voting rights;

3. no one party is relatively large enough to dominate another;

4. consideration received by equity shareholders should principally be in the form of equity shares in the combined entity;

5. no equity shareholders retain a material interest in the future performance of only part of the combined entity.

Group reconstructions

A group reconstruction may be accounted for using merger accounting even though there is no business combination meeting the definition of a merger, provided:

a) the use of merger accounting is not prohibited by companies legislation;

b) the ultimate shareholders remain the same, and the rights of each such shareholders, relative to the others, are unchanged; and

c) no minority's interest in the net assets of the group is altered by the transfer.

Acquisition accounting and merger accounting contrasted

	Acquisition method	Merger method
Results of acquired company brought in from date of acquisition.	✓	✗
Full year's results of both combining companies reflected in group accounts (i.e. as if the combining companies had 'always been together'), and corresponding figures adjusted.	✗	✓
Assets and liabilities in consolidated accounts at fair values (with increased depreciation charge as likely consequence).	✓	✗
Assets stated at cost to acquiring group.	✓	✗
Goodwill calculated as per FRS 10.	✓	✗
Minority interests calculated.	✓	✓
Reserve arising due to differences, e.g. when nominal value of shares issued exceeds aggregate of nominal value and reserves of other company.	✗	✓
Uniformity of accounting policies to be achieved for combining companies.	✓	✓

Disclosure requirements

All business combinations

The following matters should be disclosed in respect of all business combinations, whether the acquisition or merger accounting method is used:

a) the names of the combining entities (other than the reporting entity);

b) whether the combination has been accounted for as an acquisition or a merger); and

c) the date of the combination.

Mergers

In respect of each business combination accounted for as a merger (other than group reconstructions – *see above*), the following information should be disclosed in the financial statements of the combined entity for the period in which the merger took place:

a) an analysis of the principal components* of the current year's profit and loss account and statement of total recognised gains and losses into:

   i) amounts relating to the merged entity for the period after the date of the merger; and

   ii) for each party to the merger, amounts relating to that party for the period up to the date of the merger;

b) an analysis between the parties to the merger of the principal components* of the previous year's profit and loss account and statement of total recognised gains and losses;

c) the composition and fair value of the consideration given by the issuing company and its subsidiary undertakings;

d) the aggregate book value of the net assets of each party to the merger at the date of the merger;

e) details of significant adjustments to net assets to achieve consistency of accounting policies, plus details of any other significant adjustments made to the net assets of any party to the merger as a result of the merger;

f) a statement of the adjustments to consolidated reserves resulting from the merger.

Acquisitions

In respect of business combinations accounted for as acquisitions, the following information (simplified from the standard) should be disclosed:

a) the composition and fair value of the consideration given by the acquiring company and its subsidiary undertakings;

b) a table which includes a statement of the amount of purchased goodwill or negative goodwill arising on the acquisition, and for each class of assets and liabilities of the acquired entity:

   i) the book values as recorded in the acquired company's books immediately before the acquisition and before any fair value adjustments;

   ii) the fair value adjustments, analysed between revaluations, adjustments to achieve consistent accounting policies and any other significant adjustments, together with reasons for them;

---

* The turnover, operating profit and exceptional items, split between continuing operations, discontinued operations and acquisitions; profit before taxation; taxation and minority interests; and extraordinary items.

iii) the fair values at the date of acquisition;

iv) details of provisions for reorganisations and restructuring costs and related asset write-downs made in the 12 months preceding the acquisition.

The standard also encourages voluntary disclosure of the acquirer's intended expenditure on the acquired business.

FRS 6 and FRS 3

In the period of acquisition the post-acquisition results of the acquired entity should be shown as a component of continuing operations in the profit and loss account, other than those which are also discontinued in the same period.

FRS 6 and FRS 1

Cash flow statements should disclose cash paid in respect of consideration, net of any cash balances transferred as part of the acquisition. A note to the cash flow statement in the year of the acquisition should disclose the material effects of the cash flows of the acquired entity on each of the standard headings, together with details of the consideration given.

FRS 9 ASSOCIATES AND JOINT VENTURES
(Issued November 1997)

This standard replaced the very first UK accounting standard to be issued, SSAP 1, which was originally published in 1971. SSAP 1 was introduced to give a standard accounting treatment for investments in companies which, while not being subsidiaries, were subject to significant influence by the investing company. FRS 9 has extended this to include the treatment of joint ventures, where an investor shares control with one or more other entities.

Objectives

The standard's objectives are to show the effect on the financial position and performance of an investor due to its close involvement in:

1. an associate, due to its participating interest and significant influence; and/or

2. a joint venture, due to its long-term interest and joint control.

Key definitions

Associate – an entity (other than a subsidiary) in which another entity (the investor) has a participating interest and over whose operating and financial policies the investor exercises a significant influence.

Entity – a body corporate, partnership or unincorporated association carrying on a trade or business (of its own, not just part of the trades or businesses of entities that have interests in it) with or without a view to profit.

Subsidiary – an entity over which another entity has control (*see* FRS 2, p. 188).

Participating interest – a holding of 20% or more of the shares of an entity is to be presumed to be a participating interest unless the contrary is shown. The presumption is rebutted if the interest is either non-beneficial or long-term. The interest is held for the purpose of securing a contribution to the investor's activities by the exercise of control or influence arising from or related to that interest.

Significant influence – the Companies Act 1985 provides that an entity holding 20% or more of another entity's voting rights should be presumed to hold a significant influence over that other entity unless the contrary is shown. The standard requires that the investor is actively involved and is influential through participation on such policy decisions relevant to the investor such as:

a) the expansion or contraction of the business, participation in other entities or changes in products, markets and activities of the investee; and

b) determining the balance between dividend and reinvestment.

Joint venture – an entity which is jointly controlled by the reporting entity and one or more other venturers under a contractual arrangement. The reporting entity's interest is on a long-term basis.

Joint control – where none of the entities alone control the joint venture and each venturer's consent is needed for decisions on the venture's operating and financial policy.

Joint arrangement that is not an entity – if no trade or business is carried out separately within a joint arrangement, then this would not be regarded as a joint venture within the definition above. For example, where two or more companies enter into a joint marketing arrangement or agree on a shared production facility, this would not be regarded as a joint venture.

Accounting treatment

Investor's own financial statements

Associates and joint ventures should be shown as fixed asset investments, at cost less any amounts written off, or at a valuation. Dividends received and receivable are shown in the profit and loss account.

Investor's consolidated financial statements

The treatment depends upon whether the type of investment is classified as an associate, a joint venture or a joint arrangement that is not an entity. The

Table 13.1 Summary of main disclosure requirements

Level of investment	Associates	Joint ventures
Exceeds 15% of any of the investor's gross assets, gross liabilities, turnover or the three-year average of its operating result.	Aggregate share of turnover, fixed assets, current assets, liabilities due within 1 year and after 1 year or more.	Aggregate share of fixed assets, current assets, liabilities due within 1 year and after 1 year or more.
Exceeds 25% of any of the investor's gross assets, gross liabilities, turnover or the three-year average of its operating result.	Investor's share of the following should be shown: turnover, profit before tax, taxation, profit after tax, fixed assets, current assets, liabilities within 1 year, liabilities due after 1 year or more.	
In all cases, disclosure to be made of:	For each associate and joint venture, their name and details of shares held and any special rights or constraints attaching to them. Accounting period or date of financial statements used if different from those of the investing group. An indication of the nature of its business.	

chapter summary on p. 204 summarises the different accounting requirements and also includes the treatment for subsidiaries and simple investments.

Disclosures

The level of disclosure depends upon the level of investment and whether it is a joint venture or an associate. Table 13.1 summarises the main disclosure requirements.

FRS 7 FAIR VALUES IN ACQUISITION ACCOUNTING
(Issued September 1994)

FRS 7 *Fair values in acquisition accounting* bans companies from making provisions for the future trading losses of companies they acquire and the costs of any related rationalisation or reorganisation, unless outgoing management had already incurred those liabilities. In the past such devices have been used to stop costs appearing on the profit and loss account, boosting profits.

The basic principle of FRS 7 is that, when attributing fair values to assets and liabilities acquired, the fair values should reflect the circumstances at the time of the acquisition, and should not reflect either the acquirer's intentions or events subsequent to the acquisition. Thus the assets and liabilities recognised are restricted to those of the acquired entity that existed at the date of acquisition, and excludes provisions for reorganisation costs to be carried out by the acquirer and provisions for future losses. Such items are to be treated as part of the post-acquisition results of the enlarged group.

Scope

The standard applies not only in the case of a parent company acquiring a subsidiary but also where an individual company acquires a business other than a subsidiary undertaking.

Determining the fair value of identifiable assets and liabilities acquired

The identifiable assets and liabilities to be recognised should be those of the acquired entity at the date of acquisition, measured at fair values that reflect the conditions at that date. 'Fair value' is defined as: 'the amount at which an asset or liability could be exchanged in an arm's length transaction between informed and willing parties, other than in a forced or liquidation sale'.

Post-acquisition items

The following do not affect fair values at the date of acquisition, so are to be treated as post-acquisition items:

a) changes resulting from the acquirer's intentions or future actions;

b) impairments or other changes, resulting from events subsequent to the acquisition;

c) provisions or accruals for future operating losses or for reorganisation and integration costs expected to be incurred as a result of the acquisition, whether they relate to the acquired entity or the acquirer.

Application of principles to specific assets and liabilities

The standard gives guidance regarding the valuation of various types of assets and liabilities, as follows:

1. **Tangible fixed assets**

   Fair value should be based on:

   a) market value, if similar assets are bought and sold on an open market; or

   b) depreciated replacement cost.

   The fair value should not exceed the recoverable amount of the asset.

2. **Intangible assets**
   Fair value should be based on its replacement cost, which is normally its estimated market value.

3. Stocks and work-in-progress

Most stocks will be valued at the lower of replacement cost (i.e. current cost of bringing stocks to present location and condition) and net realisable value. Certain specialised stocks (including commodities) where the acquired entity trades as both a buyer and seller should be valued at current market prices.

4. Quoted investments

Valued at market price, but adjusted if necessary for unusual price fluctuations or for the size of the holding.

5. Monetary assets and liabilities

The fair value should take into account the amounts expected to be paid or received and their timing. Market value should be used where available, by reference to the current price at which the business could acquire similar assets or enter similar obligations, or by discounting to present value.

6. Businesses sold or held for subsequent resale

The investments in businesses sold or held for subsequent resale should be treated as a single asset for the purposes of determining fair values, based on either net proceeds of the sale or estimated net proceeds.

7. Pensions

The fair value of a deficiency or surplus (if reasonably expected to be realised) in a funded pension or other post-retirement scheme, or accrued obligations in an unfunded scheme, should be recognised as a liability or an asset of the acquiring group.

8. Deferred taxation

Deferred tax liabilities and assets recognised in the fair value exercise should be determined by considering the enlarged group as a whole.

Determining the cost of acquisition

The cost of the acquisition is the cash paid and the fair value of other consideration given, together with the expenses of acquisition such as fees and similar incremental costs. Internal costs, and other expenses that cannot be directly attributed to the acquisition, should be charged directly to the profit and loss account. This treatment of expenses subsequent to the acquisition gave rise to adverse comments from some commentators, who accused the ASB of ignoring the commercial realities of the transaction. They argued that within defined limits provision for planned post-acquisition expenditure should be permitted to be included in the net asset acquired (and hence avoid the need for such expenses to be shown in the profit and loss account). The ASB rejected this view on the grounds that the intention to incur revenue expenditure subsequent to the acquisition could not properly be regarded as a liability of the acquired business at the date of acquisition.

APPLICATION IN PRACTICE

The extracts shown in Figure 13.2 are taken from the annual report of Tate and Lyle plc, and show that company's consolidated balance sheet and consolidated profit and loss account, and notes relevant to the treatment of subsidiaries, associates and joint ventures.

Fig. 13.2 Tate & Lyle plc: consolidated accounts and notes

Group Profit and Loss Account
For the 78 weeks to 25 March 2000

Notes	Profit and Loss Account	For the 78 weeks to March 2000 £ million	For the 52 weeks to September 1998 £ million
	Sales	6,183	4,467
	Less share of sales of – joint ventures	(491)	(310)
	– associates	(46)	(40)
	Group sales	**5,646**	**4,117**
	Operating profit before exceptional items and reorganisation costs	370	218
	Reorganisation costs	(18)	–
2	**Operating profit before exceptional items**	**352**	**218**
3	Exceptional items	–	(15)
	of which – European Union fine	–	(5)
	– other	–	(10)
2	**Group operating profit**	**352**	**203**
	Share of operating profits of joint ventures	64	27
	Share of operating profits of associates	4	4
	Total operating profit: group and share of joint ventures and associates	**420**	**234**
3	Exceptional write downs on planned sales of businesses	(50)	–
3	Exceptional profit on sale of businesses	25	–
3	Exceptional profit on sale of fixed assets	12	13
	Profit before interest	**407**	**247**
	Interest receivable and similar income	37	32
5	Interest payable and similar charges	(139)	(100)
	Share of joint ventures' interest	(14)	(11)
	Share of associates' interest	(4)	(3)
	Profit before taxation	**287**	**165**
6	Taxation	(89)	(44)
	Profit after taxation	**198**	**121**
	Minority interests – equity	(14)	3
	Profit for the period	**184**	**124**
7	Dividends paid and proposed – including on non-equity shares	(124)	(78)
	Retained profit	**60**	**46**
	Earnings per Share		
8	Basic	**40.3p**	27.4p
8	Diluted	**40.2p**	27.1p

Fig. 13.2 continued

Balance Sheets
At 25 March 2000

Notes		March 2000 Group £ million	September 1998 Group £ million	March 2000 Tate & Lyle PLC £ million	September 1998 Tate & Lyle PLC £ million
	Fixed assets				
31	Intangible assets	1	–	–	–
9	Tangible assets	1,678	1,707	1	1
10	Investments in joint ventures:				
	– *share of gross assets*	*272*	*310*	–	–
	– *share of gross liabilities*	*(149)*	*(177)*	–	–
	– share of net assets	123	133	–	–
10	Investments in associates	11	14	–	–
10	Other investments	41	38	2,490	2,348
		1,854	1,892	2,491	2,349
	Current assets				
11	Stocks	479	388	–	–
12	Debtors – due within one year subject to financing arrangements				
	Debtors	*38*	*44*	–	–
	Less: non-returnable amounts received	*(34)*	*(40)*	–	–
		4	4	–	–
12	– other debtors due within one year	453	509	67	243
12	– due after more than one year	78	77	1	1
13	Investments	210	185	–	–
	Cash at banks and in hand	51	58	–	–
		1,275	1,221	68	244
	Creditors – due within one year				
14	Borrowings	(434)	(411)	(1,878)	(1,750)
14	Other	(530)	(567)	(49)	(69)
	Net current assets/(liabilities)	311	243	(1,859)	(1,575)
	Total assets less current liabilities	2,165	2,135	632	774
	Creditors – due after more than one year				
15	Borrowings, including convertible debt	(632)	(787)	(2)	(2)
16	Other	(12)	(11)	–	–
17	**Provisions for liabilities and charges**	(257)	(250)	(2)	(2)
	Total net assets	1,264	1,087	628	770
	Capital and reserves				
21	Called up share capital	117	117	117	117
22	Share premium account	380	376	380	376
22	Revaluation reserve	35	35	–	–
22	Other reserves	30	32	–	–
22	Profit and loss account	539	371	131	277
23	**Shareholders' funds (including non-equity interests)**	1,101	931	628	770
	Minority interests – equity	163	156	–	–
		1,264	1,087	628	770

The financial statements were approved by the Board at a meeting on 7 June 2000.

Sir David Lees
Larry Pillard } Directors
Simon Gifford

Fig. 13.2 continued

Notes to the Financial Statements

	2000 £ million	1998 £ million
10 Fixed Asset Investments		
Group		
Joint ventures – unlisted	123	133
Associates – unlisted	11	14
Other fixed asset investments:		
Listed – at cost[1]	9	8
Unlisted – at cost less amounts provided of £5 million (1998 – £1 million)[2]	11	11
Loans	21	19
Total	175	185

[1]Market value £12 million (1998 – £10 million)
[2]Directors' valuation £11 million (1998 – £11 million)

	2000 £ million	1998 £ million
Tate & Lyle PLC		
Shares in Group undertakings at cost or earliest ascribed value	1,529	1,373
Revaluation additions	7	7
	1,536	1,380
Loans to Group undertakings less amounts provided of £9 million (1998 – £9 million)	954	963
Shares in joint ventures at cost less acquisition goodwill of £nil million written off (1998 – £5 million)	–	5
	2,490	2,348

Movement in book value	Joint ventures £ million	Associates £ million	Other equity investments £ million	Loans £ million	2000 Group £ million	2000 Tate & Lyle PLC £ million
At 26 September 1998	133	14	19	19	185	2,348
Differences on exchange	12	1	–	(1)	12	(2)
Additions	–	–	6	1	7	158
Refinancing of existing joint ventures	16	–	–	4	20	–
Disposals	(30)	–	(1)	(2)	(33)	(5)
Capital repayments by joint ventures	(34)	–	–	–	(34)	–
Reduction in loans to Group undertakings	–	–	–	–	–	(9)
Retained profits of joint ventures and associates	21	–	–	–	21	–
Movement in provisions	5	(4)	(4)	–	(3)	–
At 25 March 2000	**123**	**11**	**20**	**21**	**175**	**2,490**

The provision against the Group's investment in Bulgaria was partially reversed in the period. The impairment of this asset was recognised in 1997 when difficult economic conditions halted plant operations. As conditions improved the impairment provision was reassessed in accordance with FRS11.

▶

Fig. 13.2 continued

Joint Ventures	2000 Group £ million	1998 Group £ million
Share of fixed assets	177	203
Share of current assets	95	107
Share of gross assets	272	310
Share of liabilities due within one year	(68)	(115)
Share of liabilities due after more than one year	(81)	(62)
Share of gross liabilities	(149)	(177)
Share of net assets	123	133

CHAPTER SUMMARY

FRSs 2 Accounting for Subsidiary Undertakings, FRS 6 Acquisitions and Mergers, FRS 9 Associates and Joint Ventures

Type of investment	Method used	Investor's profit and loss account	Investor's balance sheet
Subsidiary (see FRS 2, p. 188)	Acquisition accounting (see FRS 6, p. 195)	Subsidiary's income and expenditure included, minority interests adjusted.	Assets and liabilities included, minority interests adjusted.
Associate (see FRS 9, p. 199)	Equity method	Share of associate's operating result included after group operating result. Any amortisation or write-down of goodwill arising on the acquisition of the associate should be disclosed separately.	Investor's share of the net assets of its associates included and separately disclosed. Goodwill arising on the acquisition of its associates, less any amortisation or write-down, should be included in the carrying amount of its associates but disclosed separately.
Joint venture (see FRS 9, p. 199)	Gross equity method	As the equity method, but in addition the investor's share of the turnover of the joint venture is noted.	As the equity method, but the venturer's share of the gross assets and liabilities of its joint venture is also shown.

▶

Joint arrangement that is not an entity	(Not applicable)	Each party to the agreement accounts for its own share of the assets, liabilities, income and expenditure according to the terms of the arrangement, e.g. pro rata to their respective interests.	
Simple investment	(Not applicable)	Dividends received and receivable shown.	Investment shown at cost or valuation.

FRS 7 Fair Values in Acquisition Accounting

- Bans companies from making provisions for the future trading losses of companies they acquire and the costs of any related rationalisation or reorganisation.
- Fair value is 'the amount at which an asset or liability could be exchanged in an arm's length transaction between informed and willing parties, other than in a forced or liquidation sale'.

DISCUSSION QUESTIONS

1. 'Merger accounting will soon be a thing of the past.' Discuss.

2. 'Bankers regard consolidated accounts as misleading because they disguise the individual indebtedness of particular companies.' Discuss.

(*See Appendix 3* for outline responses.)

EXAMINATION QUESTIONS

1. a) How does FRS 9 *Associates and joint ventures* define an associated undertaking?
(10 marks)

b) The abbreviated balance sheets of Cable plc on 31 December 2000 and 2002 are set out below.

	2000 £000	2002 £000
Net tangible assets	300	400
Goodwill	50	50
	350	450
Ordinary shares	200	200
Revenue reserves	150	250
	350	450

Wire plc acquired 30% of the ordinary share capital of Cable plc on 1 January 2001 at a cost of £150,000. The net tangible assets in Cable plc are stated at their fair values.

Required:

i) Show how the investment in Cable plc should be stated in accordance with FRS 9 in the consolidated balance sheet of Wire Plc at 31 December 2002.

(4 marks)

ii) FRS 2 *Accounting for subsidiary undertakings* states that under the equity method of accounting, an investment in a company is shown in the consolidated balance sheet of the investing company at cost plus the share of the post-acquisition retained profits.

Using the information given show how the investment in Cable should be stated in accordance with the equity method of accounting.

(3 marks)

iii) Which of your answers in (i) and (ii) above do you consider gives the better presentation of the investment in Cable plc by Wire plc and why?

(3 marks)

ACCA (amended)

2. The merger 'pooling of interests' method of accounting is permissible in certain circumstances instead of the traditional acquisition ('purchase') method and by using the merger method a different distribution of profits policy may be available to the group.

For purposes of illustration of the two methods, suppose that one share of Company X is offered for one share of Company Y and the offer is accepted. Also assume at the time of the merger a share of Y is valued at £7 and the fair value of Y's net assets is £550,000 being a decrease of £30,000 in fixed assets and £20,000 working capital. The balance sheets of X and Y immediately prior to the merger are as follows:

	X (£000)	Y (£000)
Fixed assets	1,100	700
Current assets	300	100
	1,400	800
Creditors	400	200
	1,000	600
Share capital (ordinary £1 shares)	700	100
Capital reserve	70	–
Revenue reserves	230	500
	1,000	600

Required:

(a) identify the circumstances in which the merger method of accounting is permissible;

(4 marks)

209

(b) draw up summarised consolidated balance sheets immediately after the merger, using each of the two methods of accounting for consolidations

(10 marks)

(c) contrast the two consolidated balance sheets evaluating the consequences and effectiveness of each method of accounting.

(8 marks)

ICSA

(*See Appendix 4* for answers.)

Chapter 14

Foreign currency translation: SSAP 20

INTRODUCTION

If this book were purchased in the UK, the payment would have been made in pounds sterling. In other countries where this book may be sold, the payment would be made in the local currency, for example Singapore dollars or Malaysian ringgit. Whatever the currency, the company which publishes the book has to make appropriate accounting entries in its records in its own local currency, and has to cope with the various problems of fluctuating exchange rates and asset and liability balances held by foreign subsidiaries which are denominated in foreign currencies.

SSAP 20 addresses itself to these problems, and explains methods to be adopted both by individual companies and groups of companies for the purpose of foreign currency translation. The standard is complex, and one author estimated that it contains over three thousand alternative accounting possibilities. Examination questions are unlikely to require a knowledge of all of these!

SSAP 20 FOREIGN CURRENCY TRANSLATION
(Issued April 1983)

The explanatory note to the standard sets out the objectives of foreign currency translation as follows.

'The translation of foreign currency transactions and financial statements should produce results which are generally compatible with the effects of rate changes on a company's cash flows and its equity and should ensure that the financial statements present a true and fair view of the results of management actions. Consolidated statements should reflect the financial results and relationships as measured in the foreign currency financial statements prior to translation.'

The standard itself is split into two main areas.

1. The individual company stage, whereby a company may enter directly into business transactions denominated in foreign currencies, and may have asset and liability balances which also are so denominated.

2. The consolidated financial statements stage, whereby the results of foreign subsidiaries must be incorporated within the consolidated results of the group.

1. The individual company stage

Individual transactions

The exchange rate in operation on the date on which the transaction occurred should be used. If rates of exchange are fairly stable, however, an average rate for a period may be used.

If certain transactions are to be settled at a rate specified in a contract, or are covered by a related or matching forward contract, then the 'contracted rate' should be used.

The standard gives specific advice with regard to 'non-monetary' assets and 'monetary' assets and liabilities denominated in foreign currencies, as follows.

Non-monetary assets (e.g. plant, machinery and equity investments)
Once translated and recorded in the company's local currency*, no subsequent translations will normally be made. The exception to this is where such assets have been financed by borrowings in foreign currencies, in which case, subject to certain conditions explained later in the chapter, the amounts are translated at the end of each accounting period at the closing rates of exchange.

Monetary assets (e.g. cash and bank balances, amounts receivable and payable)
These should be translated according to the rates of exchange ruling at the balance sheet date, unless there are related or matching forward contracts, in which case the 'contracted' rate is used.

Exchange gains or losses

These arise primarily in situations where the rate prevailing at the time that a transaction is recorded differs from that used when the transaction is settled. Such gains or losses should be included in the profit or loss on ordinary activities unless they arise from 'extraordinary' events (very rare!), in which case they are included as part of such items.

In the case of exchange gains relating to long-term monetary items (e.g. long dated foreign loans), the prudence concept must be taken into consideration when deciding whether to incorporate all or part of such gains in circumstances where there are doubts as to the convertibility or marketability of the currency in question.

Gains or losses arising from group inter-company transactions should be reported within the individual company's profit and loss account, in the same way as third-party transactions.

Summary

Figure 14.1 provides a summary of the main provisions of SSAP 20 regarding individual company transactions.

---

* Defined as the currency of the primary economic environment in which it operates and generates cash flows.

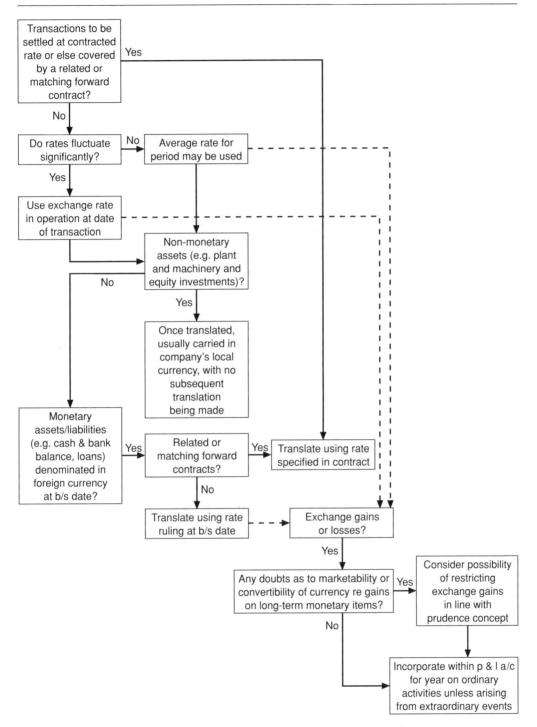

Fig. 14.1 SSAP 20 Individual company (summary of main provisions)

2. The consolidated financial statements stage

Two methods are considered for the purpose of translating financial statements for consolidation purposes: the *closing rate/net investment* method and the *temporal* method. The method chosen (usually the former) should reflect the financial and other operational relationships which exist between an investing company and its foreign enterprises.

The closing rate/net investment method

Here, the balance sheet amounts in the foreign subsidiary are translated using the rate of exchange ruling at the balance sheet date (i.e. the 'closing rate'). This method is based on the 'net investment' concept whereby it is not the value of the individual assets and liabilities which is relevant, but the value of the over-all net investment in the subsidiary. Any difference which arises if the closing rate differs from that ruling at the previous balance sheet date (or at the date of any subsequent capital injection or reduction) is shown in the statement of total recognised gains and losses, and adjusted on reserves.

Profit and loss account items

The standard allows either the closing rate or an average rate to be applied to profit and loss account items, giving the following arguments:

a) closing rate – more likely to achieve objective of translation (*see* p. 211);

b) average rate* – reflects more fairly the profits or losses and cash flows as they arise to the group throughout the accounting period.

Once the rate is chosen it should be applied consistently in future accounting periods. Where the average rate differs from the closing rate, a difference will arise which should be adjusted on reserves.

The temporal method

Although most foreign operations are carried out by organisations which operate as virtually autonomous entities, there are occasions where the foreign trade is conducted as a direct extension of the trade of the investing company, and the results of the foreign enterprise are regarded as being more dependent upon the economic environment of the investing company's local currency than on its own reporting currency.

In such cases, the 'net investment' concept is regarded as inappropriate and the transactions of the foreign enterprise are treated as though they had been made by the investing company itself in its own currency being translated by means of the 'temporal' method. The temporal method is identical with that used at the individual company stage described earlier in the chapter.

------

* 'Calculated by the method considered most appropriate for the circumstances of the foreign enterprise'

The decision as to whether the temporal method is appropriate hinges upon the relative dominance of the investing company's 'economic environment'. The explanatory note to the standard gives the following list of factors to be taken into account when arriving at the decision:

a) the extent to which the cash flows of the enterprise have a direct impact upon those of the investing company;

b) the extent to which the functioning of the enterprise is dependent directly upon the investing company;

c) the currency in which the majority of the trading transactions are denominated;

d) the major currency to which the operation is exposed in its financing structure.

Additionally, it gives three specific circumstances where the temporal method may be appropriate, where the foreign enterprise:

a) acts as a selling agency receiving stocks of goods from the investing company and remits the proceeds back to the company;

b) produces a raw material or manufactures parts or sub-assemblies which are then shipped to the investing company for inclusion in its own products;

c) is located overseas for tax, exchange control or similar reasons to act as a means of raising finance for other companies in the group.

Foreign branches

The translation method to be used depends upon the degree of autonomy which the branch enjoys:

High degree of autonomy	closing rate/net investment method
Extension of company's trade, and cash flows have direct impact on those of company	temporal method

Areas of hyper-inflation

In certain countries, a very high rate of inflation exists, which serves to distort any translation of accounts produced under the historical cost concept. In such circumstances, appropriate adjustments should be made to the financial statements to reflect current price levels before the translation process takes place.

Companies covered against exchange rate fluctuations

In the previous parts of this section, it has been seen how exchange gains and losses are normally incorporated within the company's profit and loss arising from ordinary activities. In many cases, companies enter into currency hedging arrangements by borrowing foreign currency to cushion them from any adverse effects arising from exchange rate movements. Where this cover exists, and subject to certain conditions, the standard regards it as being inappropriate to record an accounting profit or loss when exchange rates change, and requires exchange adjustments to be taken directly to reserves. It also allows the 'closing rate' to be applied to the company's equity investments, as opposed to carrying forward the original translated amounts. The conditions are:

a) in any accounting period, exchange gains or losses arising on the borrowings may be offset only to the extent of exchange differences arising on the equity investments;

b) the foreign currency borrowings, whose exchange gains or losses are used in the offset process, should not exceed, in aggregate, the total amount of cash that the investments are expected to be able to generate, whether from profits or otherwise;

c) the accounting treatment adopted should be applied consistently from period to period.

Similar provisions apply where a group has used foreign borrowings to finance group investments in a foreign enterprise or to provide a hedge against exchange risks applying to similar existing investments. One additional condition is, however, laid down in such circumstances:

d) the relationship between the investing company and the foreign enterprises concerned should be such as to justify the use of the closing rate method for consolidation purposes.

Disclosure

The following information should be disclosed in the financial statements with regard to foreign currency translation:

a) the translation methods used;

b) the treatment accorded to exchange differences;

c) the net amount of exchange gains and losses on foreign currency borrowings;

d) the net movement on reserves arising from exchange differences.

Summary

Figure 14.2 provides a summary of the main provisions of SSAP 20 regarding consolidated financial statements.

APPLICATION IN PRACTICE

Figure 14.3 provides an extract from the published accounts of Tadpole Technology plc to illustrate the accounting treatment adopted towards the translation of foreign currency.

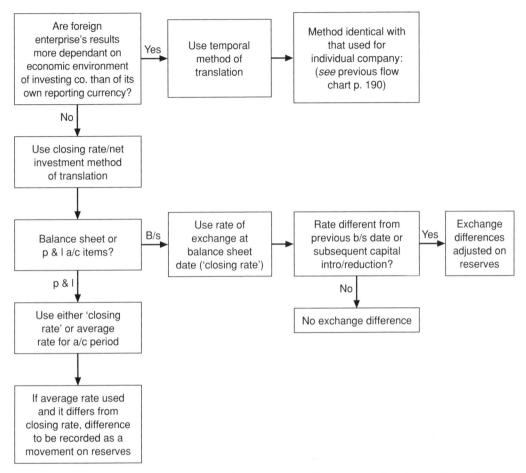

Fig. 14.2 SSAP 20 Consolidated financial statements (summary of main provisions)

Fig. 14.3 Tadpole Technology plc: foreign currencies

> #### Foreign currencies
>
> In the financial statements of individual undertakings, transactions in foreign currencies are recorded in the local currency at the actual exchange rates ruling at the date of the transaction. Assets and liabilities denominated in foreign currencies are translated at the rates ruling at the balance sheet date, exchange differences arising being taken to the profit and loss account.
>
> On consolidation, assets and liabilities of subsidiary undertakings are translated into sterling at closing rates of exchange. Profit and loss accounts are translated at average rates of exchange. Exchange differences resulting from the translation at closing rates of net investments in subsidiary undertakings, together with differences between income statements translated at average rates and at closing rates, are dealt with in reserves.

CHAPTER SUMMARY

> ### SSAP 20 Foreign Currency Translation
>
> - Individual companies: use average rate where currency is stable, otherwise use rates on date of transactions.
> - Consolidated statements: closing rate/net investment method normally used, but temporal method for autonomous entities.
> - Closing rate/net investment method requires exchange differences (shown in the statement of total recognised gains and losses) to be adjusted on reserves.
> - Temporal method – same method as for individual companies.

DISCUSSION QUESTION

1. 'The net investment method of foreign currency translation assumes that a parent company is not interested in the individual assets and liabilities of its foreign subsidiary, but in the business as a whole. However, on consolidation, the individual assets and liabilities are aggregated, line by line, which seems contradictory.' Discuss.

(*See Appendix 3* for outline responses.)

EXAMINATION QUESTIONS

1. With regard to SSAP 20 *Foreign currency translation*:

   a) Explain the closing rate/net investment method.

   (7 marks)

   b) Explain the temporal method.

   (7 marks)

   c) What factors should be taken into account in deciding whether the temporal method should be adopted? Give **two** examples of situations where this method may be the most appropriate.

   (11 marks)
   ACCA

2. a) Outline the **two** major methods of accounting for foreign currency translation, explaining clearly the objectives upon which they are based.

   (12 marks)

   b) Should exchange differences appear in the profit and loss account or be charged direct to reserves? State the reasons for your answer.

   (8 marks)
   ACCA

3. Home Ltd is incorporated in the UK and rents mobile homes to holidaymakers in this country and in Carea. The company has a head office in London and a branch in Carea where the local currency is 'mics'. The following balances are extracted from the books of the head office and its 'self-accounting' branch at 31 December 2001.

	Head office (£)	Branch (Mics)
Debit balances		
Fixed assets at cost	450,000	900,000
Debtors and cash	17,600	36,000
Operating costs	103,700	225,000
Branch current account	42,600	–
	613,900	1,161,000
Credit balances		
Share capital	200,000	–
Retained profit, 1 January 1999	110,800	–
Sales revenue	186,300	480,000
Creditors	9,700	25,000
Head office current account	–	420,000
Accumulated depreciation	107,100	236,000
	613,900	1,161,000

The following information is provided regarding exchange rates, some of which is relevant.

The fixed assets of the branch were acquired when there were 8 mics to the £. Exchange rates ruling during 1999 were:

	Mics to the £
1 January	6
Average	5
31 December	4

There are no cash or goods in transit between head office and branch at the year end.

Required:

The final accounts of Home Ltd for 2001. The accounts should be expressed in £s sterling and, for this purpose, the conversion of mics should be made in accordance with the temporal method of translation as specified in SSAP 20 entitled *Foreign currency translation*.

(24 marks)
ICSA

(*See Appendix 4* for suggested answers.)

Chapter 15

Retirement benefits: FRS 17

INTRODUCTION

FRS 17 replaced SSAP 24 *Accounting for pension costs* in December 2000 but with a phased introduction requiring full implementation for accounting periods ending on or after 22 June 2003. Under SSAP 24 (*see Appendix 2* for details), defined benefit pension schemes (where employees are promised a specific benefit regardless of the investment performance of the scheme) are valued on an actuarial basis, with the objective being to arrive at a regular pension cost each year that is a substantially level percentage of the pensionable payroll. Any variations from this regular cost are spread forward and recognised gradually over the average remaining working lives of the employees. The SSAP 24 approach had been criticised for a number of reasons, including:

- poor disclosure requirements;
- lack of transparency;
- inconsistency with international standards;
- the number of different valuation methods available;
- the number of ways of accounting for gains and losses.

The new standard brings in a market-based approach to valuation rather than actuarial values, which is in line with the international standards. This brings volatility into the measurement of surplus or deficit in the pension scheme, but unlike the international standard's approach of averaging the market values over a number of years and spreading the gains or losses forward in the profit and loss accounts over the working lives of the employees, FRS 17 requires the effect of market fluctuations to be shown in the statement of total recognised gains and losses. This has the advantages that the profit and loss charge is more stable than it would be if the market value fluctuations were spread forward, and the balance sheet shows the deficit or recoverable surplus in the scheme. The standard is very detailed, and the following represents a summary of the main points only.

FRS 17 RETIREMENT BENEFITS
(Issued December 2000)

Objective

The objectives of the standard are to ensure that:

- financial statements reflect at fair value the assets and liabilities arising from an employer's retirement benefit obligations and any related funding;
- the operating costs of providing retirement benefits to employees are recognised in the accounting period(s) in which the benefits are earned by the employees, and the related finance costs and any other changes in value of the assets and liabilities are recognised in the accounting periods in which they arise; and
- the financial statements contain adequate disclosure of the cost of providing retirement benefits and the related gains, losses, assets and liabilities.

Definitions

Key definitions include:

Actuarial gains and losses – changes in actuarial deficits or surpluses that arise because:

- events have not coincided with the actuarial assumptions made for the last valuation (experience gains and losses); or
- the actuarial assumptions have changed.

Current service cost – the increase in the present value of the scheme liabilities expected to arise from employee service in the current period.

Curtailment – an event that reduces the expected years of future service of present employees or reduces for a number of employees the accrual of defined benefits for some or all of their future service.

Defined benefit scheme – a pension or other retirement benefit scheme other than a defined contribution scheme. Usually the scheme rules define the benefits independently of the contributions payable, and the benefits are not directly related to the investments of the scheme. The scheme may be funded or unfunded.

Defined contribution scheme – a pension or other retirement benefit scheme into which an employer pays regular contributions fixed as an amount or as a percentage of pay and will have no legal or constructive obligation to pay further contributions if the scheme does not have sufficient assets to pay all employee benefits relating to employee service in the current and prior periods.

Expected rate of return on assets – the average rate of return, including both income and changes in fair value but net of scheme expenses, expected over the remaining life of the related obligation on the actual assets held by the scheme.

Interest cost – the expected increase during the period in the present value of the scheme liabilities because the benefits are one period closer to settlement.

Past service cost – the increase in the present value of the scheme liabilities related to employee service in prior periods arising in the current period as a result of the introduction of, or improvement to, retirement benefits.

Projected unit method – an accrued benefits valuation method in which the scheme liabilities make allowance for projected earnings. An accrued benefits valuation method is one which the scheme liabilities at the valuation date relate to:

- the benefits for pensioners and deferred pensioners and their dependants, allowing where appropriate for future increases, and
- the accrued benefits for members in service on the valuation date.

Retirement benefits – all forms of consideration given by an employer in exchange for services rendered by employees that are payable after the completion of employment.

Settlement – an irrevocable action that relieves the employer (or the defined benefit scheme) of the primary responsibility for a pension obligation and eliminates significant risks relating to the obligation and the assets used to effect the settlement.

1. Defined contribution schemes

In such schemes, the cost to the employer is known with reasonable accuracy, as the employer usually makes agreed contributions to the scheme and the benefits will depend upon the funds available from these contributions and the investment earnings arising from them. The accounting practice in FRS 17 for such schemes is unchanged from that in SSAP 24.

Recognition

The contributions payable to the scheme for the accounting period should be recognised within operating profit in the profit and loss account.

Disclosure

The following should be disclosed for a defined contribution scheme:

- the nature of the scheme (defined contribution);
- the cost for the period; and
- any outstanding or prepaid contributions at the balance sheet date.

2. Defined benefit schemes

In defined benefit schemes, the benefits paid will usually depend upon either the average pay of the employees during their career (or perhaps the last few years of it) or, more usually, the employee's final pay. It is impossible to know in advance that the contributions plus investment return will equal the final benefits to be paid. Any shortfall may have to be paid by the employer, either for legal reasons or else to maintain good employee relations. If a surplus arises, the employer may be entitled to either a refund of contributions or a reduction in future contributions. In view of the long-term nature of the pension commitment, actuarial valuations are needed at regular intervals (see below).

Measurement

Scheme assets

Defined benefit scheme assets are measured at their fair value at the balance sheet date. Fair value is taken as follows:

- quoted securities: mid-market value;
- unquoted securities: an estimate of fair value is made;
- property: open market value or another appropriate basis of valuation;
- insurance policies that exactly match the amount and timing of some or all of the benefits payable under the pension scheme should be measured at the same amount as the related obligations.

Scheme liabilities

Defined benefit scheme liabilities should be measured on an actuarial basis using the projected unit method (see definition above). The scheme liabilities comprise:

- any benefits promised under the formal terms of the scheme;
- any constructive obligations for further benefits where a public statement or past practice by the employer has created a valid expectation in the employees that such benefits will be granted.

The benefits should be attributed to periods of service according to the scheme's benefit formula, except where such a formula attributes a disproportionate share of the total benefits to later years of service. In such cases the benefits should be attributed on a straight-line basis over the period during which it is earned.

The assumptions (which are the directors' responsibility, based on actuaries' advice) underlying the valuation should be mutually compatible and lead to the best estimate of the future cash flows that will arise under the scheme liabilities.

The actuarial assumptions should reflect expected future events, including:

- cost of living increases;
- expected salary increases (where pensions are based on final salary);
- expected early retirement where the employee has that right under the scheme rules.

The liabilities should be discounted at a rate that reflects the time value of money and the characteristics of the liability. Such a rate should be assumed to be the current rate of return on a high quality corporate bond of equivalent currency and term to the scheme liabilities.

Frequency of valuations

Full actuarial valuations by a professionally qualified actuary should be obtained at intervals not exceeding 3 years.

Recognition

Balance sheet

- An asset (the excess of the value of the assets in the scheme over the present value of the scheme's liabilities) should be recognised to the extent that the entity is able to recover a surplus either through reduced contributions in the future or through refunds from the scheme.
- A liability (the shortfall of the value of the assets in the scheme below the present value of the scheme's liabilities) should be recognised to the extent that it reflects its legal or constructive obligation.
- Any unpaid contributions to the scheme should be presented in the balance sheet as a creditor due within one year.
- Where an employer has more than one defined benefit scheme, any total assets of one scheme must be shown separately from any total liabilities of another scheme.
- The deferred tax relating to the scheme should be offset against the scheme's asset or liability and not shown as part of other deferred tax assets or liabilities.

Performance statements

The change in the defined benefit asset or liability (other than that arising from contributions to the scheme) should be analysed into the following components.

1. Periodic costs:

- The current service cost (see definitions), based on the most recent actuarial valuation at the beginning of the period, with the financial assumptions updated to reflect conditions at that date. It should be included within operating profit in the profit and loss account.
- The net of the interest cost and the expected return on assets (see definitions) should be included as other finance costs (or income) adjacent to interest.

- Actuarial gains and losses (see definitions) arising from any new valuation and from updating the latest actuarial valuation to reflect conditions at the balance sheet date should be recognised in the statement of total recognised gains and losses for the period.

2. Non-periodic costs:

- Past service costs (see definitions) should be recognised in the profit and loss account on a straight-line basis over the period in which the increases in benefit vest. To the extent that the benefits vest immediately, the past service costs should be recognised immediately. Any unrecognised past service costs should be deducted from the scheme liabilities and the balance sheet asset or liability adjusted accordingly.

- Losses arising on a settlement or curtailment (see definitions) not allowed for in the actuarial assumptions should be measured at the date on which the employer becomes demonstrably committed to the transaction and recognised in the profit and loss account covering that date.

- Gains arising on a settlement or curtailment (see definitions) not allowed for in the actuarial assumptions should be measured at the date on which all parties whose consent is required are irrevocably committed to the transaction and recognised in the profit and loss account covering that date.

Disclosures

For a defined benefit scheme, the following key disclosures should be made (refer to the Standard for information of other, detailed disclosures):

- the nature of the scheme (i.e. defined benefit);
- the date of the most recent full actuarial valuation on which the amounts in the financial statements are based;
- the contribution made in respect of the accounting period and any agreed contribution rates for future years;
- for closed schemes and those in with a significantly rising age profile of active members, the fact that under the projected unit method (see definitions) the current service cost will increase as the members of the scheme approach retirement.

The following main financial assumptions used at the start and end of the financial period should be disclosed:

- the inflation assumption;
- the rate of increase in salaries;
- the rate of increase for pensions in payment and deferred pensions;
- the rate used to discount scheme liabilities.

APPLICATION IN PRACTICE

As the standard is in course of implementation, companies, at the time of writing, are still using SSAP 24. For examples of disclosures under that standard *see Appendix 2*, p. 236.

CHAPTER SUMMARY

FRS 17 Retirement Benefits

- Defined contribution schemes: employer usually makes agreed contributions to the scheme and the benefits will depend upon the funds available from these contributions and the investment earnings. The contributions payable to the scheme for the accounting period should be recognised within operating profit in the profit and loss account.

- Defined benefit schemes: the benefits paid will usually depend upon either the average pay of the employees during their career (or perhaps the last few years of it) or, more usually, the employee's final pay. Full actuarial valuations are needed every 3 years maximum. Actuarial gains and losses arising from any new valuation and from updating the latest actuarial valuation to reflect conditions at the balance sheet date should be recognised in the statement of total recognised gains and losses for the period.

DISCUSSION QUESTION

1. 'FRS 17 has replaced the actuarial-based valuation of pension scheme assets with a market-value based approach. Some companies have voiced concerns that this will bring unwanted volatility into the measurement of the pension surplus or deficit.' Discuss.

(*See Appendix 3* for outline responses.)

EXAMINATION QUESTION

In relation to FRS 17 *Retirement benefits*, compare and contrast (in outline) the accounting treatments for:

a) defined contribution schemes;

b) defined benefit schemes.

(20 marks)

(*See Appendix 4* for suggested answer.)

Appendix 1

Current topics and future developments

When the Accounting Standards Committee (ASC) ceased to exist on 1 August 1990, the Accounting Standards Board (ASB) adopted all SSAPs in existence at that date, though 'Statements of Recommended Practice' (SORPs) were not adopted. Several Exposure Drafts (EDs) had been issued by the ASC which had not been incorporated within new or revised SSAPs at the time of its disbandment.

At the time of writing (May 2001) the ASB has issued 19 Financial Reporting Standards (FRSs). Major documents have also been issued by the FRC, ASB and other sub-committees since their formation. Many of these have been referred to within the relevant chapters of this book, but there are a number of other areas worthy of note. These have been subdivided in this chapter as follows:

1. Financial Reporting Exposure Drafts (FREDs)
2. Discussion Papers
3. Urgent Issues Task Force Abstracts
4. Operating and Financial Review (OFR)

1. FINANCIAL REPORTING EXPOSURE DRAFTS (FREDS)

Twenty-two FREDs have been issued by the ASB from its inception to 1 May 2001. Only one was issued in the year to that date, FRED 22 *Revision of FRS 3 'Reporting Financial Performance'* (issued December 2000). Details are given in Chapter 8.

2. DISCUSSION PAPERS

Discussion papers, as the name suggests, are documents that contain draft proposals which are circulated for debate. Depending upon the feedback, they may eventually become either UITF Abstracts (*see below*), full FRSs, or definitive statements such as the Statement of Principles for Financial Reporting (*see* Chapter 2). Those current at 1 May 2001 are:

- derivatives and other financial instruments;
- business combinations;
- leases: implementation of a new approach;

- year-end financial reports: improving communication;
- share-based payment.

3. URGENT ISSUES TASK FORCE ABSTRACTS

The UITF is a committee of the ASB whose main role is to assist the ASB in areas where an accounting standard or a Companies Act provision exists, but where unsatisfactory or conflicting interpretations have developed or seem likely to develop. The UITF has up to 15 members, and a consensus must be reached by at least 11 of them before an 'abstract' can be issued. Details of all extant Abstracts can be found on the ASB's website at http://www.asb.org.uk/uitf/

4. OPERATING AND FINANCIAL REVIEW

From July 1993, the ASB recommends (but does not require) an operating and financial review (OFR) to be included in the annual reports of large companies. Areas to be covered by the OFR include:

a) commentary on the operating results;

b) review of the group's financial needs and resources;

c) commentary on shareholder's return and value.

The characteristics of the OFR are that it should:

a) be fair, giving a balanced and objective statement of good and bad news;

b) focus on matters of significance;

c) be presented in the way most likely to help the user of the annual report in gaining an understanding of the financial circumstances of the business.

No particular format is proposed for the OFR; it is left to the directors to decide upon the best way of presenting the information. Also, OFRs are not the subject of an accounting standard, but the ASB wishes to find out best practice in this area.

Appendix 2

Standards in transit

A number of standards were in the process of being replaced at the date of this edition. As some students may be examined on the 'old' standards, details are given below of SSAPs 2, 15 and 24.

ACCOUNTING POLICIES: SSAP 2

Introduction

SSAP 2 was replaced by FRS 18, which had a phased introduction from June 2001. Some syllabuses may require SSAP 2 to be examined during this change-over period.

SSAP 2 Disclosure of Accounting Policies
(Issued November 1971, replaced by FRS 18, December 2000)

The intention of the standard is to establish '. . . as standard accounting practice the disclosure in financial accounts of clear explanations of the accounting policies followed in so far as these are significant for the purpose of giving a true and fair view'. The following definition of *accounting policies* is given:

> 'Accounting policies are the specific accounting bases selected and consistently followed by a business enterprise as being, in the opinion of the management, appropriate to its circumstances and best suited to present fairly its results and financial position.'

Those accounting policies which are judged material or critical in determining profit or loss for the year and in stating the financial position should be disclosed by way of note to the accounts, with explanations being as clear, fair and as brief as possible.

Before a company determines accounting policies which are relevant to its circumstances, it must have regard both to *fundamental accounting concepts* and *accounting bases*.

Fundamental accounting concepts

The standard is frank in admitting that its purpose is not to develop a basic theory of accounting, and as such does not include a comprehensive list of all accounting concepts. Instead, four fundamental concepts are referred to, which are the broad basic assumptions that underlie the financial accounts. They have '. . . such general acceptance that they call for no explanation in published accounts and their observance is presumed unless stated otherwise.'

If accounts are prepared on the basis of assumptions which differ in material respects from any of the generally accepted fundamental concepts, the facts should be explained. In the absence of a clear statement to the contrary, there is a presumption that the four fundamental concepts have been observed.

The four concepts are:

1. going concern
2. accruals
3. consistency
4. prudence.

The definitions contained within the standard are as follows:

The 'going concern' concept
The enterprise will continue in operational existence for the foreseeable future. This means in particular that the profit and loss account and balance sheet assume no intention nor necessity to liquidate or curtail significantly the scale of operation.

The 'accruals' concept*
Revenue and costs are accrued (that is, recognised as they are earned or incurred, not as money is received or paid), matched with one another so far as their relationship can be established or justifiably assumed, and dealt with in the profit and loss account of the period to which they relate, provided that where the accruals concept is inconsistent with the 'prudence' concept (*see below*) the latter prevails. The accruals concept implies that the profit and loss account reflects changes in the amount of net assets that arise out of the transactions of the relevant period (other than distributions or subscriptions of capital and unrealised surpluses arising on revaluation of fixed assets). Revenue and profits dealt with in the profit and loss account are matched with associated costs and expenses by including in the same account the costs incurred in earning them (so far as these are material and identifiable).

The 'consistency' concept
There is consistency of accounting treatment of like items within each accounting period and from one period to the next.

---

* Also known as the 'matching' concept.

The 'prudence' concept*

Revenue and profits are not anticipated, but are recognised by inclusion in the profit and loss account only when realised in the form either of cash or of other assets the ultimate cash realisation of which can be assessed with reasonable certainty; provision is made for all known liabilities (expenses and losses) whether the amount of these is known with certainty or is a best estimate in the light of the information available.

Problems in applying the concepts

The main difficulty in applying the four concepts is the fact that decisions have to be made as to the extent to which the expenditure of one year can reasonably be expected to produce revenue in future years, i.e. whether such expenditure should be carried forward on the balance sheet or written off to profit and loss account in the current year.

The standard refers to three specific areas of potential difficulty: the treatment of stocks and work in progress, fixed asset valuation and research and development expenditure. Since SSAP 2 was issued in 1971, these matters have been covered in detail by various SSAPs, including SSAP 9 and 13, which are dealt with fully in earlier chapters of this book.

Accounting bases

Accounting policies, according to the definition given earlier, are specific accounting bases selected by the business as being best suited to a fair presentation of its results and financial position. The definition of 'accounting bases' is given as follows:

'The methods developed for applying fundamental accounting concepts to financial transactions and items, for the purpose of financial accounts, and in particular (a) for determining the accounting periods in which revenue and costs should be recognised in the profit and loss account and (b) for determining the amounts at which material items should be stated in the balance sheet.'

The standard gives a list of examples of matters for which different accounting bases are recognised, several of which have become the subject of individual standards, including depreciation, deferred taxation, hire purchase and leasing and foreign currency conversion. As more FRSs are published, the choice of accounting bases will diminish, but it is impossible to achieve a total and rigid uniformity, due to the complex nature of business activity.

Summary of SSAP 2

A summary of SSAP 2 is provided in Figure A2.1.

---

* Also known as the concept of conservatism.

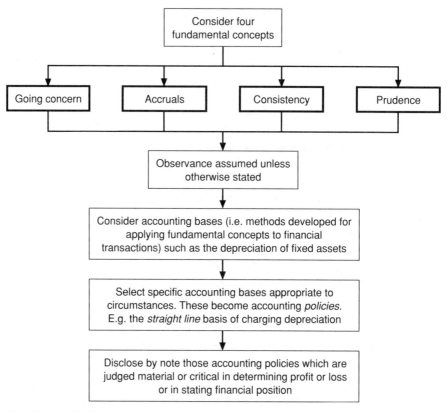

Fig. A2.1 SSAP 2

SSAP 2 and the Companies Acts

The four accounting concepts stated in SSAP 2 are given statutory force within the 1985 Companies Act, which refers to them as 'fundamental principles'. In addition, the Act lays down two other principles, as follows:

1. it is not permissible to set off amounts representing assets or income against amounts representing liabilities or expenditure, or vice versa, and;

2. in determining the aggregate amount of any item in the accounts, the amount of each component item must be determined separately.

The Companies Act 1985 also contains a provision which has a direct influence over the way in which the concepts are applied. Its effect is that the requirement to show a 'true and fair view' shall *override* the fundamental principles and all other requirements of the Act as to the matters to be included in a company's accounts or in notes to those accounts. In circumstances where a fundamental concept is abandoned, full details must be given in the accounts to comply with SSAP 2.

UITF Abstract 7, issued in December 1992, requires directors to state clearly and unambiguously when the true and fair view override is being invoked, with:

1. a statement of the treatment which the Act would normally require in the circumstances, and a statement of the treatment actually adopted;

2. a statement as to why the prescribed treatment would not give a true and fair view;

3. a description of how the position shown in the accounts is different as a result of the departure, normally with quantification.

SSAP 15 ACCOUNTING FOR DEFERRED TAX
(Issued October 1978, revised May 1985, amended December 1992 replaced by FRS 19 December 2000)

This statement, which does not apply to immaterial items, relates to the problems which arise when the tax payable on the profits of a particular period bears little relation to the income and expenditure appearing in the financial statements for that period. There are two main reasons for such an imbalance.

1. Permanent differences

Certain types of income shown in a company's financial statements are tax free (dividends and other distributions from UK companies), while certain types of expenditure cannot be offset against taxable profits (e.g. business entertainment). These give rise to *permanent* differences between taxable and accounting profits.

As these differences will not be reversed in future years, there is no requirement to consider them in relation to a deferred tax provision.

2. Timing differences

Certain items are included in the financial statements of one period, but treated in a different period for taxation purposes (e.g. interest received, which is treated on an *accruals* basis for the annual accounts, but on a *cash* basis when tax is being computed). This disparity of treatment gives rise to *timing* differences. (The standard defines deferred tax as *the tax attributable to timing differences*.) Other timing differences arise due to accelerated capital allowances,* where the allowances exceed the depreciation charged in the financial accounts.

Basis of provision

The *explanatory note* to the standard lists three principal bases for computing deferred tax.

---

* Certain capital expenditure is eligible for tax relief, which is given by means of capital allowances, at percentage rates set by the government.

1. *Nil provision* or *flow through* basis

This is based on the principle that only the tax payable in respect of a period should be charged in that period, and therefore no provision for deferred tax need be made. Those who argue in favour of this basis state that as tax liability arises on taxable profits, not accounting profits, it is necessary to provide for tax only on taxable profits. In addition, they argue that any tax liability arising on timing differences will depend upon the incidence of future taxable profits and may therefore be difficult to quantify.

2. *Full provision* basis

As its name implies, this is the opposite of the 'nil provision basis', as it is based on the principle that the tax effects (*whether current or deferred*) of all transactions of the period should be reflected in the financial statements for that period.

3. *Partial provision* basis

This is a more pragmatic approach than the other two bases, as it requires that deferred tax be accounted for only when it is likely that such a liability will crystallise. It recognises that, for a going concern, there is likely to be a *hard core* of timing differences which are being permanently deferred, as one timing difference is replaced by another before it crystallises.

Bases 1 and 2 above have the advantage that the amounts involved can be precisely quantified, but their disadvantage is that they may lead to a purely arithmetical approach being adopted, leading to a disregard of the likely tax effects of the transactions. *Basis 3 is considered preferable* as it requires an assessment of the potential liability which would result if and when the timing differences crystallise.

Method of computation

Two principal methods exist.

1. The deferral method

This method uses the tax rates current *when the differences arise*, i.e. no adjustments are made subsequently if tax rates change. Advocates of the deferral method argue that the mere fact of a change in tax rates does not indicate the potential amount of tax payable or recoverable relating to the timing differences. Any balance on the deferred tax account will therefore be shown on the balance sheet as a deferred tax credit or charge rather than as an asset or liability.

2. The liability method

Under this method, the deferred tax provisions are calculated at the rate at which it is estimated that the tax will be paid (or recovered) when the timing differences reverse. As tax rates change, therefore, the provision will be re-calculated.

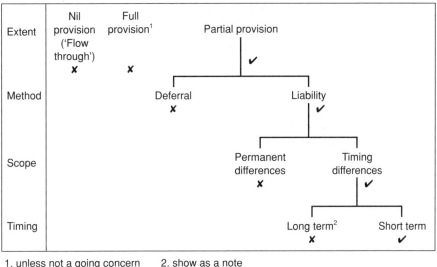

1. unless not a going concern   2. show as a note
Key: ✗ = **rejected by ASB**   ✔ = **supported by ASB**

Fig. A2.2 SSAP 15 Preferred treatment of deferred taxation

The standard favours the liability method as being consistent with the *partial provision* basis outlined earlier.

Figure A2.2 provides a summary chart of the preferred treatment of deferred taxation as laid down by SSAP 15.

Standard accounting practice

The standard comprises 22 paragraphs, divided into *General, Profit and Loss Account, Balance Sheet* and *Groups*, of which the following is a summary.

General

Deferred tax should be computed under the liability method, and accounted for only to the extent that it is probable that an asset or liability will crystallise. *Reasonable assumptions* should be used to decide on the likelihood of crystallisation, taking into account all relevant information, including financial plans or projections. A prudent approach should be adopted, particularly where there is a high degree of uncertainty over future prospects.

Profit and loss account

The amount of deferred tax relating to the company's ordinary activities should be shown as part of the tax on profit or loss on ordinary activities for the year, either on the face of the profit and loss account, or as a note to it.

The amount of any *unprovided* deferred tax in respect of the period should be shown as a note, analysed into its major components. Adjustments to deferred tax arising from a change in tax rates and allowances should be disclosed separately as part of the tax charge for the year.

Balance sheet

The deferred tax balance should be disclosed on the balance sheet or notes, and a note should be given of any transfers to or from the account.

Where amounts of deferred tax arise which relate to movements on reserves (e.g. an asset revaluation reserve), the amounts transferred to or from the deferred tax account should be shown separately as part of such movements.

The total amount of any unprovided deferred tax should be shown by way of note, analysed into its major components.

Deferred tax provisions should be shown in the balance sheet under the heading 'Provision for liabilities and charges'. Any deferred tax carried forward as an asset should be included under the heading *Prepayments and accrued income*.

Groups

A company which is a member of a group should take into account group relief which may be available when accounting for deferred tax.

SSAP 15 and SSAP 24

An amendment to SSAP 15 was issued in December 1992 to remove an inconsistency between it and SSAP 24 (Accounting for Pension Costs). The amendment allows preparers of financial statements to take into account, when provisions for pensions and other post-retirement benefits are set up, the tax relief that will be received when the benefits are actually paid. This is a relaxation of the previous SSAP 15 requirements.

Summary of SSAP 15

Figure A2.3 provides a summary of the treatment of deferred tax as laid down by SSAP 15.

SSAP 24 ACCOUNTING FOR PENSION COSTS
(Issued May 1988, replaced by FRS 17, December 2000)

The definition of a pension scheme given in the standard is:

'an arrangement (other than accident insurance) to provide pension and/or other benefits for members on leaving service or retiring and, after a member's death, for his/her dependants'.

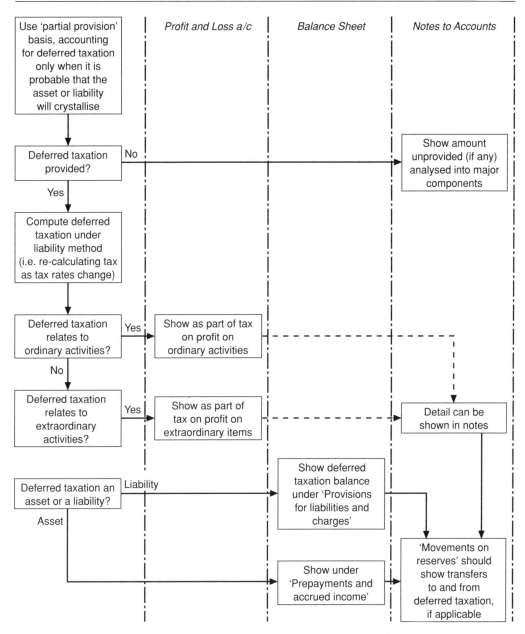

Fig. A2.3 SSAP 15

The accounting objective of the standard requires an employer to recognise the cost of providing pensions on a systematic and rational basis over the period during which he benefits from the employees' services. The standard, which does not apply to either state social security contributions or redundancy payments, applies where the employer is legally or contractually committed to the pension scheme, and also addresses circumstances such as *ex gratia* payments. Both *defined contribution schemes* and *defined benefit schemes* are covered by the standard. Their definitions are as follows:

A defined contribution scheme is a pension scheme in which the benefits are directly determined by the value of contributions paid in respect of each member. Normally the rate of contribution is specified by the rules of the scheme.

A defined benefit scheme is a pension scheme in which the rules define the benefits to be paid and the scheme is financed accordingly.

Defined contribution schemes

In such schemes, the cost to the employer is known with reasonable accuracy as the employer usually makes agreed contributions to the scheme, and the benefits will depend upon the funds available from these contributions and the investment earnings thereon. There is no need for an actuary to establish the pension cost. Such schemes tend to be smaller than defined benefit schemes (*see below*).

The accounting practice for such schemes is to charge against profits the amount of contributions payable to the pension scheme in the accounting period.

In addition, the following disclosures should be made:

a) the nature of the scheme (i.e. defined contribution);

b) the accounting policy;

c) the pension cost charge for the period;

d) any outstanding or prepaid pension contributions at the balance sheet date.

Defined benefit schemes

Here, the benefits paid will usually depend upon either the average pay of the employee during his or her career or (more usually) the final pay of the employee. It is impossible to know in advance that the contributions plus investment return will equal the final benefits to be paid. Any shortfall may have to be met by the employer, either for legal reasons or else to maintain good employee relations. If a surplus arises, then the employer may be entitled to a refund of contributions or a reduction in future contributions.

In view of the long-term nature of the pension commitment, actuarial calculations are needed to determine the pension cost charge. The choice of valuation methods and actuarial assumptions used can have a major effect on the contribution rate calculated. Such assumptions include:

a) future rates of inflation;

b) future pay increases;

c) increases to existing pensions;

d) earnings on investments;

e) number of employees joining the scheme;

f) age profile of employees;

g) likelihood of death in service;

h) number of employees leaving the scheme.

The standard states:

> 'The calculation of benefit levels should be based on the situation most likely to be experienced and not on a contingent event not likely to occur. The actuarial method selected should be used consistently and disclosed. If there is a change of method this fact should be disclosed and the effect quantified. The actuarial assumptions and the actuarial method taken as a whole should be compatible and should lead to the actuary's best estimate of the cost of providing the pension benefits promised.'

The accounting practice for defined benefit schemes is more complex than for defined contribution schemes.

1. The pension cost should be calculated using actuarial valuation assumptions and methods which are compatible when taken as a whole, and should result in the actuary's best estimate of the cost of providing the pension benefits promised.

2. The method of providing for expected pension costs over the service lives of employees in the scheme should be such that the regular pension cost is a substantially level percentage of the current and expected future pensionable payroll in the light of the current actuarial assumptions.

3. Variations from the regular costs should be allocated over the expected (or average) remaining service lives of current employees in the scheme, though this does not apply to a change caused by a significant reduction in the number of employees in the scheme. Such a change should be recognised when it occurs.

4. If a major event or transaction has occurred which has not been allowed for in the actuarial assumptions, any material deficit arising may be recognised over a period shorter than the expected remaining service lives of current employees. This applies in strictly limited circumstances which are outside the normal scope of actuarial assumptions and which have necessitated the payment of significant additional contributions to the pension scheme.

The following disclosures should be made in the accounting statements:

a) the nature of the scheme (i.e. defined benefit);

b) whether it is funded or unfunded (*see definitions below*);

c) the accounting policy and, if different, the funding policy;

d) whether the pension cost and provision (or asset) are assessed in accordance with actuarial advice, and if so, the date of the most recent formal actuarial valuation or later formal review; it should be disclosed if the actuary is an employee or officer of the reporting officer or group;

e) the pension cost charge for the period together with explanations of significant changes compared to the previous year;

f) any provisions or prepayments in the balance sheet resulting from a difference between the amounts recognised as cost and the amounts funded or paid directly;

g)* the amount of any deficiency on a current funding level basis, indicating what action is being taken to deal with it in the current and future accounting periods;

h)* an outline of the results of the most recent formal actuarial valuation or later formal review of the scheme, including:

  i) the method used, and brief description of assumptions;

  ii) market value of scheme assets at date of valuation or review;

  iii) level of funding in percentage terms;

  iv) comments on any material actuarial surplus or deficit;

i) any commitments to make additional payments over a limited number of years;

j) accounting treatment of any refunds made subject to deduction of tax;

k) details of the expected effects on future costs of any material changes in the pension arrangements of the group or company.

Ex gratia and other arrangements

An *ex gratia pension* is one which the employer has no legal or contractual commitment to provide. An example is where a long-serving employee has for some reason not been a member of the company pension scheme, but his or her employers decide to grant a pension on his or her retirement. The cost should be charged in the period in which it is granted, although it can be offset against any surplus on the pension fund. The same principle applies to discretionary 'one-off' increases in pension entitlements.

---

* These do not apply to subsidiaries which are members of group schemes.

Funding

In addition to the types of pension schemes listed above, they can also be classified by the way in which they are financed, being either:

a) **a funded scheme**, defined as a pension scheme where the future liabilities for benefits are provided for by the accumulation of assets held externally to the employing company's business, or

b) **an unfunded scheme**, where benefits are paid directly by the employer.

The same accounting principles apply to each type of scheme.

A funding plan is defined as the timing of payments in an orderly fashion to meet the future cost of a given set of benefits. Actuaries will aim at a level rate of contributions, though from time to time these might be altered due to such factors as surpluses or deficiencies on the fund.

Balance sheet disclosure

A 'net pension provision' should be created in cases where the cumulative pension cost recognised in the profit and loss account has not been completely discharged by payment of contributions or directly paid pensions. A prepayment should be shown in cases where there is an excess of contributions or direct payments when compared to the pension cost.

Group schemes

Subsidiaries which are members of group schemes should disclose this fact as well as the nature of the group scheme. It should state if its contributions are based on pension costs across the group as a whole, and also state the name of the holding company in whose financial statements particulars of the actuarial valuation of the group scheme are contained.

Foreign schemes

The pension charge should reflect obligations to pay pensions in respect of foreign operations, to be dealt with in accordance with the standard. An adjustment might be required to bring the charge into line with the basis set out in the standard, but it is recognised that it may be difficult and costly to obtain the necessary actuarial information. In such cases, the amount charged to profit and loss account and the basis of the charge should be disclosed.

APPLICATION IN PRACTICE

The 1991 annual report of Coats Viyella plc contained the note reproduced in Figure A2.4 regarding the treatment of (defined benefit) pension schemes in its accounts.

Chesterton International plc had both defined contribution and defined benefit schemes recorded in its 1995 accounts, as shown in Figure A2.5.

Fig. A2.4 Coats Viyella plc: pensions

31 Pensions

The Group operates a number of pension plans throughout the world. In the U.K. the main defined benefit arrangements is the Coats Viyella Pension Plan ('the Plan') which is open to all employees of participating Group companies provided employees are permanent, full-time and over age 20. There are other defined benefit arrangements in the U.K. for subsidiary companies which do not participate in the Pension Plan and employees who have chosen not to join the Plan, but these arrangements are not considered material to the Group position. The assets of these plans are mainly held under self-administered trust funds and hence separated from the Group's assets.

An actuarial valuation of the Plan was carried out by independent actuaries and consultants, as at 1 April 1989, using the projected unit method. The principal actuarial assumptions adopted in the valuation were that, over the long-term, the investment rate of return would be 9% per annum and would exceed future pensionable earnings increases by 2% per annum and would exceed increases to present and future pensions in payment by 5% per annum. It was also assumed that dividend increases on the equity portfolio would average 41/2% per annum. This valuation was updated as at 1 April 1991 using the same assumptions and revealed an additional actuarially calculated surplus of approximately £54m. The actuarial value of the assets at 1 April 1991 was sufficient to cover 143% of the benefits that had accrued to members at the valuation date, after allowing for expected future increases in earnings and pensions. The market value of the Plan's assets at 1 April 1991 was £634m.

In view of the surplus disclosed at these valuations, the actuaries have recommended that no contributions be paid by the Group into the Plan with effect from 1 April 1989, until the position is reviewed at the next actuarial valuation. The original actuarially calculated surplus of £141.8m was included in the balance sheet at 31 December 1988 under the transitional provisions of SSAP 24. The additional actuarially calculated surplus revealed at 1 April 1991 is being credited to profit and loss account over 13 years, being the estimated remaining working lives of the current members of the Plan as calculated in accordance with the guidelines of the Institute of Actuaries. The regular pension cost for 1991 of £12.8m has been reduced by interest of £13.3m accrued on the pension prepayment and a credit of £4.9m in respect of the spreading of the additional surplus resulting in a net credit to profit of £5.4m (1990 – £6.2m) which has been added to the balance sheet prepayment. The eligible pension costs also take account of the equalisation of benefits following the 'Barber' case judgement in the European Court of Justice.

In the U.K., the former Tootal Group operated a number of pension plans. The latest actuarial assessments of those schemes were at 31 December 1988 and 31 March 1990. The principal assumptions adopted for the valuations were a rate of return on investments of 9% and that this rate would exceed future pensionable earnings by 2%. The valuations were updated as at 31 May 1991 revealing a surplus of £63m. This surplus has been taken to reserves as part of the fair value analysis on the acquisition of the Tootal Group. For the 7 month period from 31 May the regular pension cost of £1.9m has been reduced by interest of £3.3m on the pension prepayment resulting in a net credit to profit of £1.4m.

In North America, the combined actuarial value of the major plans at the last valuation dates was 147% of the combined value of benefits accrued to members at the respective valuation dates, after allowing for expected future increases in earnings. The total market value of the assets at the last valuation was £96m. For the former Tootal Group interests in North America the actuarial surplus of the assets over the accrued benefits has been taken to reserves and is included within the acquisition balance sheet of the Tootal Group as at 31 May 1991. The remaining net surplus has not been taken

▶

Fig. A2.4 continued

to reserves but continues to be spread over the average remaining service lives of the current members in accordance with US accounting standards and in line with SSAP 24. The net pension credit to profit and loss of £1.8m has been calculated after offsetting the interest actual on the pension prepayment and the spread surplus against the regular cost of £3.6m. There are other defined benefit plans in overseas subsidiaries but, in aggregate, these are not considered material.

The net pension cost for the Group, excluding the U.K. and U.S. Plans explained above, was £10.7m (1990 – £5.8m) of which £10.6m (1990 – £5.6m) relates to overseas plans.

In addition to the surpluses in the U.K. plans referred to above, debtors includes £17.0m and creditors includes £0.5m representing the differences between pension costs charged in the accounts in respect of other plans and amounts funded to date.

Source: Coats Viyella plc 1991 accounts

Fig. A2.5 Chesterton International plc: pensions

22 Pensions

The Group operates five pension schemes, three of which are of the funded defined benefit type and two defined contribution. The assets of the schemes are held in separate Trustee administered funds.

Defined benefit schemes
The main defined benefit scheme (the Chesterton Pension and Life Assurance Scheme) is administered under trust to which the company pays an actuarially determined contribution.

The last full actuarial valuation of this scheme was carried out as at 1 July 1994 by the scheme's actuaries using the Defined Accrued Benefit method. The principal valuation assumptions were as follows:

Investment returns   9% per annum

Pensionable salary growth   6.5% per annum

Pension increases   5.5% on pensions in excess of Guaranteed Minimum Pension

This valuation showed that the market value of the scheme's assets at that date amounted to £8,798,000 and the actuarial value of the assets represented 101% of the benefits that had accrued to members, after allowing for expected future increases in pensionable earnings.

A further analysis of the fund was performed by the scheme's actuaries at 1 July 1995 using the same method and assumptions except that account was taken of lower salary increases at 2% per annum for the following three years and 6.5% thereafter.

Defined contribution schemes
The defined contribution schemes provide benefits which are directly determined by the value of the contributions paid in respect of each member. The pension cost charge represents contributions paid by appropriate group companies.

Unfunded pensions
The Group also pays pensions direct to several former employees. Full provision, based on actuarial advice, is made for the estimated liability, and is reviewed annually to allow for interest costs, changes in mortality assumptions and payments are made. The pension charge amounted to £102,000 for the year ended 30 June 1995 (1994: £158,000).

Appendix 3

Outline responses to discussion questions

Chapter 1: An introduction to standards

1. Define FRSSE. Contrast nature of small companies' ownership with those fully subject to standards. 'Red tape' issues and encouragement of entrepreneurship. Right of companies to 'opt out' of FRSSE.

2. Growing harmonisation of international practice. Most major international listed companies are likely to follow IASs after 2005 (European Union requirements will have large influence). However, there are many more unlisted companies who may see national standards as being more relevant to their circumstances. National standard-setters, whilst acknowledging the need for a set of internationally-applicable rules are likely to continue to lobby for their standards to apply within the national boundaries.

3. The statutory powers (contained in the 1989 Companies Act) serve to reinforce the need for companies to comply with best accounting practice as promulgated by the ASB. The fact that all cases have been settled without the need for court action can be see either as a triumph of negotiation over legislation, or else an admittance that directors see nothing to be gained by fighting the Panel.

Chapter 2: Principles and policies

1. Understandability is the quality that 'the significance of the information can be perceived.' This depends on the users' abilities and the way in which the information is aggregated and classified. Define other qualities (refer to Figure 2.1). Look back at the user groups listed on p. 19. Different groups will have different abilities to understand the financial information. Should relevance, etc. over-ride 'understandability'?

2. See definitions on p. 25. Give examples of each (e.g. straight-line depreciation is an estimation technique, not an accounting policy). Look at Table 2.1 to see how examples 2 and 4 change the estimation technique, but not the accounting policy.

3. Consider how prudence and consistency relate to the qualitative characteristics referred to in the Statement of Principles. If a policy is *consistent* but inappropriate, is that good accounting? If, by being *prudent*, profits or gains are deliberately understated, is that good accounting?

Chapter 3: Government grants; tangible fixed assets; investment properties

1. Old age is not of itself a reason for replacing a standard that is still appropriate. Standards are kept under review, and if no longer relevant, or out of line with the Statement of Principles, the ASB will issue a replacement standard.

2. Several standards give choices to entities as to the way in which their requirements are applied (e.g. SSAP 13's treatment of development expenditure, FRS 19's treatment of discounting deferred tax liabilities). This accords with the qualitative characteristic of relevance and allows directors a certain measure of flexibility as to the way they present their company's 'true and fair view'.

3. The tight definition of an investment property should ensure that those assets normally depreciated will be depreciated. The fact that the properties must be shown in the balance sheet at their 'open market value', with adjustments made in an investment revaluation reserve means that fluctuations in value are being recognised in the financial statements.

Chapter 4: Research and development; hire purchase and leasing; goodwill; impairment

1. The SSAP 13 criteria for capitalising development costs are stringent, and many companies may feel that they would be hard pressed to convince their auditors to allow deferral. Writing-off is a more prudent approach and overcomes problems of allocation of expenditure between the three categories of R & D identified within the standard.

2. There has been much debate regarding the potential for creative accounting for leases ever since the standard was published. Indeed, many leasing companies specifically ask their business customers the question 'do you want the asset to appear on your balance sheet?' The remedy (as currently suggested in a discussion paper) is to abandon the distinction and treat all leases equally, so that scope for manipulation would be lessened.

3. Old and established companies do not show their 'inherent' goodwill built up over generations, the reason being that it has not been objectively valued by purchase. Acquisitive companies however show goodwill paid for each company taken over. Return on Total Assets would be smaller for a company showing intangible fixed assets than for one that had internally generated goodwill. Whilst it is difficult to make direct comparisons between such companies' intangible assets, investment analysts can easily strip out goodwill values from balance sheets for the purpose of making comparisons.

Chapter 5: Stocks and long-term contracts

1. The standard requires the calculation of attributable profits to be made on a prudent basis, and only when the outcome can be reasonable foreseen.

The accruals concept requires the matching of income and expenditure for a specific period. It could therefore be argued that where the 'matched' income exceeds the 'matched' expenditure for a proportion of the contract, it is only applying the accruals concept to the contract as a whole.

2. One obstacle to the UK's use of LIFO is the fact that the UK Inland Revenue does not allow LIFO to be used when calculating a company's taxable profits. This is not an insuperable problem however, as accounting profits have to be re-calculated in any case to adjust for such items as depreciation and interest payments. More fundamental is the need for stock valuations to be *reliable*, and the fact that a LIFO stock valuation would be likely to give an outdated price to stock items could prove to be a bar to its acceptance within a future UK standard.

Chapter 6: Capital instruments and derivatives

1. The two standards on capital instruments and derivatives (FRSs 4 & 13) where published to tighten up the disclosure of complex financial arrangements which were capable of misleading shareholders and others into thinking that a company was far stronger than it really was. The ASB set out to impose a radical disclosure regime on companies, and it is no coincidence that one of the qualitative characteristics of financial statements as found in the Statement of Principles is 'Understandability'.

Chapter 7: Taxation

1. There are key differences between UK practice and the international standard, but far less than FRS 19's predecessor standard, SSAP 15. There is a clear difference of opinion regarding tax liabilities which may never materialise, and the UK standard setter is unprepared to go along with what it sees as a flawed international standard. With the former ASB chairman (David Tweedie) now in charge at the IASC, it is highly likely that a compromise will be found when the international standard comes up for review.

Chapter 8: Reporting financial performance

1. The problem with extraordinary items was that they were being manipulated by companies so that the all-important 'earnings per share' calculation could be made as high or as low as the business wanted. The old eps used a formula that showed profit *before* extraordinary items. All that a company needed to do was to reclassify 'ordinary' items as 'extraordinary', and they were taken out of the earnings formula. Many companies abused this by loading many routine overheads (e.g. for redundancy and reorganisation costs) into the extraordinary category. Investment analysts can and do re-calculate the eps figure according to formulae different from that in FRS 14.

2. The price/earnings ratio has always been a key stock market indicator, but its reliability was severely jeopardised by the laxity of the old standards SSAP 6 (abolished by FRS 3) and SSAP 3 (replaced by FRS 14). The new standard for eps recognises its importance and justifiably seeks to ensure its consistency of calculation.

Chapter 9: The substance of transactions, related parties

1. Standards cannot prevent directors from acting dishonestly, but tighter reporting requirements should ensure that the company's auditors would qualify their report to shareholders in cases where there is inadequate disclosure of transactions and related information. Prior to the issue of FRSs 5 & 8, companies could engineer financial transactions so that material assets or liabilities were left off a balance sheet, or details of related party transactions went unreported. The standards are deliberately unspecific so that directors can't exploit potential loopholes too easily.

2. The standards exercise no restraint at all on 'entrepreneurial initiatives'. They merely require full accountability to be made by means of disclosure within the published annual results.

Chapter 10: Segmental reporting

1. If information is withheld, the reasons must be stated. In practice, very few companies have taken advantage of the exemption, but examples include companies competing with divisions of other companies, where sensitive information of that competitor would not be revealed within the group accounts.

Chapter 11: Post balance sheet events; provisions and contingencies

1. It is likely that the circumstances relating to the price reductions would have occurred gradually, and encompass the balance sheet date. However, if it can be proved that the stock could have been sold at a higher price at the year-end (for example, if there are commodity market prices for raw materials) then the stock need not be written down for a subsequent fall in value.

2. Three conditions must be satisfied for a provision to be created, one of which is for the entity to have a *present* obligation as a result of a past event. The practice had grown up of aggregating present liabilities with expected liabilities of future years, including sometimes items related to ongoing operations, in one large provision, often reported as an exceptional item. The effect of such 'big bath' provisions was not only to report excessive liabilities at the outset but also to boost profitability during the subsequent years, when the liabilities were in fact being incurred.

Chapter 12: Cash flow statements

1. Cash is vital for a business to survive, as without it businesses would be unable to pay their liabilities. This would lead to creditors forcing the company into liquidation. Profit is also vital for a business's survival as profitable businesses are able to reinvest and expand whilst rewarding shareholders with appropriate dividends. Profitability does not necessarily equate to healthy cash flows, as acquisitive, profit generating businesses are often using cash balances in replacing fixed assets, buying other businesses, etc.

Chapter 13: Consolidated financial statements

1. Although the US has banned the use of merger accounting, it is still available to those companies meeting the five criteria under FRS 6. However, these criteria effectively restrict its use to a point where few companies will be able to take advantage of merger accounting. The relevant International Accounting Standard (IAS 22) also permits merger accounting where there is a genuine uniting of interests of the merging parties, subject also to stringent criteria.

2. It is true that the consolidated accounts show the group indebtedness, not that of individual companies. This may mean that a subsidiary company has significant debts that may be concealed on consolidation. In practice, groups will usually meet the liabilities of subsidiary companies where that company is not in a position to do so, and in any event, the lender can ask for the individual company's financial statements as well as that of the group as a whole.

Chapter 14: Foreign currency translation

1. There is an inconsistency, but it can be argued that the net investment method shows more realistic valuations than the alternative, temporal method, as exchange rates at the balance sheet date are being used rather than a mixture of rates – some historic (e.g. the rate on the date on which fixed assets were acquired) and some more recent.

Chapter 15: Retirement benefits

1. The ASB has attempted to reassure companies concerning volatility. The effects of the fluctuations in market values will not be part of the operating results, but will be treated in the same way as revaluations of fixed assets, i.e. by being recognised in the statement of total recognised gains and losses.

Appendix 4

Answers to examination questions

Chapter 1: An introduction to standards

1. In discussing the influence of the IASC and the EU on British published financial statements, it should be stated that the IASC has no legal status in the UK, whereas the EU's directives when incorporated into UK law have statutory force.

    However, most UK accounting and Financial Reporting Standards are in line with the relevant IAS, but where differences exist, UK companies need only comply with the UK standard. FRSs are formulated with due regard to international developments, and the ASB supports the IASC in its aim to harmonise international financial reporting. As part of this support, each FRS contains a section explaining how it relates to the IAS dealing with the same topic. In most cases, compliance with an FRS automatically ensures compliance with the relevant IAS.

    The UK accountancy bodies are members of the IASC, and through their influence in their own right and their contribution to the working of the Financial Reporting Council will endeavour to secure the widest support for international standards.

    EU directives are issued by the European Union so as to harmonise company legislation throughout the member states. In practice, the legislation is more general in scope than accounting standards, covering such matters as the qualifications of auditors and the format of published financial statements.

2. *Please see* Chapter 1, pp. 2–6.

Chapter 2: Principles and policies

1. The four qualitative characteristics of financial information contained within the Statement of Principles are relevance, reliability, comparability and understandability. User groups will benefit from their application in the following ways.

    Relevance – information is relevant if it has the ability to influence the economic decisions of the user groups and is provided in time to influence those decisions. It has predictive value or confirmatory value: the former if it helps the users to evaluate past, present or future events, the latter if it helps users to confirm or correct their past evaluations and assessments.

Reliability – information is reliable if it can be depended upon by users to represent faithfully what it either purports to represent or could reasonably be expected to represent. The information should be free from deliberate or systematic bias or material error.

Comparability – information is more useful if it can be compared with similar information about the entity for some other period in order to identify trends in financial performance and financial position, and also with similar information for other entities to establish their relative financial performance and position.

Understandability – users need to perceive the significance of the information contained within the financial statements, which depends on factors such as the way in which the effects of transactions are characterised, aggregated and classified. However, those preparing the financial statements are entitled to assume that users have a reasonable knowledge of business and economic activities and accounting.

2. Going concern refers to the ability of an entity to continue in business for the foreseeable future. It is enshrined in the 1985 Companies Act as an accounting principle. Financial statements are drawn up on the assumption that the entity is a going concern unless stated otherwise. Its importance lies in the implications for asset and other values if there was doubt over the going concern status. For example, stock values would have to be reconsidered and written down to net realisable values. Similarly, fixed assets may require substantial additional depreciation to bring values to that which they might realise in a forced sale.

The accruals concept requires the non-cash effects of transactions and other events to be reflected, as far as possible, in the financial statements for the accounting period in which they occur, and not, for example, in the period in which any cash involved is received or paid. This accords with normal double-entry bookkeeping principles and ensures that all relevant transactions are included, not simply those where cash has been paid or received in the period.

Chapter 3: Government grants; tangible fixed assets; investment properties

1. a) 'Capital-based' grants can be treated in either of two ways:

   i) by reducing the cost of the fixed asset by the amount of the grant, or

   ii) by treating the amount of the grant as a 'deferred credit', a portion of which is transferred to revenue annually.

Whilst the standard considers both treatments are 'capable of giving a true and fair view', it also points out that Counsel's opinion states that the first option is not acceptable under the Companies Act 1985.

b) The arguments in favour of each method are:

First alternative:
simplicity, as the reduced depreciation charge automatically credits the amount of the grant to revenue over the life of the asset.

Second alternative:

i)   assets acquired at different times and locations (i.e. some eligible, others ineligible) are recorded on a uniform basis, regardless of changes in government policy;

ii) control over the ordering, construction and maintenance of assets is based on the gross value;

iii) as capital allowances for tax purposes are normally calculated on the cost of an asset before deduction of a grant, adjustments to the depreciation charge shown in the profit and loss account are avoided when computing the amount of deferred taxation.

2.

	Year 1 £000	Year 2 £000
Opening book amount	3,000	3,240
Depreciation	−300	−360*
Adjusted book value	2,700	2,880
Revaluation gain (loss)		
• recognised in the profit and loss account	–	−120**
• recognised in the statement of total recognised gains and losses	540	−600***
Closing book value	3,240	2,100

* £3,240,000 over its remaining life of 9 years = £360,000 p.a.
** The fall in value when comparing the depreciated historical cost (£2,400,000) and the recoverable amount (£2,280,000)
*** The remainder of the fall from adjusted book value (£2,880,000) to estimated sale value (£2,100,000)

3. Report to managing director

a) FRS 15 states that depreciation should be allocated 'throughout the asset's useful economic life'. In the case of the existing properties, this requires a recognition that the buildings will lose value over time due to wear and tear, obsolescence, etc. Consequently, this loss must be apportioned over the estimated useful life of the buildings. If depreciation was not charged, then profit would be overstated and the financial statements would not comply with the fundamental concept of matching (accruals).

b) Investment properties are defined in SSAP 19 as: 'an interest in land and/ or buildings:

 i) in respect of which construction work and development have been completed; and

 ii) which is held for its investment potential, any rental income being negotiated at arm's length.

The following are exceptions from the definition:

 i) A property which is owned and occupied by a company for its own purposes is not an investment property.

 ii) A property let to and occupied by another group company is not an investment property for the purposes of its own accounts or the group accounts.

 iii) In the case of those held on short leases (i.e. 20 years or less) they should be depreciated in accordance with FRS 15.

c) Changes in the value of investment properties should not be taken to the profit and loss account, but should be disclosed as a movement on an investment revaluation reserve. If a deficit on revaluation exceeds the balance on the reserve then the difference shall be taken direct to the profit and loss account. Details of the valuer and basis of valuation must be stated.

4. a) The decision as to whether or not a property is classified as an 'investment' property must be taken by reference to the definition contained in SSAP 19, which states that an investment property is an interest in land and/or buildings:

 i) in respect of which construction work and development have been completed; and

 ii) which is held for its investment potential, any rental income being negotiated at arm's length.

If property is owned and occupied by a company for its own purposes, or let to and occupied by another group company, then it does not come within the definition.

The four properties given in the question can be classified as follows.

North: not an investment property as it is owned and occupied by the company.

South: not an investment property as it is let to and occupied by another group company.

East: this is an investment property, as an 'associated company' is not a 'group company', according to the definition of a group contained in FRS 2.

West: this an investment property.

To confirm the above opinions on East and West, information would be needed as to whether the properties are held for their investment potential and the rental income has been negotiated at arm's length. In addition, all construction and development work must have been completed.

b) The acquisition or disposal of investment properties does not affect the manufacturing or trading processes of the business and consequently a systematic depreciation charge is considered irrelevant. It is the current value of such properties which is relevant to the users of financial statements. The only exception is a leasehold property with an unexpired term of 20 years or less. Such properties should be depreciated, to avoid the situation whereby a short lease is amortised against the investment revaluation reserve whilst the rentals are taken to profit and loss account.

The appropriate policy for the four properties would be:

North and South: depreciate in accordance with FRS 15;
East: not depreciated;
West: depreciate over 15 years.

Chapter 4: Research and development; hire purchase and leasing; goodwill; impairment

1. a) **Applied research** is defined in SSAP 13 as original or critical investigation undertaken in order to gain new scientific or technical knowledge and directed towards a specific practical aim.

Development is defined as the use of scientific or technical knowledge in order to produce new or substantially improved materials, devices, products or services, to install new processes or systems prior to the commencement of commercial production or commercial applications, or to improve substantially those already produced or installed.

The 'explanatory note' to the standard recognises that the dividing line between the three categories is often indistinct and particular expenditure may have the characteristics of more than one category. However, the decision as to whether or not to include a particular activity as being research and development based depends upon the presence or absence of *innovation*. If the activity is merely 'routine' then it should be excluded; if it breaks new ground it can be included.

b) Whereas the development of new products or services is normally undertaken with a reasonable expectation of commercial success and a likelihood of future benefit to the company, applied research can be regarded as part of the continuing operation required to maintain a company's business and its competitive position. Applied research is not necessarily linked to any particular period rather than another.

Because of this distinction, under the matching concept research expenditure should not be carried forward, but charged to revenue in the period in which it is incurred. Provided certain criteria are met, development expenditure may be deferred and carried forward to be matched against future expenditure.

c) i) SSAP 13 states that market research would normally be excluded from research and development, presumably because it is unlikely to contain an appreciable degree of innovation.

ii) Tests of prototypes can normally be considered as research and development because it develops clearly defined existing company products.

iii) Although including the word 'research', operational research is usually concerned with techniques such as network analysis and linear programming rather than the research or development of a company's products. It would not normally be included within the SSAP 13 definitions.

iv) Testing in search of process alternatives is considered to be research and development expenditure by SSAP 13 since it is directly concerned with the production of the company's existing products. It would be classified as applied research.

2. a) A finance lease usually involves payment by a lessee to a lessor of the full cost of the asset together with a return on the finance provided by the lessor. The lessee has substantially all the risk and rewards associated with the ownership of an asset, other than its legal title.

An operating lease involves the lessee paying a rental for the hire of an asset for a period of time which is normally substantially less than its useful economic life. The lessor retains most of the risks and rewards of ownership of an asset in the case of an operating lease.

The nature of each lease will need to be determined from the terms of the contract between the lessor and lessee, as in practice all leases transfer some of the risks and rewards of ownership to the lessee, and the distinction between the two types of lease is essentially one of degree.

In preparing the financial statements of a finance company (the lessor), an asset subject to a finance lease would be recorded as follows.

The amount due from the lessee would be recorded as a debtor in the balance sheet. The amount will be the minimum lease payments, less the gross earnings allocated to future periods. The assets themselves are not recorded as fixed assets. The total gross earnings are split between those relating to the finance charge and those relating to the reduction in debt, with the former being credited to profit and loss account, and the latter reducing the outstanding balance shown as owing on the balance sheet.

An asset subject to an operating lease would be shown in the financial statements of a lessor as follows.

The asset should be recorded in the balance sheet as a fixed asset, and will be depreciated over its useful life in the normal way. The rental income from the lease will be credited to profit and loss account on a systematic and rational basis.

Disclosure should be made of the accounting policies adopted for both finance and operating leases in the accounts of the lessor.

b) The policy refers to the accounting treatment of a finance lease, whereby the risks and rewards of ownership have passed to the lessee. Instead of including the item as a fixed asset, the amount due from the lessee is included in debtors. The amount due at a point in time is the total of the lease payments, less any earnings allocated to a future period. The receipts from the lessee are divided between repayments of the debt and rental income, and the basis of the division is that over the period of the lease the rental income is a fixed percentage of the amount invested in the asset. This comprises the cost of the asset net of government grants, less rentals received to date. The 'actuarial method' referred to is an accurate approach to arriving at the interest rate implicit in a lease agreement.

The government grants are allocated over the lease period like the rentals. Because they are tax free, they may be grossed up in the profit and loss account, and the notional tax included in the taxation charge.

3. *See* answer to 2(a).

4. a) Purchased goodwill is the difference between the cost of an acquired entity and the aggregate of the fair values of the entity's identifiable assets and liabilities. Positive goodwill arises when the acquisition cost is greater than the aggregate fair values of the identifiable assets and liabilities. Negative goodwill arises when the aggregate fair values of the identifiable assets and liabilities is less than the acquisition cost.

b) Where goodwill and intangible assets are regarded as having limited useful economic lives, they should be amortised on a systematic basis over those lives. The straight line method is usually chosen.

If they are regarded as having indefinite useful economic lives, they should not be amortised. There is a rebuttable presumption that the useful economic lives of purchased goodwill and intangible assets are limited to periods of 20 years or less. The presumption may be rebutted where:

i) the durability of the acquired business or intangible asset can be demonstrated and justifies estimating the useful economic life to exceed 20 years; and

ii) the goodwill or intangible asset is capable of continued measurement (so that annual impairment reviews will be feasible).

Chapter 5: Stocks and long-term contracts

1. a) According to SSAP 9, Stock is to be stated *at the total of the lower of cost and net realisable value of the separable items of stock or of groups of similar items.* Definitions contained within the standard are:

Cost – '. . . that expenditure which has been incurred in the normal course of business in bringing the product or service to its present location and condition . . .'

Net realisable value – '. . . the estimated proceeds from the sale of items of stock less all further costs to completion and less all costs to be incurred in marketing, selling and distributing directly related to the items in question.'

The principal situations in which net realisable value is likely to be less than cost are where there has been:

i) an increase in costs or a fall in selling price;

ii) physical deterioration of stocks;

iii) obsolescence of products;

iv) a decision as part of a company's marketing strategy to manufacture and sell products at a loss;

v) errors in production or purchasing.

Furthermore, when stocks are held which are unlikely to be sold within the turnover period normal in that company (i.e. excess stocks), the impending delay in realisation increases the risk that the situations outlined in (i) to (iii) above may occur before the stocks are sold and needs to be taken into account in assessing net realisable value.

The comparison of cost and net realisable value needs to be made in respect of each item of stock separately. Where this is impossible, groups or categories of stock items which are similar will need to be taken together. If this were not the case, then material distortions could arise in the overall valuation.

b) **Raw materials**: lower of cost and net realisable value for each separate item of stock:

Material X	£1,200
Material Y	£240
Material Z	£530
	£1,970

Work in progress: 200 half completed petrol caps. £4,470 was the total cost for 2,000 complete and 200 half complete petrol caps. Excluding the administrative overheads, the cost per 'equivalent unit' is £4,200 ÷ 2,100 = £2, which is lower than the net realisable value. The valuation of the work in progress is therefore $200 \times (\frac{1}{2} \times £2) = £200$.

Finished goods: value $2,000 \times £2 = £4,000$.

2. a) **Lytax Limited: profit and loss account for the year ended 31 October X3 (extracts)**

	£000
Turnover (W2)	1,162
Cost of sales (W2)	1,154
Gross profit	8

b) **Lytax Limited: balance sheet as at 31 October X3 (extracts)**

	£000
Stocks	
Long-term contract work in progress	
Net cost less foreseeable losses (W4)	308
Applicable payments on account (W4)	94
	214
Debtors	
Amounts recoverable on contracts (W3)	108
Creditors: amounts falling due within one year	
Payments on account (W3)	165
Provisions for liabilities and charges	
Provision for foreseeable losses	45

Workings

1. Foreseeable profit/loss

	1	2	3	4	5
	£000	£000	£000	£000	£000
Contract price	1,100	950	1,400	1,300	1,200
Costs incurred to date	664	535	810	640	1,070
Estimated further costs to completion	106	75	680	800	165
Estimated costs after completion	30	10	45	20	5
	800	620	1,535	1,460	1,240
Profit/(loss) foreseen at 31 October X3	300	330	(135)	(160)	(40)
Cumulative profit/(loss) on each contract	218*	250†	(135)	(160)	(40)

2. Profit and loss entries

	Total	1	2	3	4	5
	£000	£000	£000	£000	£000	£000
Cumulative cost of sales		580	470	646	525	900
Cumulative profit (W1)		218	250	–	–	–
Turnover		798	720	646	525	900
Previously credited		560	340	517	400	610
Year X3 turnover	1,162	238	380	129	125	290
Cost of sales						
Cumulative		580	470	646	525	900
Add Foreseeable loss (W1)		–	–	135	160	40
		580	470	781	685	940
Costs previously charged		460	245	517	400	610
Foreseeable loss previously charged		–	–	–	70	–
Year X3 cost of sales	1,154	120	225	264	215	330

Profit/(loss)	Total	1	2	3	4	5
	£000	£000	£000	£000	£000	£000
Cumulative		218	250	(135)	(160)	(40)
Previously credited/charged		100	95	–	(70)	–
	8	118	155	(135)	(90)	(40)

* $\dfrac{580}{800} \times 300$

† $\dfrac{470}{620} \times 330$

3. Amounts recoverable on contracts

	Total £000	1 £000	2 £000	3 £000	4 £000	5 £000
Cumulative turnover		798	720	646	525	900
Progress payments						
Received		615	680	615	385	722
Awaiting receipt		60	40	25	200	34
Retentions		75	80	60	65	84
		750	800	700	650	840
	108	48				60
Excess payments on accounts			80	54	125	
Set off against balance on contract WIP			65	29	–	
Net payments on account	165		15	25	125	

4. Contract work in progress

	Total £000	1 £000	2 £000	3 £000	4 £000	5 £000
Costs incurred		664	535	810	640	1,070
Cost of sales transfers		580	470	646	525	900
Foreseeable losses (W1)		–	–	135	160	40
	263	84	65	29	(45)	130
Transferred to provisions	45				45	
Net cost less foreseeable provisions	308					
Excess payments on account (W3)	94	–	65	29	–	–
	214	84	–	–	–	130

Chapter 6: Capital instruments and derivatives

The finance cost is:

Total payments: $(100,000 \times 120\%) + (5 \times 5,000)$	=	145,000
Less Net proceeds $(110,000 - 2,000)$		108,000
Finance cost		37,000

Year	Balance b/f (£)	Finance cost (6.544%) First half-year (£)	Interim dividend	Balance (£)	Finance cost (6.544%) Second half-year (£)	Final dividend	Balance c/f
2002	108,000	3,534	(2,500)	109,034	3,567	(2,500)	110,101
2003	110,101	3,603	(2,500)	111,204	3,638	(2,500)	112,342
2004	112,342	3,676	(2,500)	113,518	3,715	(2,500)	114,733
2005	114,733	3,754	(2,500)	115,987	3,795	(2,500)	117,282
2006	117,282	3,837	(2,500)	118,619	3,881	(2,500)	120,000
		18,404	(12,500)		18,596	(12,500)	

Total finance cost = 18,404 + 18,596 = 37,000
Total dividends = 12,500 + 12,500 = 25,000

Chapter 7: Taxation

1. Although question 1 is not specifically related to SSAP 5, it provides useful practice at understanding the basic book-keeping underlying the VAT entries.

Value Added Tax Account

30 August Cheque to Customs and Excise	4,700	31 July Balance b/f	4,700
31 October VAT on standard rated purchases	11,915	31 October VAT on standard rated sales	17,500
VAT on zero-rated purchases	1,787		
Balance c/d	3,798		
	22,200		22,200
		1 November Balance b/d	3,798

Sales Account

	31 October Invoices:	
	standard rated	100,000
	zero rated	10,000
	exempt	5,000
		115,000

Purchases Account

31 October Invoices:

standard rated $\left\{80{,}000 \times \dfrac{100}{117.5}\right\}$ 68,085

zero rated $\left\{12{,}000 \times \dfrac{100}{117.5}\right\}$ 10,213

exempt $\underline{2{,}300}$

                                          $\underline{80{,}598}$

2. a) Timing differences are differences between an entity's taxable profits and its results as stated in the financial statements that arise from the inclusion of gains and losses in tax assessments in periods different from those in which they are recognised in financial statements. Timing differences originate in one period and are capable of reversal in one or more periods.

b) Examples of timing differences that are *not* to be provided for are those arising when:

- a fixed asset is revalued without there being any commitment to sell the asset (though if the asset is continuously revalued to fair value, with changes recognised in the profit and loss account, then deferred tax would be recognised);
- the gain on sale of an asset is rolled over into replacement assets;
- the remittance of a subsidiary, associate or joint venture's earnings would cause tax to be payable, but no commitment has been made to the remittance of the earnings.

Chapter 8: Reporting financial performance

1. a) Earnings per share (eps) is widely used by investors as an indicator of a company's performance, being more reliable than measures such as dividend yield. By relating earnings to shares outstanding in a period, the user of the information can assess the impact on earnings of company expansion where shares have been issued in exchange for acquiring new businesses.

    In the case of a group of companies with ordinary and preference shares, the earnings figure to be used is the net profit (or loss) of the period after tax, extraordinary and exceptional items, minority interests and after deducting preference dividends.

b) i) The company should disclose two figures for eps, the basic figure and the fully diluted figure. The calculation of diluted earnings per share is based on the following formula:

Net profit (or loss) after tax, extraordinary and exceptional
items, minority interests and preference dividends, plus post-tax effects
of dividends, interest or other income or expense relating to the dilutive
potential ordinary shares[1]

Weighted average number of ordinary shares outstanding
during the period plus the weighted average number of all potential
ordinary shares, deemed to have been converted
at the beginning of the period[2]

Notes:

1. e.g. interest on convertible loan stock which would be saved if the
   conversion rights are exercised by the stockholders.
2. or date of issue if not in existence at the beginning of the period.

ii) The eps will be calculated by the earnings being apportioned over
the number of shares ranking for dividend after the capitalisation. The
corresponding eps for the previous period should be adjusted. The
formula is:

Net profit (or loss) after tax, extraordinary and exceptional items,
minority interests and preference dividends

Weighted average number of ordinary shares, including those issued by
way of bonus, outstanding during the period

iii) The eps is calculated by the earnings being apportioned over the
average number of shares outstanding during the period, weighted
on a time basis.

c)
	£000
Total pre-rights share capital	6,000
Rights issue (1.5m × £1.50)	2,250
	8,250

Theoretical ex-rights price: $\dfrac{8,250,000}{4.5m} = £1.83$

or

Holding pre-rights	2 shares @ £2	=	£4.00
Rights to	1 share @ £1.50	=	£1.50
	3		£5.50

$$\frac{£5.50}{3} = £1.8$$

Weighted average number of shares in issue, after allowing for notional
bonus element in rights issue:

$$\frac{6}{12} \times 3,000,000 \times \frac{£2.00}{£1.83} = 1,639,344$$

$$\frac{6}{12} \times 4,500,000 = \underline{2,250,000}$$
$$\underline{3,889,344}$$

$$\text{Earnings per share} = \frac{\text{Earnings for year}}{\text{Weighted ave. no. of shares}}$$

$$= \frac{£750,000}{3,889,344} = 19.3p$$

2. a)

	£000	£000
Profit on ordinary activities after taxation		2,502
Less Minority interest	90	
Preference dividend	45	
		135
Basic earnings		2,367

Theoretical ex-rights price:

Pre-rights	12m shares @ £1.50	=	£18m
Rights	3m shares @ £1.00	=	£3m
	15m		£21m

$$\frac{£21m}{15m} = £1.40$$

Shares in issue, after allowing for notional bonus element in rights issue:

$$\frac{3}{12} \times 12,000,000 \times \frac{£1.50}{£1.40} = 3,214,285$$

$$\frac{9}{12} \times 15,000,000 = 11,250,000$$
$$14,464,285$$

$$\text{Basic earnings per share} = \frac{£2,367,000}{14,464,285} = 16.4p$$

b) eps for previous year = 15p

$$\text{adjusted by factor:} \quad \frac{\text{Theoretical ex-rights price}}{\text{Actual cum-rights price}}$$

$$15p \times \frac{£1.40}{£1.50} = 14p$$

c) The basic eps figure (16.4p) will be stated on the face of the profit and loss account, together with the adjusted eps (14p) for the previous period. The basis of calculation should be disclosed, revealing the amount of the earnings and the number of shares used in the calculation.

Chapter 9: The substance of transactions, related parties

Off balance sheet financing, as the name suggests, is a means whereby a company can arrange that some or all of its finance does not appear on its balance sheet. Its purpose is to disguise the company's true financial position so as to either mislead existing investors or present a false picture to attract funds from new investors. Gearing (i.e. debt to equity) levels are distorted, and could influence lending decisions on the false assumption that companies are low-geared when in reality their debts are much greater than the balance sheet discloses. Examples given within the standard include sale and repurchase of stock, discounting bills receivable and sale and leaseback schemes.

The standard's objective is to ensure that the *substance* of a company's transactions is reported in its financial statements, as opposed to merely its legal form. The commercial effect of the company's transactions, and any resulting assets, liabilities, gains or losses, should be 'faithfully represented' in its financial statements. A key step in determining the substance of a transaction is to identify whether it has given rise to new assets or liabilities for the company and whether it has increased or decreased its existing assets or liabilities.

Chapter 10: Segmental reporting

1. a) If the financial statements of a large, diverse, multinational company were presented without a segmental analysis, users would have considerable difficulty in assessing the proportions of profits and turnover derived from the separate product areas and geographical sectors. Without this information, assessment of factors such as risk, growth and profitability would be restricted to a view of the business as a whole, whereas the overall picture may mask individual weaknesses within particular areas. For example, an electronics group may have both domestic and military divisions both trading internationally. Its trade may be with both stable countries and military regimes. By showing a breakdown by segments, the user can make meaningful analyses which would be impossible if only overall consolidated figures were available.

Readers of financial statements fall into several distinct groups who may regard the provision of segmental information in different ways.

Shareholders will want to ensure that profitability and growth is occurring in all sectors, and that management is taking action if individual sectors are performing badly.

Employees may view the information in terms of job security and the relative strength of their own segment compared with others within the business.

Government can use the statistical data provided to get a more accurate portrait of company performance within specific geographical and business areas.

b) A group may resist disclosing detailed segmental information for various reasons, including confidentiality, cost or the difficulty in compiling and presenting the information.

As with the relevant provisions of the CA 1985, SSAP 25 gives an exemption from disclosure where such disclosure would be 'seriously prejudicial to the interests of the reporting entity'. For example, a company may have been operating in a geographical area which is subject to trade and other sanctions imposed by other countries. Disclosure of trading links (past or current) with that specific area may be prejudicial to the wider interests of the company, and expose the company itself to the risk of boycotts and sanctions.

The cost of compiling and presenting the information may be prohibitive, particularly for a diverse multinational group. The costs of providing the additional information may outweigh the benefits, but compliance with SSAP 25 is nevertheless essential if the company is to avoid an audit qualification. There is a danger of 'information overload', where users of the financial statements may be confused by being presented with even more detailed analysis.

It is up to the directors to decide how many different classes of business the company has and how many markets it has traded with. This may lead to subjective choices being made which deliberately mislead users so as to protect the best interests of the company's management.

Chapter 11: Post balance sheet events; provisions and contingencies

1. a) i) A post balance sheet event is defined in SSAP 17 as 'those events, both favourable and unfavourable, which occur between the balance sheet date and the date on which the financial statements are approved by the board of directors.'

ii) Adjusting events are post balance sheet events which provide additional evidence of conditions existing at the balance sheet date.

iii) Non-adjusting events are post balance sheet events which concern conditions which did not exist at the balance sheet date.

iv) A contingent liability is either a possible obligation that arises from past events and whose existence will be confirmed only by the occurrence of one or more uncertain future events not wholly within the entity's control; or a present obligation that arises from past events but is not recognised because:

1. it is not probable that a transfer of economic benefits will be required to settle the obligation; or

2. the amount of the obligation cannot be measured with sufficient reliability.

v) A contingent asset is a possible asset that arises from past events and whose existence will be confirmed only by the occurrence of one or more uncertain future events not wholly within the entity's control.

b) Four examples of adjusting events are:

i) The subsequent determination of the proceeds of sale of assets purchased or sold before the year end.

ii) A valuation which provides evidence of a permanent diminution in value.

iii) The renegotiation of amounts owing by debtors, or the insolvency of a debtor.

iv) The discovery of errors or frauds which show that the financial statements were incorrect.

Four examples of non-adjusting events are:

i) Issues of shares and debentures.

ii) Opening new trading activities or extending existing trading activities.

iii) Closing a significant part of the trading activities if this was not anticipated at the year end.

iv) Decline in the value of property and investments held as fixed assets, if it can be demonstrated that the decline occurred after the year end.

c) i) Contingent liabilities should not be recognised by an entity. In other words, no transfer should be made out of the profit and loss account. However, a contingent liability is disclosed (i.e. as a note to the accounts) unless a transfer of economic benefits is remote.

ii) Contingent assets also are not recognised within the profit and loss account due to the possibility of overstatement of profit by an amount which may never be realised. However, they are disclosed where an inflow of economic benefits is probable. If the realisation of profit is virtually certain, then it is not regarded as a contingent asset and therefore can be recognised.

2. i) Assuming the amount is material, this would appear as a contingent gain, with the details appearing as a note. There is no certainty that the painting will reach the suggested price, so the estimated gain must not be recognised in the financial statements. If the auction house is reputable then the gain need not be considered as remote.

ii) As the amount will probably have to be paid, a provision should be made in the financial statements for £200,000, with the £100,000 counter-claim being shown as a contingent gain in the notes to the financial statements. The counter-claim can only be offset against the £200,000 if legal opinion confirms that the company is virtually certain of success against the subcontractors.

iii) The £50,000 unpaid and more than three months old should be provided for, as the company is legally obliged to repurchase the debts. There is a contingent liability of £150,000 on the factored debts not yet paid but within the 90-day period, and this should be disclosed by way of note.

iv) The manufacturer should take legal advice, but a threat to sue is sufficiently remote to warrant no action being taken by the company. The situation should be reconsidered if a formal letter is received from the player setting out the precise basis of the claim.

Chapter 12: Cash flow statements

	£000	£000
Cash flow from operating activities (Note 1)		271
Returns on investments and servicing of finance (Note 2)		(14)
Taxation (W1)		(54)
Capital expenditure (Note 2)		(39)
Equity dividends paid (W2)		(34)
Cash inflow before financing		130
Financing (Note 2)		(134)
Decrease in cash in period		(4)
Reconciliation of net cash flow to movement in net debt (Note 3)		
Decrease in cash in the period	(4)	
Repayment of long term loan	150	
Change in net debt		146
Net debt at 1.1.01		(222)
Net debt at 31.12.01		(76)

Notes to the cash flow statement
Note 1 – Reconciliation of operating profit to operating cash flows

Operating profit			210
Depreciation charges			59
Loss on sale of fixed assets			9
Increase in stocks			(2)
Increase in debtors			(8)
Increase in creditors			3
Net cash inflow from operating activities			271

Note 2 – Analysis of cash flows for headings netted in the cash flow statement
Returns on investments and servicing of finance

Interest paid			(14)

Capital expenditure

Payments to acquire tangible fixed assets (W3)		(45)	
Receipts from sale of tangible fixed assets (W3)		6	
			(39)

Financing

Issue of ordinary share capital		16	
Repayment of long term loans		(150)	
			(134)

Note 3 – Analysis of changes in net debt

	At 1.1.01 £000	Cash flows £000	At 31.12.01 £000
Cash at bank	28	(4)	24
Debt due after 1 year	(250)	150	(100)
Total	(222)	146	(76)

Workings

(1)

	Taxation		
		b/f	43
Cash =	54	P & L	62
c/f	51		
	105		105

(2)

	Dividends		
Cash =	34	b/f	8
c/f	10	P & L	36
	44		44

(3)

	Fixed assets		
b/f	780	Disposals (=)	27
Additions	45	c/f	798
	825		825

	Depreciation		
Dep'n on disposals (=)	12	b/f	112
c/f	159	P & L	59
	171		171

	Disposals		
Cost	27	Depreciation	12
		P & L (Loss)	9
		Proceeds(=)	6
	27		27

Chapter 13: Consolidated financial statements

1. a) FRS 9 *Accounting for associates and joint ventures* defines an associate as an entity (other than a subsidiary) in which another entity (the investor) has a participating interest and over whose operating and financial policies the investor exercises a significant influence.

Terms contained within this definition can be explained as follows:

Entity – a body corporate, partnership or unincorporated association carrying on a trade or business (of its own, not just part of the trades or businesses of entities that have interests in it) with or without a view to profit.

Subsidiary – an entity over which another entity has control.

Participating interest – a holding of 20% or more of the shares of an entity is to be presumed to be a participating interest unless the contrary is shown. The presumption is rebutted if the interest is neither non-beneficial nor long-term. The interest is held for the purpose of securing a contribution to the investor's activities by the exercise of control or influence arising from or related to that interest.

Significant influence – the Companies Act 1985 provides that an entity holding 20% or more of another entity's voting rights should be presumed to hold a significant influence over that other entity unless the contrary is shown. The standard requires that the investor is actively involved and is influential through participation on such policy decisions relevant to the investor such as:

i) the expansion or contraction of the business, participation in other entities or changes in products, markets and activities of the investee; and

ii) determining the balance between dividend and reinvestment.

b) i) Share of Cable's net tangible assets
    (30% × 400)   120
    Share of Cable's goodwill (30% × 50)   15
    Goodwill arising on acquisition:
    $\left(£150 \times \dfrac{100}{30}\right)$ 500

    Fair value $\dfrac{350}{150} \times 30\%$ $\dfrac{45}{}$
                                                                   180

ii) Cost of investment   150
    Post acquisition profits
    30% × (250 − 150)   30
                                                                   180

iii) The valuation of the associated company investment in (i) above is at the fair value of the assets at the balance sheet date, less the original goodwill paid. This suggests that the investing company exerts significant influence over the assets and the profits derived from them. The method gives more information regarding the split of Cable's assets between tangible assets and goodwill than the FRS 2 approach as shown in (ii).

The method used under FRS 2 as shown in (ii) above gives the same value. It states the investment at cost plus retained post acquisition profits, and suggests a much less active role by the investing company, sharing profits but not controlling assets.

The FRS 9 approach shown in (i) above is considered preferable.

2. a) FRS 6 requires acquisition accounting to be used for any business combination where one party is being acquired by the other. Merger accounting is restricted to, and required for, those business combinations where the use of acquisition accounting would not properly reflect the true nature of the combination. With FRS 6, the restrictions are such that the use of merger accounting in future will be 'very rare'.

FRS 6 defines a merger as:

'. . . a business combination in which, rather than one party acquiring control of another, the parties come together to share in the future risks and benefits of the combined entity. It is not the augmentation of one entity by the addition of another, but the creation of what is effectively a new reporting entity from the parties to the combination.'

The five criteria for merger accounting

Merger accounting can only be used if the combination meets the following five criteria:

1. neither party is portrayed as acquirer or acquired by their boards or management or by any other party to the combination;

2. all parties participate in the formation of the management structure and the selection of personnel; decisions are made by consensus rather than by the exercise of voting rights;

3. no one party is relatively large enough to dominate another;

4. consideration received by equity shareholders should principally be in the form of equity shares in the combined entity;

5. no equity shareholders retain a material interest in the future performance of only part of the combined entity

b) **Acquisition method**

X Ltd Consolidated Balance Sheet

		£000
Fixed assets (1,100 + 670)		1,770
Goodwill		150
		1,920
Current assets (300 + 80)	380	
Creditors (400 + 200)	(600)	
		(220)
		1,700
Share capital (700 + 100)		800
Capital reserves (70 + 600)		670
Revenue reserves		230
		1,700

Workings: Goodwill:

Value of consideration given	
100,000 shares @ £7 each	700,000
Assets and liabilities acquired, at fair value	(550,000)
	150,000

Share premium:	
Value of consideration, as above	700,000
Less Nominal value of shares issued	(100,000)
	600,000

Merger method
X Ltd Consolidated Balance Sheet

	£000
Fixed assets (1,100 + 700)	1,800
Current assets (300 + 100)	400
	2,200
Creditors (400 + 200)	(600)
	1,600
Share capital (700 + 100)*	800
Capital reserve	70
Revenue reserves (230 + 500)	730
	1,600

c) The major consequence of adopting the merger method of accounting has been to increase the amount of distributable reserves when compared with those arising under the acquisition method. This is of obvious benefit to the existing (and new) shareholders of X Ltd, as under the acquisition method pre-acquisition profits are not available for dividend.

The Financial Reporting Standard FRS 6 lays down detailed criteria for determining whether the merger method can be applied, and this acts as a safeguard for the interests of creditors of the companies being merged. The argument against merger accounting that it creates 'instant distributable reserves' is counter-balanced by the fact that the combined total is no higher than that of the distributable reserves of the individual companies immediately prior to the merger.

Chapter 14: Foreign currency translation

1. a) Under the closing rate/net investment method of foreign currency translation, the balance sheet amounts in the foreign subsidiary are translated using the rate of exchange ruling at the balance sheet date (i.e. the 'closing rate'), with the exception of equity capital, which is translated at the rate when acquired. Profit and loss account items are translated at either the closing rate or the average rate for the year. This method is based on the 'net investment' concept whereby it is not the value of the individual assets and liabilities which is relevant, but the value of the overall net investment in the subsidiary. The objective of consolidation is to present information which is useful to decision makers in the parent company's country, but without necessarily presenting the results as though the parent company and its subsidiaries were a single entity.

---

* i.e. X's original share capital plus the 100,000 shares issued for Y.

b) Whilst most foreign operations are carried out by organisations which operate as virtually autonomous entities, there are occasions where the foreign trade is conducted as a direct extension of the trade of the investing company, and the results of the foreign enterprise are regarded as being more dependent upon the economic environment of the investing (i.e. parent) company's local currency than on its own reporting currency.

In such cases, the 'net investment' concept (upon which the 'closing rate' method of foreign currency translation is based) is regarded as inappropriate, and the transactions of the foreign enterprise are treated as though they had been made by the investing company itself in its own currency, being translated by means of the 'temporal' method. The temporal method is therefore based on the premise that the objective of consolidation is to present the results of the parent company and its subsidiaries as though it were a single entity.

Under the temporal method, monetary assets, current liabilities and long-term liabilities are translated at the rate of exchange prevailing at the end of the year, but non-monetary assets and depreciation are translated at the exchange rate at the date of purchase. Equity capital is translated at the exchange rate when acquired. Profit and loss account items are translated at the average rate for the year.

c) The decision as to whether the temporal method is appropriate hinges upon the relative dominance of the investing company's 'economic environment'. The explanatory note to the standard gives the following list of factors to be taken into account when arriving at the decision:

i)   the extent to which the cash flows of the enterprise have a direct impact upon those of the investing company;

ii) the extent to which the functioning of the enterprise is dependent directly upon the investing company;

iii) the currency in which the majority of the trading transactions are denominated;

iv) the major currency to which the operation is exposed in its financing structure.

Two example of circumstances where the temporal method may be appropriate are where the foreign enterprise:

i)   acts as a selling agency receiving stocks of goods from the investing company and remits the proceeds back to the company;

ii) produces a raw material or manufactures parts or sub-assemblies which are then shipped to the investing company for inclusion in its own products.

2. a) *See* answer to 1(a) and 1(b) above.

b) For individual companies, exchange gains or losses arise primarily in situations where the rate prevailing at the time that a transaction is recorded differs from that used when the transaction is settled. Such gains or losses should be included in the profit or loss account as part of the profit or loss on ordinary activities.

In the case of exchange gains relating to long-term monetary items (e.g. long dated foreign loans), the prudence concept must be taken into consideration when deciding whether to incorporate all or part of such gains in circumstances where there are doubts as to the convertibility or marketability of the currency in question.

Gains or losses arising from group inter-company transactions should be reported within the individual company's profit and loss account, in the same way as third-party transactions.

For consolidation purposes, exchange gains or losses are adjusted directly on reserves.

3. Using the temporal method of foreign currency translation, the trial balance of the Carea branch is as follows:

	Mics	Rate	Debit(£)	Credit(£)
Fixed assets at cost	900,000	8	112,500	
Debtors and cash	36,000	4	9,000	
Operating costs	225,000	5	45,000	
Difference on exchange*			7,850	
Sales revenue	480,000	5		96,000
Creditors	25,000	4		6,250
Head office current account	420,000	Actual		42,600
Accumulated depreciation	236,000	8		29,500
			174,350	174,350

The final accounts of Home Ltd for 2001 are as follows:

Profit and loss account for the year ended 31 December 2001

		£
Sales revenue (186,300 + 96,000)		282,300
Operating costs (103,700 + 45,000)	148,700	
Exchange losses	7,850	
		(156,550)
Net profit		125,750

---

* Balancing figure.

Balance Sheet as at 31 December 2001

Fixed assets, at cost (450,000 + 112,500)	562,500	
Less Depreciation (107,100 + 29,500)	(136,600)	
		425,900
Debtors and cash (17,600 + 9,000)	26,600	
Less Creditors (9,700 + 6,250)	(15,950)	
		10,650
		436,550
Share capital		200,000
Retained reserves (110,800 + 125,750)		236,550
		436,550

Chapter 15: Retirement benefits

a) Defined contribution schemes: in such schemes, the cost to the employer is known with reasonable accuracy, as the employer usually makes agreed contributions to the scheme and the benefits will depend upon the funds available from these contributions and the investment earnings arising from them.

The contributions payable to the scheme for the accounting period should be recognised within operating profit in the profit and loss account.

b) Defined benefit schemes: the benefits paid will usually depend upon either the average pay of the employees during their career (or perhaps the last few years of it) or, more usually, the employee's final pay. It is impossible to know in advance that the contributions plus investment return will equal the final benefits to be paid. Any shortfall may have to be paid by the employer, either for legal reasons or else to maintain good employee relations. If a surplus arises, the employer may be entitled to either a refund of contributions or a reduction in future contributions. In view of the long-term nature of the pension commitment, actuarial valuations are needed at regular intervals.

In the balance sheet, assets should be recognised to the extent that the entity is able to recover a surplus either through reduced contributions in the future or through refunds from the scheme. Liabilities should be recognised to the extent that they reflect its legal or constructive obligation.

The current service cost, based on the most recent actuarial valuation at the beginning of the period, should be included within operating profit in the profit and loss account. Actuarial gains and losses arising from any new valuation and from updating the latest actuarial valuation to reflect conditions at the balance sheet date should be recognised in the statement of total recognised gains and losses for the period. (*See* Chapter 15 for a more detailed summary of requirements.)

Index

Revision briefings

Cut out these pages to help with pre-exam revision.

FRS 1 Cash flow statements

Standard layout with the following headings:

- Operating activities
- Dividends from joint ventures and associates
- Returns on investments and servicing of finance
- Taxation
- Capital expenditure and financial investment
- Acquisitions and disposals
- Equity dividends paid
- Management of liquid resources
- Financing

FRS 2 Accounting for subsidiary undertakings

- Parent subsidiary relationship exists if majority shareholding owned or 'dominant influence'.
- All of subsidiary's income and expenditure included in consolidated profit and loss account, but minority interests (if any) adjusted.
- All of subsidiary's assets and liabilities included in consolidated balance sheet, but minority interests (if any) shown separately.

FRS 3 Reporting financial performance

- Introduced changes to the profit and loss format (continuing/discontinued activities, acquisitions).
- Introduced a statement of total recognised gains and losses, a note of historical cost profits and losses and a reconciliation of movements in shareholders' funds.
- Abolished extraordinary items.

FRS 4 Accounting for capital instruments

- Definition: all instruments that are issued by reporting entities as a means of raising finance, including shares, debentures, loans and debt instruments, options and warrants that give the holder the right to subscribe for or obtain capital instruments. In the case of consolidated financial statements the term includes capital instruments issued by subsidiaries except those that are held by another member of the group included in the consolidation.
- Capital instruments are to be classified as liabilities if they carry an obligation to transfer cash or other resources.
- Liabilities should be classified as current or non-current according to their contractual maturity dates unless where the same lender is committed to refinance the debt on the same terms.
- Liabilities should be recognised in the balance sheet at the amount received less any issue costs. The finance costs should be allocated to accounting periods so as to achieve a constant rate on the amount outstanding.

FRS 5 Reporting the substance of transactions

Four main areas:

- the substance of transactions – has the transaction given rise to new assets or liabilities and has it changed the entity's existing assets and liabilities;
- recognition of assets and liabilities in the balance sheet – if sufficient evidence of the existence of the item and the item can be measured at a monetary amount with sufficient reliability;
- disclosures, e.g. where assets are not available for use as security against liabilities;
- quasi-subsidiaries – definition: 'a company, trust, partnership or other vehicle that, though not fulfilling the definition of a subsidiary, is directly or indirectly controlled by the reporting entity and gives rise to benefits for that entity that are in substance no different from those that would arise were the vehicle a subsidiary.'

FRS 6 Acquisitions and mergers

Merger accounting only permissible if five criteria met.

Otherwise 'acquisition accounting' used.

FRS 7 Fair values in acquisition accounting

- Bans companies from making provisions for the future trading losses of companies they acquire and the costs of rationalisation or reorganisation.
- Fair value is 'the amount at which an asset or liability could be exchanged in an arm's length transaction between informed and willing parties, other than in a forced or liquidation sale.'

FRS 8 Related party disclosures

- Definition of related party transaction: the transfer of assets or liabilities or the performance of services by, to or for a related party irrespective of whether a price is charged.
- Disclosure of transactions to be made include the names of related parties, their relationship and description of the transactions and amounts involved.

FRS 9 Associates and joint ventures

- Associate if another company has a participating interest and significant influence of more than 20% of share capital.
- Joint venture is jointly controlled and long-term.
- Associates accounted for by equity method, with share of associate's operating result included after group operating result in consolidated profit and loss account. Share of associate's net assets shown in consolidated balance sheet.
- Joint ventures accounted for by 'gross equity method' which is the same as the equity method, but the share of the joint venture's turnover and gross assets and liabilities is noted.

FRS 10 Goodwill and intangible assets

- Internally generated goodwill not included in accounting statements.
- Positive purchased goodwill amortised if not expected to be maintained indefinitely – usually not exceeding 20 years.
- No amortisation if goodwill is expected to be maintained indefinitely.
- Annual impairment review for non-amortised goodwill, otherwise only in year after acquisition.

FRS 11 Impairment of fixed assets and goodwill

- Impairment = reduction in the recoverable amount of a fixed asset or goodwill below its carrying amount.
- Various reasons for potential impairment, e.g. losses, cash outflows, obsolescence, damage to asset, etc.
- Impairment losses (and reversals of impairments) recognised in profit and loss account in the majority of cases.

FRS 12 Provisions, contingent liabilities and contingent assets

- Provisions (liability of uncertain timing or amount) recognised if there is a present obligation arising from a past event, a probable transfer of economic benefits and a reliable estimate can be made.
- Neither contingent liabilities nor contingent assets can be recognised, but can be disclosed by note if there is the likelihood of a transfer of economic benefits.

FRS 13 Derivatives and other financial instruments: disclosure

- Requires entities to provide a discussion of the major financial risks they face in their activities and how they manage their exposure to these risks.
- Numerical disclosures analysing borrowings, fair values of financial instruments etc. must be made.

FRS 14 Earnings per share

- Basic formula:

$$\frac{\text{Net profit (or loss) after tax, extraordinary and}}{\text{exceptional items, minority interests, and preference dividends}}$$
$$\text{Weighted average number of ordinary shares outstanding during the period}$$

- Formula if there has been a bonus issue or share split: as basic eps, but divisor includes ordinary shares issued by way of bonus or share split during the year.

- If there has been a rights issue at less than fair value, previous year's eps must be adjusted by the factor:

$$\frac{\text{Fair value per share immediately before the exercise of rights}}{\text{Theoretical ex-rights fair value per share*}}$$

*calculated as follows:

$$\frac{\text{Pre-rights fair values of shares + Proceeds from rights issue}}{\text{Shares outstanding after rights issue}}$$

- *Diluted earnings* refers to the effect of potential conversion rights of loan stocks, warrants etc. into ordinary shares at future dates. Formula is:

$$\frac{\text{(numerator as in basic eps) plus post-tax effect of dividends, interest or other}}{\text{income or expense relating to the dilutive potential ordinary shares}}$$
$$\text{(divisor as in basic eps) plus the weighted average number of all potential ordinary}$$
$$\text{shares, deemed to have been converted at the beginning of the period}$$

FRS 15 Tangible fixed assets

- Cost of a tangible fixed asset is purchase cost plus directly attributable costs.
- Administration and general overheads excluded from cost.
- Finance costs can be included if entity chooses.
- Revaluations only if entity adopts such a policy, in which case full valuation on properties every 5 years, interim in year 3.
- Allocate depreciation on a systematic basis over asset's useful economic life.

FRS 16 Current tax

- Current tax relating to a gain or loss that is or has been recognised in the statement of total recognised gains and losses should also be recognised in that statement.
- Other current tax should be recognised in the profit and loss account.
- Dividends and interest received is shown gross (before any withholding tax), with the related tax suffered being shown as part of the total tax charge for the period.

FRS 17 Retirement benefits

- Defined contribution schemes: employer usually makes agreed contributions to the scheme and the benefits will depend upon the funds available from these contributions and the investment earnings. The contributions payable to the scheme for the accounting period should be recognised within operating profit in the profit and loss account.
- Defined benefit schemes: the benefits paid will usually depend upon either the average pay of the employees during their career (or perhaps the last few years of it) or, more usually, the employee's final pay. Full actuarial valuations needed every 3 years maximum. Actuarial gains and losses arising from any new valuation and from updating the latest actuarial valuation to reflect conditions at the balance sheet date should be recognised in the statement of total recognised gains and losses for the period.

FRS 18 Accounting policies

- Contrasts accounting policies with estimation techniques.
- Two concepts have 'pervasive role': going concern and accruals.
- Relevance, reliability, comparability and understanding are objectives for judging appropriateness of policies.

FRS 19 Deferred tax

- Deferred tax must be fully provided for on most types of timing differences.
- Timing differences *not* to be recognised include a fixed asset revalued without there being any commitment to sell the asset, and when the gain on the sale of an asset is rolled over into replacement assets.
- Deferred tax relating to a gain or loss that is or has been recognised in the statement of total recognised gains and losses should also be recognised in that statement.
- Other deferred tax should be recognised in the profit and loss account.

SSAP 4 Accounting for government grants

- Revenue-based grants are credited against expense in same period.
- Capital-based grants reduce fixed asset cost: net amount is depreciated.

SSAP 5 Accounting for Value Added Tax

- Registered traders show amounts exclusive of VAT, except where irrecoverable.
- Non-registered traders show amounts at VAT-inclusive prices.
- VAT owed/owing included within debtors/creditors.

SSAP 9 Stocks and long-term contracts

- Stock stated at lower of cost and net realisable value.
- Cost is expenditure incurred in normal course of business in bringing the product or service to its present location and condition.
- LIFO, base stock and replacement stock (except in certain circumstances) are not acceptable valuation methods.
- Long-term contracts: attributable profit can be recognised in the profit and loss account by recording turnover and related costs as contract activity progresses. Foreseeable losses must be recognised immediately.

SSAP 13 Accounting for research and development

- Research always written off to profit and loss account, unless relating to fixed assets which would be capitalised.
- Development expenditure must meet 'DECORATE' criteria (see p. 56) to be carried forward as deferred asset – otherwise write off.
- Entity can choose whether to treat development expenditure as a deferred asset or to write it off.
- Amortise when commercial production starts.

SSAP 17 Post balance sheet events

- A post balance sheet period is between balance sheet date and the date on which the board of directors approve the financial statements
- Adjusting post balance sheet events provide additional evidence of conditions existing on the balance sheet date and require figures to be adjusted accordingly.
- Non-adjusting post balance sheet events are material events that occur in the post balance sheet period and are sufficiently important to be brought to the attention of users by way of note.

SSAP 19 Accounting for investment properties

Investment properties are:

- land or completed buildings;
- have more than 20 years lease life;
- not owned or occupied by the entity for its own purposes;
- not let to and occupied by another group company;
- rented out at arm's length;
- not depreciated.

SSAP 20 Foreign currency translation

- Individual companies: use average rate where currency is stable, otherwise use rates on date of transactions.
- Consolidated statements: closing rate/net investment method normally used, but temporal method for autonomous entities.
- Closing rate/net investment method requires exchange differences (shown in the statement of total recognised gains and losses) to be adjusted on reserves.
- Temporal method – same method as for individual companies.

SSAP 21 Accounting for leases and hire purchase contracts

- Treatment depends on whether operating or finance lease.
- Operating lease: period of time substantially less than useful economic life, lessor retains most risk and rewards.
- Finance lease: lessee pays full cost to lessor, plus finance charge. Lessee has most risk and rewards.
- Operating lease – lessee's books: rentals charged to profit and loss account. Lessor's books: asset capitalised and depreciated, rental income shown in profit and loss account.
- Finance lease – lessee's books: asset capitalised and depreciated. Liability to lessor also shown. Lessor's books: debtor (due from lessee) shown as asset, gradually reducing over lease life. Profit and loss account shows finance charge.

SSAP 25 Segmental reporting

- If entity has two or more classes of business or operates in two or more geographical segments, it should define them and report for each class:
  - turnover, split between that arising from external customers and that arising from other segments;
  - profit or loss;
  - net assets.